PRAISE FOR

"In *No Woman Left Behind*, Kate Grant shares her journey of overcoming setbacks and red tape to help women access life-changing fistula surgeries, offering inspiration and insights for anyone determined to make a difference"
—Secretary Hillary Rodham Clinton

"Kate Grant has enabled 100,000 surgeries to transform the lives of women who were facing a bleak future. *No Woman Left Behind* is an inspiring and empowering story. Read it!"
—Peter Singer, Emeritus Professor, Princeton University, co-founder The Life You Can Save

"In *No Woman Left Behind*, Kate tells moving stories about dedicated doctors and generous donors that step up and step in to help ensure that women survive and thrive after giving birth. She shines a bright light of hope on the resilient women who emerge as heroes in their own stories. If you are passionate about maternal health and care about creating a world where women can thrive in motherhood like I do, this book is for you!"
—Christy Turlington Burns, founder & president, Every Mother Counts

"Where a woman delivers a child can be the difference between life, death, and disability. It is easy to ignore suffering when the problem exists a continent away, for poor women living in Africa or Asia. Grant's book is a call to action for compassionate advocates, and a stunning tale of how deeds triumph over platitudes. *No Woman Left Behind* is a powerful plea to be our sister's keeper, and a guide-book to change the world, one woman at a time."
—Dr. Denis Mukwege, founder, Panzi Hospital and winner of the Nobel Peace Prize

"*No Woman Left Behind* is part bildungsroman, expedition diary, and call for action against a terrible affliction. Our guide stares down the particular cruelty of vaginal fistula in the world's remotest corners—stares down, too, her own flaws and presumptions as she relentlessly rattles the doors of donors to ease the suffering. It's a bracing tale in these uneasy times of redemption for both the afflicted and those committed to their cure, and how to live a life with meaning."

—BROOKE GLADSTONE, host of NPR's On the Media

"*No Woman Left Behind* is a stirring story of how a talented social entrepreneur found her true purpose and defied the odds to build an organization that has changed women's lives worldwide. This book will fill you with hope."

—DAVID CALLAHAN, founder and publisher of
Inside Philanthropy

"Few have heard of obstetric fistula, but it is a serious health condition plaguing tens of thousands of women injured in childbirth around the globe. Most live in poverty without access to medical care; others are victims of brutal rapes and sexual violence perpetrated by armed combatants as a tool of war. For those afflicted, it is often isolating, debilitating and a source of shame. Repair surgery is the answer, but too often inaccessible. Join the author, Kate Grant, on her remarkable journey of hope to help women suffering from fistula and her powerful call to action."

—MELANNE VERVEER, former US Ambassador for
Global Women's Issues

NO
WOMAN
LEFT
BEHIND

NO WOMAN LEFT BEHIND

A Journey of Hope to Heal Every
Woman Injured in Childbirth

KATE GRANT

Founding CEO, Fistula Foundation

Published 2025
Printed in the United States of America
Print ISBN: 978-1-64742-897-6
Hardcover ISBN: 978-1-64742-670-5
E-ISBN: 978-1-64742-898-3
Library of Congress Control Number: 2025900960

For information, address:
She Writes Press
1569 Solano Ave #546
Berkeley, CA 94707

Interior Design by Tabitha Lahr
Front Cover Image: Sumy Sadurni/GGImages Media
Cover Design: Leah Lococo
Copyright: Abraham Verghese, Foreword

Photos in the insert are from the author's collection, except for the following: author with Hillary Clinton, courtesy of the White House; Dr. Denis Mukwege with patients, Paula Allen; Dr. Shershah Syed, Dr. Sajjad Siddiqui with fistula patient, Naseema, PC Khaula Jamil; author with Frances Alonzo, courtesy of Voice of America; Sarah Omega, Lindsey Pollaczek in West Pokot, Dr. Hillary Mabeya with blueprint, Gynocare Hospital Grand Opening, Georgina Goodwin; Louis CK, courtesy of Saturday Night Live; patients at CCBRT, Roshni Lodhia; Brooke Gladstone, Peter Singer, with author, Rachel Kenaston.

She Writes Press is a division of SparkPoint Studio, LLC.

Names and identifying characteristics have been changed to protect the privacy of certain individuals.

In memory of
Lois and Bob Grant,
my parents

For Bobby Houston,
my son

There is no such thing as not worshipping.
Everybody worships.
The only choice we get is what to worship.

—DAVID FOSTER WALLACE

Don't let anybody, anybody convince you
this is the way the world is and therefore must be.
It must be the way it ought to be.

—Toni Morrison

CONTENTS

PART ONE: Lost and Found

PART TWO: True North

PART THREE: A Million Reasons

PART FOUR: In It to End It

I've tried to relay my experiences honestly. I've changed names and details to protect people's feelings. I've left a few things out and sometimes told things out of order to not bore you silly. Any errors are mine.

FOREWORD

By Abraham Verghese

I was born and raised in Addis Ababa, Ethiopia, where my expatriate parents had been recruited as schoolteachers. I recall that the parents of one of my schoolmates were both surgeons, Reg and Catherine Hamlin. At some point I discovered that they were also pioneers in the treatment of fistula in women, though I had no idea what a fistula was. That changed when I entered medical school in Addis Ababa and learned firsthand about obstetric fistula.

The patients with fistula often came from miles away seeking care for an injury that created relentless misery. They continuously leaked urine or feces or both, as a result of trauma during childbirth. Their profound suffering was impossible to forget. Fistula is a condition that is exceedingly rare in the west, and when it occurs, the cause is cancer or radiation injury, not the complication of a delivery. Countries where fistula is common tend to be those where, particularly in the rural areas, women get little or no prenatal care; indeed, to get any sort of medical care they must trek vast distances by foot, by donkey, and then bus. In such places it is the rule for women in labor to do so at home while attended by a relative, or an untrained midwife, or no one at all. The typical fistula patient is one in whom labor stalls; for many of them, malnutrition and rickets in childhood have left them with a narrow pelvis that makes the passage of the baby difficult, if not impossible. Many hours and days after the first contraction, it becomes clear that the baby is not coming out except by a cesarean section or by applying forceps; by then the baby has typically succumbed to the stress. Once the family realizes they need help, poor roads and absent public transport add more hours to that task—that is if they get help at all. If the mother survives, the hours that her bladder, rectum, and vagina were entrapped between the baby's skull and her own unyielding pelvic bone results in a terrible birth injury. When things heal in a fashion, she is left with an opening—a fistula—between the bladder and the vagina, or between the vagina and the rectum. It is bad enough to be incontinent, but the woman often suffers rejection by the husband and in laws; she becomes ostracized by society because constant dribbling makes it impossible to stay dry. I would guess many others succumbed to recurrent urinary infection; some women are driven to take their own lives.

I left Ethiopia in the 1970s, when Emperor Haile Selassie was deposed and a harsh military regime took over. After many years in practice, in 2008 I wrote my first novel *Cutting for Stone*. It was set partially in Ethiopia, and it involved characters who were or would become physicians. Given my vivid memories of patients with fistula, it is no surprise that one of the characters in the book becomes a fistula surgeon. *Cutting for Stone* did exceedingly well, staying on the *New York Times* bestseller list for many weeks. By this time, I was living in the Bay Area and inevitably I learned of the Fistula Foundation which is based there. I was inspired by what it did, and I also became a friend and admirer of Kate Grant. I witnessed her fierce empathy for women with fistula and steadfast belief in the surgeons whose work she championed.

When Nicholas Kristof of the *New York Times* wrote about fistula and the work of the Fistula Foundation, many more people became aware of the scourge of fistula. I've rejoiced from the sidelines, as the Foundation has grown tremendously, helping more and more women year after year. Recently, an incredibly generous gift to the Fistula Foundation by MacKenzie Scott has enabled it to further multiply its efforts. For those of us who have long believed in the work done by the Foundation—by Kate, her staff, her board, and the surgeons they support—this transformative gift feels like a kind of vindication, proof that sometimes the efforts of good people are eventually recognized.

The time has never been more right for Kate to tell the story of the women who have suffered too long in the shadows, and that of the many people who work tirelessly to help them get life-transforming care. It is inevitably also Kate's own story of growth and transformation during a journey of a lifetime. I hope you will enjoy it as much as I have.

PROLOGUE

Addis Ababa, Ethiopia, August 1994

Put your ear down close to your soul and listen hard.

—ANNE SEXTON

An ancient cab, the color of moss, speckled with rust, hugged the curb outside my hotel. I got in and asked the driver if he could take me to the Fistula Hospital. We made our way onto the road, nestled behind a bus that belched gray clouds of diesel smoke into the crisp morning air. Out the window I could see a snaky train of haggard women, skinny men with a few missing limbs, and bony kids on foot. Ethiopia had recently emerged from decades of a brutal communist dictatorship and endured a famine of biblical proportions; think rock stars singing "We are the World." The human toll of that brutal history was trudging by us.

A few days earlier at Dulles Airport, a silver-haired stranger had asked me with a smirk "Are you a mercenary, a missionary, or a misfit?" when I'd told him I was headed to Africa. The answer should have been easy. I'd spent my twenties largely unburdened by introspection, enjoying the spoils of my Madison Avenue career. In search of a more meaningful path, I'd landed in Washington, DC, working on Capitol Hill. I liked to think of myself as a pragmatic idealist out to save the world. But maybe I was kidding myself. Maybe I was just a misfit trying to escape the rat race.

I was in Ethiopia as part of a "Co Del"—short for Congressional Delegation—and the embassy suggested that I visit the hospital. "It's for women, you'll find it interesting," was all I'd been told. I mulled over the word *fistula*. It meant nothing to me. I had a vague memory that Italy occupied Ethiopia in the 1930s. Was fistula a proper name, and the hospital was named for a "Mario Fistula" or some other long-dead Italian who may have endowed the place?

Then, the car darted off the main road, making a hard right turn. We drove past a small green sign with white lettering that said "Addis Ababa Fistula Hospital" in English and Amharic and a wall topped with broken glass stuck in cement. A large open metal gate led into a courtyard.

As I got out of the cab, the lush green lawn and purple bougainvillea surrounding the hospital surprised me. Large trees shaded the two-story, white-washed, tin-roofed building from the morning sun. The chaotic noise of horns and car engines on the main road was gone. The only sound was the soft murmur of conversations that emanated from women in ragged clothes sitting on benches in front of the building.

I opened the front door and stepped into the cavernous entrance. The unmistakable smell of disinfectant was a sharp contrast to the strong smell of urine I noticed while walking by the women who occupied the benches outside. The ward looked like something out of a history book from the days of Florence Nightingale, with row after row of beds.

An older white woman wearing a doctor's coat and practical flats walked toward me. She smiled and said, "Hello, I'm Catherine Hamlin. It's lovely to have you visit us."

Her sparkling blue eyes and Australian accent put me at ease. She was slender and towered over me and everyone else. As she escorted me to a few plastic chairs off to the side of the ward, she asked about my trip and then offered me tea.

Before I could expose my complete ignorance about fistula, Dr. Hamlin explained what it was. "Dear, a fistula is a hole between an internal organ and the outside world that shouldn't exist." She paused, then continued. "And in the case of all the women here, the cause is unrelieved obstructed labor. The hole is between the bladder, vagina, and sometimes the rectum, leaving a woman incontinent. Surgery is their only hope." Ok. Got it. The smells both inside and outside now made sense.

We were soon joined by an Ethiopian woman that Dr. Hamlin introduced as Mamitu Gashe, who she explained was a former fistula patient who now helped with fistula surgery. Mamitu was short in stature but had a giant smile and big expressive eyes. She gently shook my hand.

I asked Dr. Hamlin how she had ended up in Ethiopia. She explained, "I came here in 1959 with my husband, Reg. He, too, was a doctor, and we thought we'd stay a few years." She laughed then added, "Things worked out differently than we'd planned. We continued to meet patients with fistula. They had often been turned away by other hospitals because of their odor and the stigma from their incontinence. We felt we needed to do something for them."

That something was the hospital we were sitting in. She said it had opened in 1974 and was the only hospital in the world dedicated to treating women with obstetric fistula. She added, "In places like the US and Australia, most babies are born in a hospital and obstructed births are treated with a C-section. This means where you live, fistula is almost unheard of."

She then suggested that we take a tour of the floor and meet one of the patients. When we got closer to the bed, I smiled at the young woman. Her expression was blank, and I figured she had reason to be wary of me. She was striking, with high cheekbones, large brown eyes, and skin the color of coffee with cream.

"This is Hanna," Dr. Hamlin said. "Mamitu, can you ask Hanna to tell us what happened to her?"

Mamitu turned to Hanna and asked her a question in Amharic. I waited for the translation, which took a while because Hanna had a lot to say. "She married a young man from her village when she was seventeen and soon become pregnant, but after five days of labor at home, she delivered a stillborn baby boy. She awoke to find herself in a urine-soaked bed. She hoped it would go away, so she stayed in bed as much as she could. But it wouldn't stop. Her husband hated her smell and built a separate small hut for her to live in. It was so lonely. That was about five years ago. But when her mother heard there was a hospital in Addis to help her, she sold a goat to pay for the bus fare. It took several different buses to finally reach Addis."

Mamitu then asked Hanna another question, and a smile radiated across her face. While I didn't understand Amharic, it was clear something good had finally happened to Hanna. Mamitu explained, "She said arriving at the hospital and seeing other women with her problem made her feel less alone and less sad."

Dr. Hamlin added, "We were able to close her fistula yesterday. It was an easy operation, and she should be able to go home in two weeks once she's healed."

I shook Hanna's hand and squeaked out the only word I knew in Amharic, "Ameseginalehu,"—it means thank you.

Dr. Hamlin and Mamitu took me around the rest of the hospital. Like Hanna, most of the patients seemed quite young. She was only seventeen when she developed a fistula. What was I worried about at her age? My lack of a prom date? The growing realization that I'd never be pretty like my sister, as smart as my dad, or as charming as my mom? I definitely wasn't mourning a stillborn child, facing rejection by my husband, or struggling to find treatment for holes in my vagina and bladder.

As we walked back toward our seats, Dr. Hamlin said with a tender tone, "They come to us often malnourished and usually clinically depressed." She stopped and turned to me, looking into my eyes, "There are so very many of them. They will break your heart." The compassion in her voice and the intensity of her gaze was riveting. I could feel her love for her patients in the tenderness of her words. I gazed at the vast ward of patients that were going to get a new shot at life because of this humble giant. A lump rose in my throat and my eyes started welling up.

But then, Dr. Hamlin's black dog began nipping at my heels trying to play. It made me laugh and the threat of tears vanished. After a few more minutes, it was time for me to go. Dr. Hamlin had a hospital to run. As we walked toward the door, she joked that she was a "professional beggar" with her constant need to raise funds to keep the place going.

"It must be a challenge," I said, thinking that was obvious.

I knew I'd just met a few people I'd never forget: Dr. Hamlin, Mamitu, and Hanna. I wished I had money to write a big check to help keep the place running. But, at that point, what I had was residual debt from grad school and a ten-year-old Honda that badly needed new tires.

Within a few weeks, I was in Cairo for a once-in-a-decade International Conference on Population and Development, the ICPD, along with thousands of delegates from the 179 members states of the United Nations. The conference produced a 104-page Programme of Action. Years in the making, it was essentially the world's blueprint for addressing poverty, covering critical problems like accessibility of contraception, education, and safe drinking water. But absent from that ambitious, detailed document was the word "fistula." In 1994, the world did not acknowledge the plight of a million women like Hanna, let alone have a plan to help them.

———————————————

The day a woman gives birth is the day she is most likely to die or be grievously injured. The biggest difference in health outcomes between rich and poor in our world is in the odds of death due to pregnancy or childbirth. As Justin Trudeau proclaimed, "poverty is sexist." For a woman in sub-Saharan Africa that lifetime risk is 1 in 41. For an American woman it is 1 in 2,700; for a woman in the EU, it is 1 in 11,500. For every woman who dies, an estimated twenty are injured, some seriously. We tell ourselves that all lives have equal value, but this data reveals a very different story.

The late Egyptian public health leader Professor Mahmoud Fathalla said it powerfully: "Women are not dying because of diseases we cannot treat. They are dying because societies have yet to decide their lives are worth saving." That negligence also causes disabling injuries, like fistula. The most immediate victims of the losses of life and health are women. But the ripple effects stretch far and wide: to children deprived of mothers; families missing wives, sisters, and daughters; communities and nations cheated out of the contributions of multitudes of women. It doesn't have to be this way.

Fistula Foundation was founded in 2000 to help support Dr. Hamlin's work in Ethiopia, powered by volunteers for the first few years. Since then, we've expanded to fight fistula globally. Caring people in more than seventy countries have contributed $150 million and counting to support dedicated surgeons in countries across sub-Saharan Africa and Asia. These valiant doctors have enabled more than one-hundred-thousand courageous women like Hanna to get their lives back. Our small but mighty largely female team now support more surgeries for women with childbirth injuries than the United Nations or USAID, the US Government's foreign aid program.

This book is the unlikely tale of how we got here. Part of that story is mine about finding the path that brought me to the Foundation. I've run into dead ends that I thought were through streets, fallen flat on my face, confronted obstacles I created and shortcomings I tried to deny. But my work has given me rewards that money can't buy and taken my heart to places my younger self didn't know were possible. That's in large part because of the people I've been so fortunate to meet and learn from along the way.

I have had the great privilege of partnering with extraordinary men and women on the frontlines of healthcare in Africa and Asia. They've built hospitals, braved murderous violence and oppressive forces of patriarchy, and provided women with a new shot at a healthy life. They've shown me the saving grace of gratitude and the matchless joy of working with others to accomplish goals bigger than ourselves.

I've been inspired by courageous patients who face a formidable injury that too often relegates women to lives as outcasts. I've met deeply empathetic people who step up to help women they likely will never meet receive life transforming surgery. I wanted to try to share their stories and mine with you.

PART ONE:

LOST

AND

FOUND

1. IT'S ALL WORTH IT

*If you can see your path laid out in front of
you step by step, you know it's not your path.
Your own path you make with every step
you take. That's why it's your path.*

—John Irving

EIGHT YEARS EARLIER, 1986

The elevator door opened. Bright morning sunlight flooded the reception area through a skylight the size of a volleyball court. I walked past overstuffed teal sofas, which contrasted perfectly with the tan floor tiles made of leather. I am not kidding. On Friday nights a crew who spoke mostly Spanish showed up to polish them like shoes. I was in the office of the ad agency Foote, Cone & Belding, FCB, in San Francisco.

It was the "greed is good" 1980s, and out of college I'd wound up in a training program at the Chicago ad agency, Leo Burnett. They'd created charming cultural icons like the Keebler elves and the Jolly Green Giant, along with dubious characters like the Marlboro Man. Then I joined FCB. It had been named Agency of the Year by *Advertising Age* and was producing Clio-award winning commercials for clients like Levi Strauss. The place ran on a combination of adrenaline and testosterone; all the senior leaders were men.

3

When I got to my office, my secretary Barbara greeted me with a smile and a mock-up of a print ad for my review. Advertising was the beating heart of American capitalism, and this day, like most, whizzed by with meetings, memos, and phone calls, pretty much nonstop. I'd become a devoted practitioner of the industry's dark arts that make people feel real emotions for trivial branded products. To do that, we used sophisticated research to hack the psyches of unsuspecting consumers. There was almost nothing at FCB that made me question my career path. The exception was a sign one of the copywriters I worked with had on his wall:

In the ad game, the days are tough, the nights are long, the work is emotionally demanding, but it's all worth it because the rewards are shallow, transparent, and meaningless.

Every time I read it, I had a sinking feeling in my gut.

I had what I was supposed to want: A job that paid more than my younger self imagined, a closet full of dress-for-success clothes, and expense-account funded trips to New York and LA. But at a place deep inside that I didn't fully understand, my soul hungered for something more. I'd been frenetically grasping brass rings since my first spelling bee in second grade, my fierce work ethic a birthright of my striving parents and their parents before them. I was constantly driving forward but had not thought much about where I was headed.

An idea had been stalking me with growing intensity, generating waves in equal measure of fear and excitement. It started when I'd bought an outdated copy of *Let's Go Europe* off the sale table at a local bookstore. It now sat on my nightstand, and I read it dreaming of places I'd never been. I'd worked every summer to help pay for college at a series of forgettable jobs and seen precious little of the world beyond our shores. This was my potentially reckless plan: I should quit my job and travel around the world.

But the voice in my head that I'd been raised listening to always shouted back *Are you nuts?*

A few weeks later, on a rainy Sunday morning, I walked into Greens restaurant on the waterfront to meet my friend Linda for brunch. She was smart and confident, looked a bit like Sigourney Weaver, and was the only woman I knew who looked good with a perm.

"Let's sit next to the window," Linda said.

We made our way over to a table for two. I barely noticed the view because I was focused on my pitch for Linda.

"I've got an idea. How about if we take a break from our jobs and travel around the world for six months? Seriously, wouldn't that be great?"

Linda laughed with a warmth that brightened the gloomy day. "You're kidding, right?"

"No, I'm not! Think about it. We don't have kids, or mortgages. Our thirties are years away. The timing is perfect."

She asked, skeptically, "How would that even work?"

"Easy. We put our stuff in storage and try to get a leave of absence from our jobs."

"But what if they say no? Then what?"

"Well, we'll get other jobs." As I said that my stomach tightened. I didn't want to leave FCB and face unemployment. But I kept my spiel going: "We can travel on the cheap. I think we can do it for $25 a day. Start in Europe and make our way around the world. *All* the way around."

She just sat there staring at me, shaking her head.

Then she said, "Let me think about it."

Linda had a great sense of humor and knew how to have fun. Together with my sister, Shelley, we'd hiked up Mount Tam, skied at Lake Tahoe, and partied until the wee hours at clubs in The City. But this was a new scale of adventure.

Two days later she called and said, "I'm in."

The next week, I talked to the head of FCB who said he'd consider hiring me back, but "no promises." I went out for drinks with my boss Ned. He was my favorite person at the agency and I was excited to talk to him about our trip. A New Yorker by birth, he'd cut his teeth on the real Madison Avenue and exuded the savvy confidence of someone who'd been around a few blocks in the Big Apple. He was sarcastic, had interesting takes on all things political. He reminded me of Woody Allen, but unlike Woody, he had a wife his own age, two teenage kids, and a big house in Marin. When the bottle of chardonnay was nearly empty, he confessed that he felt like he'd wasted his life. He said he wished he'd become a journalist or a high school history teacher instead. I'd always thought his cynicism was only black humor, but as it turned out his gloom ran far deeper.

"Don't end up where I am," he said. "It's not too late for you to do something different with your life."

Rays of late afternoon sunshine sparkled off pricey cars speeding by me as I merged onto Highway 280, the freeway that connected San Francisco with what is now Silicon Valley. I was on my way to my parents' house in Sunnyvale about 40 miles south planning to talk to them about the trip over Sunday dinner. Nestled in the hills beside 280 were the high-income towns of Hillsborough, Woodside, Portola Valley, and Los Altos Hills with their commanding views of San Francisco Bay. By contrast, Sunnyvale and the surrounding communities, were in the solidly middle-class flatlands of the valley, home to track houses, high performing public schools, and in later years the tech revolution that would change the world and my hometown forever.

A few decades earlier, Sunnyvale had largely been orchards, but those had been plowed over to make room for homes to house families like ours. The population of Sunnyvale went from less than ten thousand in 1950 to more than ninety-five thousand in 1970. Bye-bye orchards.

I got off the freeway and drove up Fremont Avenue past rows of single story homes that were as familiar to me as old friends, then parked in the driveway of the place I'd called home throughout my childhood.

I gazed at our ranch house, grey with white trim and a red front door. It was edged by flowerbeds that were as well kept as my dutiful parents. Though the place was nothing special, I knew it was pure luxury compared to the humble dwellings in Butte, Montana, where my parents had grown up. Back then it was a tough mining town referred to as the "Pittsburgh of the West." It drew immigrants like my grandfather, who toiled in the city's copper mines. My mom's grandfather had homesteaded a cattle ranch that my cousins still run an hour outside of Butte in a place called Wise River. It's breathtaking, truly one of the most beautiful places on earth and makes me want to sing "God Bless America" at the top of my lungs every time I visit. But my dear parents, growing up in hardscrabble Butte, with the mountain peaks off in the distance, had a life that was more like poverty with a view.

I'd put off the visit for weeks.

I always had their love, but I too rarely had something I craved: their approval.

I knew my parents believed the trip was a bad idea. Having lived through the Depression and a world war, they always lived frugally, as if either of those things could happen again. They re-soled shoes, clipped coupons, and could have originated the idea of re-use and repair. For them, the trip was the kind of thing that irresponsible people did, spending their savings on a lark instead of say, a down payment on a house. This was 1986, so only about 3% of Americans even had passports. No one my parents knew had traveled around the whole world.

Sunday dinner seemed like my best shot at warming them up to my crazy idea. Mom was always at her best entertaining. After I was born, she quit her teaching job and took understandable pride in her lovely dining room, the fine china, table linens, and artwork—possessions that gave her the symbols of the economic stability and status she so hungered for as a kid. Like Dad, she was the first in her family to graduate from college. At that point only about one in twenty American women had.

Dad exuded a stoic energy as he sat at the head of the Danish modern table he'd made for their first apartment. Like my mom's dad, his had only finished sixth grade. Dad's motto was luck comes to those who apply for it early, meaning you made your own luck by your own choices. Through sheer tenacity, he made it to grad school, then landed at NASA, working as an aeronautical engineer (aka a rocket scientist). In that Sunnyvale track house, my parents were living out their version of the Great American Dream, raising a quartet of tightly spaced children. And unlike me, my parents never took for granted the prosperity they'd worked so hard to achieve.

I picked at Mom's pot-roast and then downed a few big gulps of red wine. As I looked into the adjacent family room, I thought of all the fights that had taken place there during my teenage years.

As the oldest girl in our big extended family, by the time I hit high school, I'd had my fill of babysitting, laundry, cooking, dishes and housecleaning. I didn't know much at that point, but I was sure of one thing: I didn't want to be a housewife. I came of age during the 70s and the world was shifting under our feet. We fought about a range of things—from the length of my skirts to Watergate and everything in between. I managed to shatter argument by argument any semblance of their previously obedient daughter and become the family black sheep in the process.

I have a vivid memory of her in a sleeveless cotton shift ironing Dad's pale blue button-downs with a can of spray starch. She implored me to pay attention when she showed me how to press the shirt. I pushed back saying I didn't care. Mom became exasperated and said something like, "You'll never keep a husband if you don't know how to press his shirts properly."

I screamed back, "Then I never want to get married!"

I look back now and feel a stab in my heart thinking of how I must have hurt my mom's feelings as I rejected the person she worked so hard to become. And of course, at the time, I was far too self-absorbed to appreciate her toil that kept our family going.

When it came time to pick a college, that too had been a fight. I wanted to go to Berkeley. For my parents, a college education was not a path to enlightenment. It was a means to an end: a job that kept you off a factory floor or out of a mine shaft; soul-crushing jobs which paid too little and could lead to an early grave. They were two God-fearing, rock-ribbed Republicans. Understandably, lefty Berkeley scared the bejesus out of them. They were afraid the place would turn me into a radical feminist or worse yet, a Democrat, and were so relieved when I emerged four years later heading to a good job not a commune.

I sat there, glancing down the table at Dad, as Frank Sinatra's "Fly Me to the Moon" played on their stereo. Finally, Mom asked cheerfully, "So tell us about this trip you are planning to take."

"Well, Linda and I will leave around Memorial Day, first stop Spain, last stop Fiji. We'll be home in time for Christmas."

Dad looked concerned and asked, "How are you going to pay for this?"

"I've been saving money, just like you taught me. I won't go into debt. We have a budget." I was trying to sound more confident than I truly was.

Dad picked up on my angst and asked, "What if you run out of money?"

"We've got a cushion of 20 percent for unexpected expenses." (What I didn't tell him was this was also for purchasing stuff we'd want, like shoes in Rome, or silk scarves in Thailand.)

"What about your job?"

"So, I asked for a leave and the head of FCB said he'd like to bring me back." I conveniently left out the "no promises" part.

Dad crossed his arms over his chest. After a long pause, Mom changed the subject.

The day of our departure, Shelley gave me a beautiful leather journal to record highlights of our journey. I'd asked her to join Linda and me on the trip, but she had a new job and said she couldn't afford it. One of my big regrets is that I didn't twist her arm to come with us and drain my savings to make the offer impossible to turn down.

As we said our goodbyes at the airport, Dad hugged me tight. When he let go, he sputtered out the words, "Good luck," as his voice cracked. He was blinking fast and tears spilled over from his eyes. Dad was old-school, "real men don't cry." I had only seen him do so once before, when his father died. This was before there were cell phones, so they'd have no idea where I'd be for the next seven months.

2. ANOTHER WORLD

I think of luxury as a matter not of all the things you have,
but of all the things you can afford to do without.

—Pico Iyer

I stared at the ceiling illuminated only by the reflected light from a streetlamp outside the window. I glanced at the alarm clock. It was 3 a.m. and I was wide awake. Jet lag. We had landed in Madrid late the previous afternoon. Armed with no reservations and *Let's Go Europe* as our new bible, we'd found this simple hotel room for $20 a night. It had two twin beds with scratchy sheets and a musty smell like my grandmother's attic. I lay there wondering what the coming months would hold as waves of anxious excitement flowed through me. When morning light finally began to peek through the blinds, I fell back asleep.

Three months in Europe gave us an opportunity to see what could be called the highlights of Western Civilization. In Seville, we walked among the remains of Roman aqueducts and partied with a group of minor league bull fighters. In Florence, we looked into the steely eyes of David and up into the soaring ceiling of the Renaissance Duomo. In Rome, we toured the ruins of the ancient Forum, gazed at the splendor of Michelangelo's Sistine Chapel, and gorged on plates of cheap pasta while flirting with charming Italians. In Paris, we toured the Louvre and, in a day, saw centuries of art. In

Germany, we toured Dachau and glimpsed the remains of Nazi evil and returned to Munich for a cold stein of beer. We went behind the "iron curtain," past Checkpoint Charlie into East Berlin, the faces of resigned Germans as gloomy as the Stalinist architecture.

We took a student tour of what was then the Soviet Union. A bright American man who had a crush on Linda and was fluent in Russian became our own personal translator, so we largely bailed on the tour and set out on our own. When we got beyond the tourist attractions, the destitution compared to the US was shocking. We walked through a hospital in Moscow that looked like it was from the nineteenth century. We searched for Western publications but, right out of Orwell, all we found was *Pravda*—"truth" in Russian—which reported anything but that. I'd landed in Moscow, a good Berkeley liberal, thinking the image of the USSR as an "evil empire" was Reagan-era propaganda. I left feeling luckier than ever to be an American, believing Adam Smith truly was a genius and Karl Marx a fool.

After hiking through the Alps, we flew to Israel. In Jerusalem, we saw Jews praying at the Western Wall. In Jericho, Muslims bowed their heads to the ground worshipping Allah. In Bethlehem, Christians prayed where Jesus was born. We floated with other tourists in the Dead Sea and sweltered riding camels around the pyramids in Egypt before making our way by ferry to Athens. Next stop, Asia.

The two of us and our backpacks were squeezed like puzzle pieces into the tuk-tuk as it weaved its way through Delhi's chaotic traffic. It was a rickety three-wheeled contraption that felt like a cross between a beat-up golf cart and a tricycle. The narrow streets were dense with people, motorcycles, cars, buses, and trucks. Angry car horns, screeching brakes, and Bollywood music from boom boxes blared. The smells were as overpowering as the noise, a wild combination of sweat, incense, and manure. Gentle cows ambled among people and vehicles, giving clear meaning to the phrase "holy cow." A blaze of women in colorful saris seemed to be always in motion, while men enjoyed tea and laughter in tiny shops at the cusp of dark lanes.

We settled into a tiny inn in Old Delhi, where we saw few tourists. It was cheap and everything seemed to be coated in grime, including us. We stuck to our budget and did not escape to the comfort of posh hotels designed for rich foreigners, and so were immersed in the frenzied energy of this exotic city. One morning, two guys about our age that we met in a small restaurant asked if we wanted to join them for a ride around the city on their motorcycles. Because we were young and stupid, we said yes. Because we were lucky, we came back in one piece after a dizzying and death-defying day.

The next morning, we walked with a gritty stream of humanity to the main train station. Our plan was to travel into the countryside of Rajasthan. In front of the station was a multitude of thin, raggedy kids some with sunken eyes, clad in dirty, tattered clothing. Many of them were barefoot, which was concerning because sidewalks were often littered with garbage and the occasional broken bottle. I quickly emptied my pockets of change. It was surprising to see people pass them with casual indifference, as if they were a mural rather than children in need of help. When we got into the station it felt like the population of a small town was waiting on the platform with us.

Once we finally got on the train, a young Canadian woman with short black hair and a wide smile sat down next to Linda and struck up a conversation. She said she was an aid worker with a children's charity whose name I can't remember. I asked her about the kids we'd seen at the station. With a weary tone, she told us that India's malnutrition rate was about 50 percent, so a lot of Indians grow up to be "stunted," which she explained was the clinical term for small stature. I realized that this was why at a mere five foot six I towered over most women and a lot of men. She also told us that many of the kids we saw begging were likely street kids. This meant they were living without parents to look after them. She said that they sometimes sniffed glue since it gave them a high and took away their appetites but also could cause long-term brain damage.

When we got to the town where we planned to spend our first night, we checked into a guest house. Linda said she wanted to stay in to write in her journal, and I think needed a break from me, so I decided to go for a walk. It was a steamy afternoon yet the winding streets were clogged with vendors selling everything you could think of—fruit, rice, cooking oil, even haircuts. A wild symphony of familiar sounds: children's laughter, buzz saws, motor bikes firing, and the ubiquitous car horns filled the air. I passed a mound of burning trash that smelled like rubber. I finally got beyond the packed urban center and came upon a cropping of small homes that looked more like sheds, or what we'd call shacks. As I walked farther, it felt like I'd landed in some alternate universe where time had stood still a century or more ago, so the modern conveniences we mindlessly relied on didn't exist.

Gone was drinkable water flowing from a tap. In its place were women with jerry cans on their heads, carrying water they'd fetched presumably from streams or wells.

Gone were home toilets. Instead, I could spot individual men, and less often women, squatting in fields to do their business.

Gone were cars for every family, replaced by lines of pedestrians, adults on bikes, and entire families of four or five riding on a single motor scooter.

Gone were washers and dryers. Instead, I saw women near a stream beating clothes against rocks that would then be left out to dry on nearby bushes.

And, as we'd seen in Delhi, men were sometimes relaxing, while women seemed to be in continual motion tending fields, farm animals, and children.

Next we traveled to Nepal and trekked for several weeks in the Annapurna region in the west of the country. We camped part of the time, and on other nights stayed in simple tea houses for $5 a night.

We'd wake to the sound of roosters crowing and see fog blanketing the deep valleys. The stark, breathtaking beauty of the snowcapped Himalayas inspired awe in both of us.

At the same time, the dirt-floored homes, with no running water or electricity, the few schools, and kids that too often looked unwell with runny noses and hungry smiles made it impossible for me to forget how fortunate we were. One man told us that the brisk wind that beat against us and the omnipresent red, blue, and yellow prayer flags would take his prayers to heaven. I wondered if he prayed for more food, electricity, or healthcare for his family. From there we went on to what was then Burma, now Myanmar, and then to Thailand and Indonesia, where the poverty was in many ways like what we saw in India and Nepal.

I remembered a proverb I'd seen in Nepal: "What the eye doesn't see, the heart doesn't feel." I'd grown up a member of the great American middle class. I took all of it for granted—plenty of good food, free public education, safe drinking water, a flushing toilet—the way you do the air you breathe. Yet for the last few months we'd spent our days surrounded by people whose lives revolved mainly around getting those basic needs met. A profound realization finally seeped through to my dense, privileged soul: I had won a lottery I'd never entered or even thought of. I'd been born in the richest country on earth in the second half of the twentieth century.

At our last stop, Fiji, I contacted FCB and found out that my job was waiting for me when I got back. While I was relieved to not face unemployment, I had a gnawing sense of dread. The voice in my head that led me on the trip was now asking anxious relentless questions: *Is Ned right that I should do something else while I can? What would that even look like?*

———————+———————

If I were a braver, better person than I am, another Malala Yousafzai or Greta Thunberg, I would have walked away from advertising and joined the Peace Corps or some such outfit trying to change the world. But that's not what happened.

At least not yet.

3. LET'S GO CRAZY

San Francisco, Fall 1989

No matter how difficult and painful it may be,
nothing sounds as good to the soul as the truth.

—MARTHA BECK

I gave Beast one last belly rub as she purred, arched her back, and rolled over. I put on my banana-yellow Nikes, grabbed my Walkman, popped on the headphones, pushed play, and Madonna's "Material Girl" blasted me awake for my walk to FCB. As I locked the door to my apartment, I had no idea that I'd never spend another night there.

A little after five that afternoon, my desk chair jolted and I rolled forward. The floors, walls, and ceiling were shaking. It was like the whole building was being held in the palm of a giant with Parkinson's. I instinctively ran to the door of my office. I froze. I'd been told that door frames were the most secure place to be during an earthquake. I had no clue if that was true, but there I stood. I watched as a vase of wilting red roses that my boyfriend, Rich, sent for my birthday the week before slid from one side of my desk to the other. I could hear shrieks from the cubicles.

And then the violent tremor stopped.

While the lights were still on and there was no damage evident, I was spooked and decided to head home. I walked outside and right then my friend Beth from FCB pulled up and asked if I wanted a ride. I jumped into her black BMW as we made our way up Bay Street heading toward my place in the Marina.

When we got to the top of the hill overlooking the Golden Gate Bridge, Beth gasped. Off in the distance we could see bright orange and red flames that gave way to billowing plumes of smoke that towered over the buildings in the Marina near my apartment. About six blocks from my place, the traffic that had been inching along came to a stop. I told Beth goodbye and got out of the car.

I started walking fast. The streets were chaotic as frantic people like me rushed to get home as sirens blared. Fire trucks heading toward the fire zoomed by.

Two blocks from my place, I came across what had been a three-story building on a corner. It was now collapsed into a frightening one-story heap in the street.

I started sprinting. A gray cloud was enveloping most of the sky and my lungs filled with the smoky air.

I could see Divisadero Street right ahead of me. It was a main drag that ran from Pacific Heights through the Marina and dead-ended into the Bay. It was half a block from my building. But as I got to the corner, I stopped short. The massive inferno was devouring a large three-story apartment building in the next block. I'd never seen a fire that massive, except in movies. A giant fire hose was pointed at the building to try to douse the rising flames. It was held by a line of people standing several feet apart, their faces illuminated by the blaze. As I gazed down the line, I realized this human chain was bringing water from the Bay. So far, the fire was a few buildings away from mine.

When I got to my apartment building, I bounded up the stairs and opened my door. I flipped the light switch, but there was no power. Several pictures had come off the walls in the hallway leading to the living room and shards of glass were all over the floor. Out the living room window, flames were firing into the twilight sky in the next block. I heard a faint meow coming from the bedroom and found Beast under the bed, trembling. I could smell gas and realized I should get out of there. I grabbed Beast's carrier from the closet and stuck her inside. What if the place burned down? What was irreplaceable? *THINK!* I pulled a suitcase from the closet and stuffed photo albums, my jewelry box, my passport, and a scrapbook inside. I snapped up Beast's carrier and darted out the door.

I walked up Divisadero in the opposite direction of the fire. Eventually, a German woman, who I'd never see again, pulled up in an old Volvo station wagon. She asked me if I needed a ride, and then drove me to Beth's place near Golden Gate Park, where Beth greeted me with a big hug and a glass of wine.

I called my parents and learned that everyone in our family was fine. I tried to reach Rich who was in New York for a commercial shoot. I was surprised he didn't pick up, given the time difference; it was close to midnight in New York. I left a message at reception and gave him Beth's number. My last thoughts before I drifted off into a fitful night of sleep on her couch: did my building burn to the ground? And where was Rich?

———————————⁂———————————

Soon after I returned from our trip, Joe Cocker's "You Can Leave Your Hat On" was blaring at an FCB party when Rich asked me to dance. He was tall, with gentle green eyes, and an easy smile. The attraction was overpowering and I fell hard and fast. Any fleeting dreams of saving the world's poor didn't stand a chance. Over the coming weeks we became inseparable. He was a creative director and a rising star at the agency. With the soul of an artist, he quoted the verses of Walt Whitman and the ballads of Bruce Springsteen in equal measure, and knew more about design, architecture, and fashion than I ever would. Cliché, I know, but he drove a Porsche. A not-small part of me liked being on his arm. I think I believed I somehow looked better when I was next to him, like you might feel wearing anything by Prada that you can neither afford nor quite pull off. I looked up to him and my mantra soon became, "I don't know, what do you think?"—seven words that seemed like an aphrodisiac to him. He thought I was foolish to even consider leaving advertising— "people would kill for your job." And, so of course, I listened to him. My idealistic aspirations surrendered without a fight.

As milky morning light started to peek through the living room window, Beth came bounding in. She said she'd just heard on NPR that the fire in the Marina had been contained, with only the one massive building near mine destroyed by the fire. My first feeling was relief. My home hadn't burned to the ground. My second feeling was a sinking sadness when I realized Rich hadn't called. That afternoon, I got a belated unsatisfying voicemail: "Sorry I missed your call last night. I had told the front desk to hold all calls so I could sleep and had a 7 a.m. start for the shoot today. . ."

The National Guard let me and other Marina residents into our apartments, but for only ten minutes. A guy from FEMA took me through the alley to the back of my building and showed me that it had come off the foundation and was leaning on the building next to it. He had no idea how long it would be before I could get the rest of my things, but he guessed it would be a few weeks at least.

Beast and I moved into a furnished corporate apartment, paid for by FCB, since I had the unfortunate distinction of being the employee hurt most by the earthquake. My new home smelled of Pine-Sol and was a bland, modern one-bedroom—everything the color of sandpaper. It came complete with silk plants, shag carpeting, and pictures of San Francisco landmarks, in case you forgot where you were. It was like living in a Macy's showroom.

Rich visited the next weekend but got in late on Friday and left early on Sunday. We talked every few days, but the calls had a pinched quality to them. I was a needy mess. What I wanted was support. What I got too often when I called his hotel was, "I'm sorry, there's no answer. May I take a message?"

Before the quake, I had been such a good sleeper that I could have fallen asleep in an MRI machine. Now, I found myself wide awake in the middle of the night, staring at the popcorn ceiling telling myself it was the dismal apartment that was screwing up my sleep. One night I dreamt that Rich was walking out of the movie theater in the Marina and I ran toward him. As I got closer, he gave me a blank stare like he didn't know me and kept walking. You don't need to be Carl Jung to analyze that one.

I was not, as they say, thriving. The lack of sleep made me sluggish and cranky. I had the energy and appetite of a chemo patient. I'd grown so absent-minded, I did bone-headed things like forgetting my purse in a restaurant, miraculously turned in by an anonymous saint. Another day I went to work with mismatched shoes—one black, one navy, which is what I got for being so unimaginative that I had the same pump in different colors.

I decided to spend a night at Rich's place even though he was still in New York. During the last two years we rarely spent a night apart when we were both in town, so his place felt more like home than the Macy's showroom. Maybe there I'd finally be able to get a good night of sleep. Like Rich, his apartment was tasteful and curated: old Persian rugs, neatly organized bookshelves, Art Deco pieces mingled with eighteenth century antiques.

But right after I arrived, the phone rang. Before I could get to it, the call went to the answering machine. I could hear the voice of Julia, a New York college friend of Rich's whom I'd met once. She was an interior decorator and willowy, though not beautiful, or at least that's what I told myself. Her tone was warm and a tad too friendly when she said, "I've left something for you and I think you'll like it a lot," then she giggled and hung up. *Wait! Left what for him? Where?*

My mind was reeling. I was trying to make excuses for the message. None of them worked. I called my friend Diane, who was like the big sister I never had, street smart, strong-willed and always supportive. I played the message for her. She agreed it sounded suspect and suggested I ask Rich about it. I called him, and he insisted that Julia was "just a friend." He said I was burnt out from all that had happened and was misreading the situation. That night as I was brushing my teeth, the face that stared back at me in the bathroom mirror had the sunken eyes of a refugee and skin as ashen as paper.

I didn't know the term "gaslighting" at the time, but it now seems to fit. *I'm not staying in NYC and cheating on you; you're exhausted and anxious...* The thing with gaslighting is it can make you nuts. And not the Prince "Let's Go Crazy" kind, the losing-your-mind variety. I had two opposing thoughts in my head and only one of them could be true. I so wanted to believe that Rich was not being unfaithful to me. But I was crumbling under the weight of the truth I was denying.

And that's where the therapist came in.

Diane was a big fan of therapy. Her childhood home sounded like a ton of fun for the adults in her neighborhood. There were lots of martini-fueled bashes with Tony Bennett and Nat King Cole crooning on 45s. Until her dad killed himself. I admired her courage in facing pain I can't begin to fathom. Me, not so much. Lois and Bob were dependable Presbyterians. My dad's drink of choice was skim milk. They were both long on "get back on the horse" perseverance and short on emotional introspection. Our tribe's approach to problems: if sheer determination didn't work, bury your troubles in denial. If all that failed, blame the problem on someone else. But, at this point, the "stiff upper lip" approach wasn't getting me anywhere.

The next week, I got to the therapist's office and plopped myself down in a waiting room. I was nervous about going and relieved to be the only person there. I was filled with shame. *Why couldn't I solve my own problems?*

At 5:30 p.m. the door opened, and the therapist, Melody, walked over to introduce herself. She was forty-something with confidently graying shoulder-length hair and round tortoise glasses. As I sat down on the sofa in her office, I started to relax. In a kind and caring tone, she asked me why I had come to see her. I stayed calm for the first few minutes like a journalist reporting the facts about the earthquake, the fire, and my lousy sleep. But when I began to tell her about the phone message, my voice cracked. My words started to battle with jagged sobs and I reached for the tissues.

Melody listened with great patience as I described all this turmoil and my refusal to accept the obvious. As I blathered and wept, I wondered if Melody thought I was a lunatic. Though my thrifty self-questioned if it was worth $100 to pay a stranger to essentially watch me fall apart, we agreed to meet again the next week.

———————————

Amid this darkness, Rich suggested we get away to sunny Mexico for Thanksgiving so I could rest. After all, this was entirely about me being a depleted head case. I consented, but even with mariachi music and salty margaritas, it was a gloomy week. There weren't raised voices or angry outbursts. It was worse. The feeling I had was sadness, like there was something dead and rotting in the room. I was withdrawn, unlike my normal boundaryless-rescue-dog self. Something fundamental had shifted in me. A steel wall was shielding my heart from this person who had already broken it.

When we got back, I lugged my wounded self into Melody's office where I cried less and talked more. I had started off casting myself the victim, filled with righteous anger, like I'd been hit by a drunk driver. But as Melody dug deeper another truth became clear. I was trying so hard to be the person Rich wanted me to be —caring about things like fashion and interior design—that I'd contorted myself into somebody I wasn't. The charade had eaten away at my self-confidence. Worst of all, I'd lost myself focusing on him. And who could blame Rich for wanting to be with Julia who wasn't pretending to be someone she wasn't. The brutal truth was the relationship with Rich also enabled me to escape from the far more troubling worry that like Ned, I was wasting my life in advertising.

No surprise here, we broke up.

The earthquake had cracked my world wide open, and it was now in pieces. In a few short months I had lost my home and a relationship that had provided the scaffolding for my career. My future was rushing toward me even if I had no idea what it looked like.

4. JUMPING OFF

Some women choose to follow men, and some women
choose to follow their dreams. If you're wondering
which way to go, remember your career will never wake up
and tell you that it doesn't love you anymore.

—LADY GAGA

I walked into the Career Center on the UC Berkeley campus. I sat in the reception area mulling over the dreary conclusion that I'd spent the last decade basically devoted to selling stuff I didn't give a fig about—cruises, breakfast cereals, jeans, fast food, and showerheads. I realized more promotions would mean more clients, like winning a pie-eating contest and being given a pie. All for a fat paycheck and nights at five-star hotels. But what would I do if I left advertising? That was the open question.

I tried to think of people I admired who'd jumped off one ladder and gotten on another; I didn't have to look farther than my siblings. My brother Eric had done something similar. The ceiling of his childhood bedroom was barely visible, because hanging from it were numerous planes that he'd built from models. He graduated from Berkeley with a degree in economics. I was awed when he quit a finance job to follow his heart becoming a US naval aviator, and was now a senior United pilot. My sister Shelley had ditched her career in retail, gotten a graduate degree in Chemistry, and decided to teach at a public school in a low-income community. While I had no talent for science and wouldn't make a good pilot, I thought that maybe the guy I was about to see could help me find my way.

Finally, the receptionist said I could go back to the last office on the left, belonging to Dr. Herman Weissman. Nearing retirement, Weissman bore a passing resemblance to Paul Giamatti and exuded a calm warmth as he greeted me. The office was cluttered with over-stuffed bookshelves and an old wood desk too large for the space. I sat down on an upholstered chair the color of mud that had seen better days.

Peering over his reading glasses, he listened with great patience as I droned on about my fear that I was wasting my life in advertising, my concern about the poverty I'd seen in Asia, and my confusion about what I should do next. When I paused, he sighed and quoted Kurt Vonnegut: "A step backward, after making a wrong turn, is a step in the right direction." Very Zen. This was Berkeley . . .

Then he said, "I think your skill set could be very useful in the nonprofit or public sector, to help address the poverty you saw in Asia that still seems to haunt you." While I was not sure he was right, I appreciated his encouragement.

"I don't know much about either nonprofits or government," I said, wondering what a career in either would even look like.

"Have you considered going back to graduate school? A program in public policy could be a powerful way to redirect your career."

I had only a vague sense of what a public policy program entailed, but he lent me catalogs from a couple graduate schools and suggested I reach out to a few others. I called the schools and asked them to send me admission packages. When the glossy things arrived in the mail, I savored their profiles of grads that now ran major nonprofits and lead government agencies focused on problems like feeding the hungry or educating the illiterate. I took a week off and visited a handful of graduate schools and came away exhilarated by the potential paths each offered. In early January, I mailed off the applications and waited. What did I have to lose? I still had a job if I didn't get in.

A few weeks later, I had a work trip to Los Angeles with my new boss, who I considered a bit of an empty suit and was nothing like Ned. He was bald, fit and always impeccably groomed. It was rumored that the reading glasses he wore occasionally in client meetings were fake, a prop to make him appear smarter than he was. After a full day at a production company, we went to dinner in a posh restaurant at the Four Seasons Hotel with a trying client who wanted to adjourn to the bar. Boss and I said we needed to call it a night . . . early flights home tomorrow . . . yada yada yada.

In the elevator, Boss asked me if I wanted to have a nightcap in his suite. I didn't really want to, but instead I found myself saying, "Sure." While I'd been hit on a couple times before by drunken clients at agency dinners, I'd known Boss and his wife for years, so this seemed safe.

But once the door shut, Boss pulled me close to him. As the space between us disappeared, he attempted a sloppy French kiss that tasted like scotch. I gently brushed him aside with a nervous "you're so silly" laugh. I said I was exhausted and left. Amazing that during this encounter, my first worry was about wounding his ego.

Those instincts proved right, because in subsequent weeks I found myself getting shut out of key strategy sessions and client dinners. Maybe he was embarrassed, but this triggered basic passive aggressive behavior from me. I would come to the office, read my mail, and then tell Barbara that I was going to a meeting. She'd ask where, and I'd say downstairs. Then I'd get in the elevator and go to Il Fornaio, a restaurant off the lobby. I'd sit at the coffee bar and read *The New York Times* front to back for an hour or two. I'd focus on the articles about all things international, soaking up detail about the world I hoped to enter. I was quietly quitting; there but not really there, starting to torch a bridge I hoped would soon be in my rear-view mirror. But I was also nervous. *What will I do if this grad school idea doesn't pan out?*

By mid-March, my purgatory was getting old. One night, I was rushing to meet Diane for dinner. On the way, I stopped at my place, unlocked the mailbox and saw two envelopes from schools I'd applied to: one big and thick and the other a thin business-class envelope. I grabbed both and headed to the restaurant.

I spotted Diane and nearly ran over. I said, "Look what I've got," as I waved the envelopes, then slapped them down on the table and sat down.

Diane said, "Oh my god, the big one is from Harvard! Open it! Big usually means acceptance."

After I skimmed the cover letter to myself, I nearly yelled "You're right!" and I handed it to her.

Diane picked up the skinny envelope and said, "The other one's from Princeton. Aren't you going to open it?"

"I will. But I know it's going to be a rejection because it's only a letter."

"Who cares? You got into Harvard!"

So, I opened the letter. I got to the second paragraph, and I shrieked—a blood curdling scream. Diane said later that she thought I'd bitten into glass.

"What's wrong?"

I stammered, my heart soaring, "Nothing... I got in and I've got a fellowship covering tuition plus a stipend."

If I ever had any doubt that luck was real, this annihilated it.

The next day, I told Ned I was history. He seemed nearly as happy as I was.

I wrote a one-line memo giving my creepy boss two weeks' notice and tried to not look back.

5. AN EDUCATION

Nothing really wonderful can happen to you
unless you take uncomfortable risks.

—SCOTT GALLOWAY

O ut the plane's narrow window I could see the sun rising over the Indian Ocean. The faint outline of the turquoise water and a white beach nestled alongside the city became visible. As our plane descended, the pilot announced we'd soon be landing in Dar es Salaam.

My first year at Princeton, the field of International Development captured my imagination. As the name suggests, it is the study of the human and economic development of countries that helped me understand the poverty I'd seen in Asia. I decided to spend the summer between my first and second year working for the United States Agency for International Development (USAID) in Tanzania. I'd be managing a social marketing program to push condoms to help prevent the spread of HIV/AIDS which was ravaging the continent. At that point, there was no treatment, so HIV/AIDS was a death sentence. Condoms were the only thing, other than abstinence, to prevent it. I was excited about the summer ahead, hoping to put some of my Madison Avenue skills to good use.

After making it through customs, I went outside to look for a driver from USAID. I spotted a young man wearing a suit too big for his stick figure frame, holding a sign labeled "Kate Grand." Groggy from two long plane flights, "grand" was not at all how I felt. He introduced himself as Jonathan. I was glad he wasn't chatty because I wanted to drink in my new surroundings. I'd lucked out and gotten free housing. I'd be house-sitting for one of the staff at USAID who was on home leave, sharing the place with another woman, an intern for the World Bank named Erin.

I'd learned in one of my classes that Tanzania had remained peaceful since gaining its independence in the early '60s. But they'd endured a failed socialist experiment and thirty years later the economy was in worse shape than ever.

As our car headed away from the airport, I saw a steady line of people walking on the side of the road toward what I assume was town, with a few men here and there on bikes. People were also setting up shop for the day at wooden stalls with tin roofs on the edge of the road as skinny dogs roamed nearby. On the sides of low-rise buildings handwritten billboards hawked things like phone calls, laundry soap, and Coke.

At a stoplight, a boy not much taller than the window of the car pleaded with me to buy his gum, candy, or chips. I pulled out some schilling and bought a pack of no-name spearmint gum. Soon we were driving through what I assumed was the downtown commercial area with office buildings, all still closed. The facades looked dilapidated. Storefronts were tattered and dingy, in need of paint and a good handyman. It felt like a neighborhood in San Francisco that had been untended for decades—like out of a sci-fi thriller.

Soon, the beautiful beach that I'd seen from the plane came into view on my right. On my left, the storefronts gave way to scruffy green hedges that obscured large houses. After a short while, the car stopped at an open gate and a guard with a wooden club sitting at a small booth waved us in. We drove slowly toward a massive two-story white block made of what I assumed was concrete with a large lawn surrounding it. It had all the charm of a low-security prison.

When I knocked on the front door, Erin answered in her robe and introduced herself with a smile. She was tall and lanky, like a basketball player, with shoulder-length red hair. As I walked in, I was struck by the enormity of the living room. After some small talk about my flight, Erin offered to show me around.

First stop, the kitchen, where she introduced me to our cook and housekeeper, Sarah. *Really? We have a servant.* When we got out of earshot, Erin assured me that Sarah's salary was picked up by the family that was away for the summer. I was shocked that she made only $50 a month. Then Erin took me upstairs to my bedroom where a giant mosquito net was suspended above the bed. On the landing there was an imposing metal floor-to-ceiling gate. If closed, it would have blocked entrance to the floor.

"What's with the gate?" I asked.

"It's a Mau Mau Gate."

"A what?"

"It's left over from the Mau Mau rebellion in Kenya decades ago, back when it was a British colony. The gate is so you can lock yourself in here if there was, you know, an uprising. Or more likely these days, a simple break-in. That's what the guard downstairs is for, too. Also, above the bed, there's a button you can press, and armed security will show up if someone gets past the guard."

I said, "The beach looks great. I want to go for a short run."

"Yeah, that's not a good idea." Erin pointed to a big bandage on her knee. "I tried that last week when I got here. I went for a run on the road near the beach. A guy came out of nowhere, shoved me to the ground and yanked off my shoes." At this point she also raised her elbow to show me another bandage.

"Your shoes! That must have been so scary," I said, stunned.

"Beginner's mistake. I won't let it happen again."

"I thought this was supposed to be a safe neighborhood. Doesn't the ambassador live near here?"

"Yep, he lives a couple houses down." She pointed across the tall hedge at the side of the house. "I've heard when he goes for a run, he takes a Marine guard with him."

"Bummer. I was thinking it would be great to be near the beach, but now you're saying it's not safe. Then what do you do for fun?"

"So far, I've been spending my free time at the American Club. They have a pool and a bar. They make a decent burger. It's not bad."

And so began my summer in Tanzania.

On my first day of work, I went out for a short walk after lunch to see downtown. As I came to the corner, ready to cross the street, I noticed a little boy sitting down in the shadow next to a bank building. He looked to be about five or six with shorn hair, large expressive eyes, and smooth skin the color of milk chocolate. As I waited for the traffic to pass, I smiled at him, and he said "Jambo (hello) Miss, what's your name?" From then on, I was "Miss Kate." I asked him his name and he said, "Joseph, like in the Bible, but people call me Joe."

I gazed down at him and noticed that his shriveled legs were curled under him. My guess was he'd been a victim of polio—something eradicated decades ago in the US, but still inflicting its crippling lifelong injuries on too many kids in Africa. He was sitting on a board about the dimension of a kitchen towel that had small wheels the size of golf balls underneath it at the corners. It looked like the thing my dad put under his back so he could roll beneath our station wagon to do repairs. As Joe inched toward me to talk further, I realized that he used his board with wheels as a makeshift wheelchair. We chatted about the warm weather and as we did, a lump in my throat emerged and my eyes welled with tears. His welcoming smile and playful eyes were such a jarring contrast from his disabled body. I did my best to say a cheerful goodbye and I put some change into the little bowl he had in front of him.

As in Asia, poverty was here every day before my eyes. With AIDS killing adults in the prime of their lives, kids were often left destitute, cared for by stretched-too-thin grandparents. I heard it referred to as "slim disease" because as it progressed, those infected grew increasingly emaciated.

I'd spent my entire professional life in a fast-moving, dog-eat-dog business. Normal work hours were only suggested, since you did whatever you needed to do to get a job done or you were out. The USAID Mission had a different ethos. People arrived promptly at 7:30 a.m. and were out by 4:00 p.m. By 4:05, you could have rolled a bowling ball down the main hall and you wouldn't have hit a soul.

I got to work to try to strengthen their condom marketing program. I remember holding up a cracked cardboard package containing two condoms with crooked printing proclaiming the Tumaini brand, "trust" in Swahili. The side of the package split apart when I tried to open it. How was anyone supposed to have confidence the condom would prevent them from acquiring a deadly virus when the package crumbled before you could get it open? And yet, even getting the necessary approvals to produce new packaging was a bridge too far that summer.

Worse than this, a large shipment of condoms paid for by US taxpayers was sitting in the port. There are provisions in US law that require that goods donated by USAID must be produced in the US. So, the condoms had been shipped all the way to Tanzania from the manufacturer back home. The Tanzanian government was demanding that duty be paid on them. The US government couldn't and wouldn't do that. A stalemate had developed. The condoms sat there. Prolonged heat and rubber are not a winning combination. There was talk that they were likely rotting and would have to be destroyed. And those condoms cost multiples more than what they would have if sourced in Asia. Welcome to the foreign aid bureaucracy!

I began to wonder if the US government's basic approach to foreign aid was sound. It directed a lot of aid through the local government, which seemed like a good idea on the surface. I kept asking myself, did US foreign aid shore up governments like the one in Tanzania, making it less accountable to their own citizens? Can these programs be reformed to make them work better? Is there a better way to help alleviate poverty than through big government programs like the one I was working on?

On the Fourth of July, the ambassador had a big barbecue at his residence, a palatial home designed for huge bashes like this one. There were American flags all over the place, hot dogs on the grills, and white-jacketed waiters serving drinks. I struck up a conversation with a gray-haired American with world-weary energy who said he was a former journalist. He'd fallen in love with a Tanzanian woman and decided to retire there. His tanned, deeply lined face reminded me of an old baseball mitt, and after a few beers, he let loose with what he thought of foreign aid and the party all around us.

"This is a joke. You know that, right? Most of the money spent by US taxpayers on foreign aid either stays in the US or goes to pay for parties like this and the house you are staying in. Look around: other than a few government officials, what do you see? Mostly white people. Notice that most of the Africans here are waiting on us?"

That wasn't entirely true. There were a number of Tanzanians at the party, but I got his bigger point. He asked about my background. When I told him what I used to do, he said that advertising was an honest way to make a living because you weren't pretending to be saving the world.

I wanted to debate him, but I wasn't sure who he knew, so, I kept my mouth shut.

But the conversation left me with a disquieted feeling, that he might be right, both about foreign aid and about advertising.

That summer I was lonely, stuck in emotional solitary confinement. This was before cell phones or the internet. Calls to the US cost $10 a minute, so long calls with my boyfriend from Princeton or friends and family in California were cost prohibitive. I hungered for news and would buy a "pre-read" *New York Times* sold by enterprising young men downtown. The papers had likely been left on arriving plane flights since at that point you couldn't buy *The Times* in Dar.

Erin, my housemate, left after a few weeks to take a job in Ethiopia. So, it was just me in that monstrous house. Sarah lived in a shack behind it that depressed me because it looked like a mini ghetto. She only spoke to me when I spoke to her and she seemed to know only a little English. I tried to learn a bit of Swahili, but that proved hopeless since I'm pathetic at learning new languages.

On weekends, I would go to the American Club and sit outside by the pool under a giant umbrella to keep my skin that's the color of Wonder Bread out of the intense equatorial sun. I stayed out there because I found the club tedious. The conversations gravitated toward common denominator topics. The Major League Baseball standings. The upcoming US presidential election. The merits of Steven Spielberg films. The rising cost of housing in DC. It was like I was in a country club in suburban Maryland, but with cheaper beer and better service.

The other popular topic was Dar's crime. Everyone seemed to have an experience to share like Erin's. The troubling part was the tendency of too many Americans to judge Africans harshly. This was, after all, The American Club. We were doing things right, whereas the Africans were acting irresponsibly or worse.

The summer wasn't without a couple of adventures. I made it to a game park one weekend and saw elephants in the wild. Another weekend, I went out to Zanzibar, an island off the coast, with white-washed buildings, curving streets, and water the color of Windex. The natural beauty aligned with my dreams about Africa, but my hopes for my work life went unrealized.

When I landed in Dar, I had aspirations of working hard with dedicated people at USAID to help stop the spread of AIDS. What I found were well-meaning public servants, not warriors. They worked their eight hours and went home to their big, subsidized houses with generous pensions to look forward to after twenty years as a foreign service officer. They seemed resigned to the status quo. In fairness to them, pushing forward a mammoth federal bureaucracy that was encased in decades of red tape was likely a fool's errand. While I didn't miss thinking about how to make ads, I did miss the "jump how high" energy and the adrenaline rushes from working hard with a bunch of creative, driven people. Had I made a mistake leaving that all behind?

I also had a romantic notion of working alongside Africans. That proved to be a fantasy too, because most of the Africans I met were in the service of well-off foreigners like me. There weren't many single white women on the streets at that point. While I'd traveled in the Middle East and Asia with Linda, I had never been to a place where I stood out so much. I heard some version of the phrase "Jambo rich girl" so many times I lost count. And, of course, I was wealthy by comparison. I might have thought of myself as a cash strapped grad student, but the reality was different. My monthly stipend was more than the average yearly income of a Tanzanian, only $500.

I hated feeling like a wealthy outsider. But, let's face it, that's exactly what I was: living in that massive house, protected 24–7 by a guard, with a servant. And the house that looked a bit like a prison started to feel like one. I had no unmet material needs, while most Tanzanians struggled to afford what I'd gotten that summer largely for free. I had a brewing sense of shame and guilt because I knew I was not helping these people in any meaningful way.

I never got used to seeing Joseph. He looked healthier than other kids I'd seen. I found out that he lived with his grandmother who sold fruit in the market and that his parents had "gone away." I didn't know what that meant and I was afraid to ask. Had they died of AIDS like so many young adults in Africa? Even with his bright smile, I'd walk away feeling gloomy, cursing the cruel fate of this poor kid likely destined to beg on the streets the rest of his life.

It was becoming very clear I was never going to be another Mother Teresa.

When I got back to Princeton, I reached out to someone who'd impressed me at an HIV/AIDS conference that spring, Dr. Seth Berkley. He worked in the health division at the Rockefeller Foundation in New York, exuded brilliant, irrepressible energy and looked a bit like Art Garfunkel. Seth was launching something called the International AIDS Alliance to put small grants in the hands of community groups where they could do the most good. I wrote to him and said I'd work for him one day a week for free as an intern and he took me on.

I was set to graduate after the next fall, so I started to look in our nation's capital for where there were jobs for new MPAs (Master of Public Affairs). I spent a week in October seeing pretty much anyone who would talk to me at the World Bank, NBC News, various NGOs, and Capitol Hill. The last meeting of the week gave me my first big break.

6. IMPOSTER

*The best way to accelerate growth is
to embrace, seek, and amplify discomfort.*

—Adam Grant

After I cleared security at Rayburn House Office Building, one of the massive structures lining Capitol Hill, a receptionist walked me back to meet an alum whose title was "Professional Staff Member, House Foreign Affairs Committee." I had no clear idea what he did, and *Professional* in front of *Staff Member* seemed redundant. Do they have unprofessional staff? His office was a glorified cubicle with a small couch in a warren of similar digs.

As I sat down, I noticed a clock on the far wall with small flashing lights beneath it that was visible to all the cubes. I asked about it, and he explained that the lights indicated when the House was in session and flashed when votes were being cast. The place bustled with energy that reminded me of FCB, but here the focus was how to wisely exert US power. He told me he advised members of the Foreign Affairs Committee on defense spending, something I guess I should have cared about, but didn't. But, as he talked about his work researching policy issues, helping craft legislation, traveling to conferences and military bases for fact-finding, with a "no two days are the same" schedule, he got my attention. This varied workday seemed like a good fit for my attention-challenged self.

He asked what I wanted to do. When I described my interest in foreign aid and global poverty, he called over the wall to his colleague.

"Hey, have we filled Carol's job?"

"No, not yet," came back.

Turned out, Carol had had responsibility for USAID oversight and had left to take a job at the World Bank. Within a couple weeks I was back in DC for a set of interviews for her former position, including one with the committee's chair, Congressman Lee Hamilton. That interview was cut short when a phone call interrupted it. President Bill Clinton was on the line.

I got the job and arrived in Washington during January's winter gloom. At that point, I had only a vague notion of how Congress worked, informed in part by grad school classes on political theory and by the old movie *Mr. Smith Goes to Washington* where the stakes were high and a principled hero saved the day. In other words, I was a complete political novice. Most people I met on the Hill worked on political campaigns and for members of Congress, often for years. They were at home with the "ends justify the means" world I'd just entered. I had a growing case of imposter syndrome.

One of our main goals that year was to try to rewrite the Foreign Assistance Act of 1961, the legislation that had created USAID which I'd seen in action in Tanzania. The Act was over one thousand pages long, thicker than a couple of Russian novels, but I was up for this challenge—or at least thought I was.

Within a month after arriving, I got an invitation to speak on a panel on foreign aid reform. The audience would be about six-hundred dedicated nonprofit people working on international development issues. I wrote my talk, ran it by my boss, and practiced it at home. I said the Foreign Assistance Act was outdated, larded with red tape, and we were going to fix it. I held up a fat binder as a prop. The idealists in the crowd clapped enthusiastically. Then a senior staffer from the Senate took the podium. In the polite tone and measured terms of such events, she said that what I'd proposed was about as likely to happen as Congress reinstating Prohibition. She had a great reputation, and I clearly didn't know what I was talking about. And she was a liberal Democrat! My optimism was not only misplaced; it was delusional. I wanted to disappear. (She was right: that piece of legislation that advances US interests and had been written at the height of the Cold War—think John F. Kennedy and the Cuban Missile Crisis—largely still guides US foreign aid programs.)

A major international event that year was the much-anticipated UN Conference on Population and Development, the ICPD for short. This was the biggest conference ever held in which the world would agree on a plan for tackling global poverty. Women's reproductive rights, particularly both access to contraception and control over planning and spacing of children, was a central issue. I believed the committee should hold a hearing. Some of my colleagues weren't so sure that was needed, but Congressman Hamilton consented and I got to work developing an agenda of speakers.

I was thrilled, thinking the hearing would be a great way to demonstrate the centrality of reproductive rights to global development. While Congressman Hamilton stayed in the chair for the entire session, out of the forty-five members of the committee, there were rarely more than a couple members in the room during the testimonies. The sparse audience was comprised almost entirely of staffers from the organizations speaking. There wasn't much discussion either. You know the expression "preaching to the choir." In this case, it felt like a church service with no one in the pews. I was astounded and sad that the rights of the half of humanity—women—that take 100 percent of the risks to bring all of us into the world was not a bigger draw.

That summer a team of us Hill staffers took off for a whirlwind Co-Del to Africa, ahead of my travel to the ICPD in Cairo in September. We started with Ethiopia, where I made that memorable visit to the Addis Ababa Fistula Hospital and met my first fistula patient, Hanna. After Ethiopia, we would head to Kenya, then to what was then Zaire and is now Democratic Republic of Congo (DRC), Mozambique, and South Africa.

———————————·———————————

The roar of the airplane's engines was all I could hear. I was standing on the tarmac of an airfield in Entebbe, Uganda with my five Co-Del colleagues. Soon we were ascending a large wide ramp up the back into the hull of a giant C-130 Hercules cargo plane. The thing was like a warehouse with wings, loaded with grain, blankets, and cooking oil. The plane was destined for the refugee camps outside of Goma, Zaire, where at least a million Hutu refugees had fled neighboring Rwanda when the Tutsis retook power. In the months before, the Hutus had committed genocide, slaughtering an estimated eight-hundred-thousand Tutsis. While the US and other nations were far too slow to act to stop the carnage, US aid was now focused on helping the Hutu refugees. We sat on narrow jump seats and finally put on headphones to protect our ears.

After we landed, we traveled by jeep along a narrow valley where the Hutus were making camp. In the distance, a volcano at the base of neighboring Lake Kivu puffed smoke into the air. Everything and everybody—men, women, children, livestock, makeshift tents—seemed to be coated in gray dust. The looks on the faces of the refugees were blank, with the thousand-mile stares you'd expect from people who had witnessed or even participated in their neighbors being hacked to death with machetes. If there was hell on earth, I was pretty sure this was it.

The scale of the humanitarian operation to bring supplies to nearly a million displaced people was breathtaking. It gave me increased appreciation for what US power could do when directed in the right place; in this case helping feed and house multitudes of hungry, traumatized people. As for us, we lived on MREs, the meals-ready-to-eat that feed US military personnel in combat or emergency situations. We picked up a couple of French MREs and, no kidding, they came with plastic cups of red wine.

I spent an afternoon in a small camp for about fifty children ranging in age from toddlers to middle-school-age kids that had been separated from their parents or relatives. It was run by a collection of nonprofits like CARE and Save the Children. The kids were largely quiet, with their emotional neediness and trauma expressed in their silence. I held small kids, brushed hair, and fed them snacks. The intensity of my feelings surprised me. Growing up I'd had my fill of babysitting, but here I found my soul ignited with compassion for these kids. Was my biological clock finally ticking?

From there, we went to South Africa, to Mozambique, and then to Cairo to attend the UN Conference. It proved to be a dizzying conclave, with delegates hammering out a detailed plan of action to address poverty. Name drop alert: I got to meet Ted Turner and Jane Fonda. Turner was a big supporter of the UN and, with Jane as his inspiration, would donate a cool billion dollars to found the UN Foundation. It was clear he was passionate about the environment, women's empowerment, and Jane. Congresswoman Connie Morella invited me to spend a day with them visiting family planning clinics in Cairo, along with Jane and her daughter, Vanessa. Fonda displayed commendable humility; I don't think the people we met at those clinics had any idea that they were guiding around a two-time Oscar winner.

We returned to DC by mid-September. The vibe on the Hill was anxious. Nothing was getting done on foreign aid reform or much else. The fear was that after forty years in power, the Democrats would lose the House in the upcoming November election. And that's exactly what happened: Newt Gingrich with his "Contract with America" won. The election stunned many of my Democratic colleagues who'd been on the Hill for decades. For them, it was as if New York had elected Sean Hannity as mayor.

Me, not so much.

I was the most junior person on our team and the least qualified. I was toast.

The morning after the election I was calling anyone I'd met in the past year who could help me find a new job. Several weeks later, I landed a better one, truth be known, in the Executive Branch. I'd be the Special Assistant to the Administrator of USAID, Brian Atwood, and for good measure got the title Deputy Chief of Staff.

7. THE ROOM WHERE IT HAPPENED

*No country can ever truly flourish if it stifles
the potential of its women, and deprives itself
of the contributions of half its citizens.*

—Michelle Obama

It was 7:45 a.m. I'd just pulled up to the entrance to the State Department's garage and slowed down long enough to flash my pass to the guard. One of the many perks of my new job was a reserved parking spot in the small lot under the building. Soon I was speed walking down the linoleum tiled hallway in the bowels of the State Department before getting into the private elevator that will whisk me to my boss's office—a suite really. As I got off the elevator I walked past my assistant to my own office. It was larger than my apartment's living room, came with a sofa, and was a world away from my windowless cubicle on the Hill. In DC's pecking order, I had taken a huge step up. My boss, the head of USAID, reported to the Secretary of State and the Head of the National Security Council, who both reported to the President.

Problem was, like on the Hill, I was trying to look and act the part of an experienced staffer. In other words, I was still faking it.

Republicans now controlled both houses of Congress. It meant we were at war, with the battles fought in "gotcha" hearings on Capitol Hill and with dueling articles in *The Washington Post*. On one side, the head of the Senate Foreign Relations Committee had called for abolishing USAID with no more taxpayer money "going down foreign ratholes," (a direct quote from chair, Senator Jesse Helms), while our side generally defended the status quo. Lost in the political melee: any hope for real reform.

I spent a good part of my day in meetings. These sometimes included fascinating people like Eunice and Sargent Shriver, Pamela Harriman, or an imposing Russian oligarch whose name I can't remember. More often they involved an array of ministers of this and that from countries that received US foreign aid. I'd write memos to summarize points of view of warring bureaucratic factions when the way forward wasn't clear-cut and try to make my boss's demanding job slightly easier. I was working harder day in and day out, week after week, than I ever had before. Yet somehow, I always felt like I was a step behind. My sister Shelley sent me a blowup of a picture from *I Love Lucy* with Lucy and Ethel in the fudge factory with the headline "Speed 'em up."

I usually was the least important person in any meeting. What I had was proximity to power, so people would be exceptionally kind to me, particularly if they wanted something from my boss. The aggressive niceness was off-putting at first, and then I got used to it and tried not to let it go to my head. I could often gauge how much someone wanted from my boss, by how charming they were to me.

We traveled frequently to places like Nairobi or Jakarta where USAID had big missions. In these places the USAID Administrator was greeted like a head of state because so much money flowed through the agency to developing country governments. We'd touch down in, say, Lima, Peru, and the schedule for the next few days would be packed. We'd be flying in helicopters to look at drug control programs in the morning, then trudging through fields to see new drip irrigation systems before capping the day off with a formal dinner and a speech. It was a disorienting combination of places and people, power and poverty.

I walked up to the guard's booth at the front gate. I was nervous and not sure what to expect. This was, after all, The White House. Once inside, the wood-paneled room was filling up with the forty or so people on the US's delegation to the upcoming UN Beijing Conference on Women. It felt like a place where serious work happened, and a big part of me couldn't believe I was there. What would my grandfathers with their sixth-grade educations make of this?

From what I'd seen on the Hill, too often issues that impacted the lives and livelihoods of women and girls such as lack of access to contraception, education, political power, and economic resources were left out of foreign policy discussions. The Conference provided a way to focus the world's attention on women. I'd asked Brian if I could attend as part of the US delegation and was thrilled when he supported the idea. The inclusion of First Lady Hillary Clinton on our delegation meant that the whole conference would get more attention globally.

The delegation included household names like the soon-to-be first female Secretary of State Madeleine Albright, and a group of staffers like me.

After inspiring remarks by Madeleine Albright, and Hillary's Chief of Staff, Melanne Verveer, Hillary stepped up to speak. I'd only seen her on TV and I was prepared to be disappointed. In my last job, I saw a stream of speakers at hearings and listened to a litany of remarks from Members of Congress. Some read verbatim speeches prepared by a staffer; others would improv, too often awkwardly, from talking points. I thought Hillary might be the same. But as she started speaking it was clear she was in in a league all her own. Without notes or a staffer whispering in her ear, she spoke in flawless paragraphs, and projected a deep knowledge about the nuances of policies ranging from the education of girls to domestic violence against women.

———————·———————

A few weeks later, it was wheels up for the long plane ride to China. I'd brought a beat-up copy of Betty Friedan's *The Feminine Mystique* that I picked up at a used bookstore. I had always meant to read it but never had. In it, she mentioned "the problem that doesn't have a name." Then, of course, she described it: the malaise of middle-class white women in the '50s and '60s—often college-educated but confined to domestic roles; women that could have been my dear mother. Then Betty Friedan walked down the aisle, saw me reading her book, and stopped to chat. She seemed offended that I had not read it before. I guess I can understand how she felt. Women my age had benefited from those second-wave feminists who helped enable us to work without blatant legal discrimination. Even so, she offered to autograph my book.

With the fall of the Soviet Union a couple years earlier, the US was the sole remaining superpower so Clinton's remarks were the most anticipated of the conference. Though official delegates hammered out language for the final declaration that was eventually approved, I'd argue that the most significant part of the conference took place in only twenty minutes—the time Hillary had the floor.

None of us staffers had seen her speech, but the buzz was that it was going to be great. When we got to the giant auditorium, we'd passed snaking lines of women trying to get into overflow rooms, forced to watch her speech from monitors. With our delegation badges, we got right into seats reserved for us. The audience was a sea of color, with some people dressed in traditional clothing of their native lands. After I sat down, I looked up and saw that the balcony above us was also packed.

After Clinton's name was announced, she graciously greeted the dignitaries on the stage and a hushed, nervous silence fell on the room as she took the podium. Clad in a pink suit, cream blouse, and pearls, she looked as if she could have been the wife of a Methodist minister or a headmistress at a conservative girls' school.

She started by describing the vital role women play in families and societies but underscored that 70 percent of the world's poor are women. She asserted that for too long, women's rights had been ignored and that "it's time to break the silence to no longer discuss women's rights as separate from human rights." Clinton labeled bride burnings, sex slavery, and genital mutilation as human rights' abuses, not only pesky women's issues. These were not Betty Friedan's "problems that have no name." These were brutal, traumatizing assaults.

Then, to make the point clear, she went for the political jugular with this:

> It's a violation of human rights when babies are denied food or drowned or suffocated or their spines broken, simply because they are girls. . . .

> It's a violation of human rights when women are forced to have abortions or are sterilized against their will.

While Clinton hadn't mentioned them by name, everyone knew she'd just called out the Chinese on their home turf, in front of the world, for forcing women to abort babies and for turning a blind eye to the slaughter of baby girls. This was the opposite of a typical UN speech edited to death by everyone up and down the bureaucratic chain of command, designed to not offend anyone by not saying anything worth listening to. And then came the line for which the speech would be remembered:

> *If there is one message that echoes forth from this conference, let it be that human rights are women's rights and women's rights are human rights, once and for all.*

The next thing I know I am on my feet as is everyone in the American delegation around me. There are high-fives, hugs, and overwhelmed tears. I looked out over the audience that had been placid twenty minutes earlier. Now delegates representing virtually every nation on earth were giving our Clinton a standing ovation, one big "you go girl!"

This was a display of US power and values at its very best. It felt like history in the making as a battle cry for a generation was born that day. I have never been prouder to be an American than I was at that moment.

What would the world be like if women and girls had the same opportunity for a healthy future as men and boys?

I pulled out of the State Department garage at 7:40 p.m. If I made most of the lights, I'd get across town to my polling place on Capitol Hill right before it closed. At 7:55 p.m., I got my ballot and went into the booth. The major party choices for president were Bill Clinton and Bob Dole. This should have been easy. But I just stared at the ballot. A worker announced it was 8 p.m. and the polls were closing. I hurriedly checked Ralph Nader's box. While I admired Nader, I didn't want him to be president. I was losing it.

I left the polling place and went for a long walk around the Capitol grounds, plopped myself down on the steps and gazed out at the Mall. I had a commanding view of the city. All three branches of government conceived by our visionary founders more than two-hundred years earlier were within walking distance of each other and, at that moment, me. Having traveled to many countries where the rights I took for granted were nonexistent, such as the ability to criticize a president with impunity, I loved my country. I knew how lucky I was to have been born here. But my head throbbed. Rather than feeling inspired, I simply felt depleted. I realized I had not eaten since downing a yogurt at my desk around noon. I felt like I hadn't seen the light of day in weeks.

I asked myself: Have I made any difference whatsoever in the last three grueling years? Have my efforts helped the poor in Africa or Asia to lead better lives? The simple truth? No. I was a small, insignificant, overworked cog in a large lumbering machine. And lurking in the back of my mind was the haunting question, *did I make a big mistake leaving Madison Avenue?*

I'd arrived in Washington brimming with naive optimism, believing that reform of the kind of foreign aid I'd seen in Tanzania was possible. But I had learned that about 80 percent of US foreign aid stayed in the US paying for government employee salaries, contractors, and for US-manufactured goods like contraceptives, wheat, and those condoms rotting in the port in Tanzania. Often it was Americans rather than the poor in developing countries who benefited most from US foreign aid.

I'd loved my time in graduate school, because we got to wrestle with how policy tools could solve critical problems. This, I learned, had little to do with "how the sausage was made." It was like going from studying at the Cordon Bleu to working at a meat processing plant. A lot of good comes out of that "sausage making," like health care for the elderly, a defense establishment that keeps us safe, environmental protection so we can drink clean water out of the tap. There are people who have the stomach and tenacity for the blood sport of politics, but I wasn't one of them.

My life was consumed by my job. The little time I had left was spent with a lovely guy who was as overworked as I was. If I stayed in Washington, I could easily wake up at fifty with Beast or another cat, a few war stories about political battles waged, and not much else.

I realized I was done—not only with my job at USAID, but with DC.

8. HAPPILY, EVER AFTER

*This thinking you can have every single
thing you want in life is not the thinking of
a feminist. It's the thinking of a toddler.*

—ARIEL LEVY

gazed at the glistening water of Lake Como below when a trim
waiter in a white jacket offered me an aperitif. I was standing on
the terrace of the Rockefeller Foundation's Bellagio Center in Italy.
It was an elegant marble tiled mansion, with wide hallways, and
tasteful artwork adorning the walls. If the location sounds vaguely
familiar, that may be because it's where George and Amal Clooney
have a home. But, with its fifty acres, the Rockefeller facility makes
the Clooneys look like paupers. It felt like it could have fallen out
of an episode of *Succession*, a place meant for plutocrats.

I had reached out to my old boss, Seth Berkely, and was delighted
when he hired me to help him with his ambitious plan: the ouster
of the current Director-General of the World Health Organization
(WHO) who many felt had let the agency stall and the health of the
world's poor suffer. This was a tall order because it's a political position
voted on by the members of the WHO executive board who are all
part of the UN. Seth's idea was to use the mantle of the Rockefeller
Foundation to host a series of meetings all over the world that would
focus on setting an agenda for global health subtly pointing out ways
the WHO was stumbling. The invitees were ministers of health,

heads of major medical schools and hospitals, and other luminaries and the meetings were held in places like the Philippines, Zimbabwe and Egypt. I had spent the previous six months darting around the globe helping Seth organize those meetings that culminated in this conference at Lake Como.

I was joined on the terrace by a physician who was a former minister of health from a South American country. He radiated a self-assured warmth. I asked him about the disconnect of us meeting in this over-the-top place to address the health of the world's poor. He smiled, and with an engaging Spanish accent said, "The last time I was here, Kate, the title of the conference was 'Suffering Societies.'" He laughed coyly as if he were letting me in on an inside joke.

On the one hand, it was a treat to spend a week in this ritzy place. On the other hand, a practical part of me wondered how much good could be done if Rockefeller sold the facility. They'd likely bring in hundreds of millions of dollars, if not more, and could use the money to help alleviate poverty and the unnecessary misery that goes with it. It felt corrupt for the Foundation to treat its community to such astonishing luxury. But there I stood, enjoying the view, the drink, and a conversation with a charming South American doctor.

The plan was that we'd produce a detailed report of our findings. Having just left political DC, my small contribution was to suggest we also develop a single paged "manifesto." It was signed by all eighteen participants from fourteen countries. *The Lancet*, the leading international health journal, published the thing under the benign headline "Supporting the World Health Organization at a Critical Juncture." It was coupled with a stinging editorial titled "WHO: where there is no vision, the people perish." (Students of the Bible will recognize this statement as Proverbs 29:18.) The next year, WHO's Director-General was gone. I'm convinced this would not have happened without Seth, *The Lancet*, and its visionary editor, Dr. Richard Horton.

When Seth left Rockefeller the next year, so did I. I took a position with a new project called the Women's Lens on Global Issues working with Joan Dunlop, the founder of The International Women's Health Coalition. The goal was to use the galvanizing energy from the Beijing Women's Conference to develop a constituency of US women that would support programs to improve human development and the status of women such as family planning and girls' education. We held a series of conferences in US cities to gain the perspective of women's groups. Then we commissioned research to prove that US women had a different view of the world and would support these "soft power" initiatives. But there was one big insurmountable problem. When we got the research results back, it turned out women did not have a different view of the world than men. So much for our Women's Lens! This would have been heartbreaking for me, but at this point my heart was focused somewhere else.

———————————⊥———————————

When I was working at Rockefeller, one of my colleagues set me up on a blind date with a PhD-smart consultant. The plan was for him to meet me at my apartment. When I opened the door to greet him, my first thought was *you are out of my league*. He was built like the college quarterback he once was and looked a bit like Alec Baldwin about the time he starred in *30 Rock*. He was newly single after a long marriage. I was coming out of years of perpetual work in DC. Our first date was twelve hours long as we trekked the length of Manhattan, from my apartment in Chelsea up to The Whitney Museum and back and kept a conversation going with lunch and dinner in between.

Our second date lasted four days. We fell in love the way the starving devour a meal—with zeal, but without much thought. Here in midlife, we had the passion of the young with the wisdom to match. And, as a backdrop for a love story, is there a more romantic city in the US than New York?

He proposed, complete with a beautiful ring. We were married the next year, and even got an announcement in *The New York Times* that made my mom happy. The year after that, I gave birth to our son and named him Robert, aka Bobby, after my dad. Then we moved back to California at the peak of the tech boom for me to start a job at Yahoo to help build a corporate philanthropy and community relations program.

The next year, the curtain came down on my marriage. I joined a dubious sorority: the "left for a younger woman club." I was replaced by a woman with old money and new everything else. In four years, we'd lived through a tumultuous Cliff Notes version of *You've Got Mail* and *Kramer v. Kramer*. We divorced the year after that.

Here are my lessons from that whirlwind chapter:

1. Think twice about getting engaged to someone you've known for less time than an average baseball season.
2. Make sure that getting married on Valentine's Day really makes sense. (Yes, dear reader, that's what this fool-for-love did, giving me a yearly reminder of my hubris.)
3. If your heart calls for motherhood, have the baby because that you will never regret.

PART TWO:

TRUE
NORTH

9. TAPE IN THE MACHINE

The moment you know with certainty
that your intention is fully aligned with what you
believe, all bets are off. You've already won.

—OPRAH WINFREY

From 1986 to 2011 *The Oprah Winfrey Show* was "must-see-TV" for many American women. While Oprah would do more than 4,500 shows in those twenty-five years, the one with Dr. Catherine Hamlin in January 2004 was the most consequential for women with fistula and for me.

Winfrey did with fistula what she had done with so many other issues, from domestic violence to institutional racism: she shined her bright, engaging light on it, opening minds and hearts in the process. Thanks to Oprah, Dr. Hamlin streamed into living rooms around the country with her radiant kindness, discussing her work to heal women injured in childbirth and too often left as outcasts.

When describing fistula and the gender discrimination that underlies it, Dr. Hamlin said: "If men were getting fistula, something would have been done years and years ago, I think."

Oprah added: "If a man had a hole in his penis, you're darn right about that. I mean, all the men would rise up . . . If there was a problem with men with a hole in their penises, there would be a Hole in the Penis Committee developed immediately to fix that." The woman had a way with words. She had earned a devoted following and within weeks, a bit more than three million dollars in donations had poured into the Fistula Foundation's San Jose office to support Dr. Hamlin's work.

The waiter placed a steaming plate of *doro wat*—a spicy chicken stew that's the national dish of Ethiopia—between us. Seated in front of me was Ric Haas, the founder of Fistula Foundation, formed to support Dr. Hamlin's hospital. I had reached out to Ric to do a case history on the Foundation's experience with Oprah and their website, as part of my job with Network for Good, a group I'd joined after leaving Yahoo. Network for Good was founded by AOL, Cisco, and Yahoo to help nonprofits raise money by making it easy for donors to give money online.

I was excited to meet Ric and hear about the Foundation, as powerful memories from my visit to the Fistula Hospital came flooding back. He was understandably shocked to learn that I had been to the hospital in Addis and met Dr. Hamlin, since Ethiopia is not exactly a vacation hot spot. His face lit up as he talked about the work being done to transform women's lives. He explained that he and his daughter, Shaleece, a talented photographer, had visited in 2000. Like me, they were moved by what they saw. Unlike me, they came home and started the Foundation to support the hospital. But they soon discovered how hard it was to raise money, even with a cause as compelling as fistula. He told me that Oprah and her viewers had changed everything, enabling him to think about hiring permanent staff.

In the coming weeks, one conversation led to another, and Ric asked me to join the board, and several months later to take on the role of executive director. I was just emerging from the darkest chapter of my life—my divorce—so I jumped at the idea. I gave no thought to how Ric and I would work together. Ric was passionate about Catherine Hamlin and fistula treatment, and I was too.

Ric had built a career as a successful financial planner and had earned the trust of his clients. In HR speak, he was an *individual contributor* and was accustomed to making decisions on his own. He had used his money to start the Foundation, which I admired. Without him, it wouldn't exist.

I began the first week mainly listening to Ric describe what he wanted to do so I could understand his priorities. I remained excited that together we could do a lot to help Dr. Hamlin and women like Hanna. I was striving to get to a place with Ric where my experience and ideas could be useful to building the Foundation.

But we started hitting bumps.

At first, we disagreed about small things: the stationery, color scheme, website design, and whether we should pay a writer to do the newsletter. I tried, as my dad used to advise, "to go along to get along." But keeping my opinions to myself was like forcing a two-year-old to sit still. There was so much potential with the Oprah windfall to build a powerful organization to help women with fistula. But it wasn't clear that Ric wanted my views on how we should run things, if they differed from his own.

We'd started discussing staffing and potentially hiring more people. This is a bigger deal than, say, the color of the stationery, because staffing is where nonprofits spend a lot of their money, paying people like me. Ric wanted to staff a second office in New York with two people. He saw it as an expansion opportunity. There were a lot of wealthy generous people in New York. Sounds good.

But I didn't see it that way.

For me, opening a second office with no clear long-term funding stream was risky and would leave us with an obligation for rent and salaries that would limit our ability to fund fistula treatment. To be fair, one could argue that I am neurotic about money with my happy places including Costco, used bookstores, and your average garage sale. I was raised by two people who saw waste as a secular sin, and I'd inherited their thrift.

When we met on the topic, I laid out my arguments like cards when you are convinced you have a winning hand. I tried to be respectful of Ric's perspective and convey my concerns with appropriate tact. But maybe my memory is too rosy. I could have behaved something closer to "I'm right, and you'll understand once you listen to me." Your basic pain in the neck.

The next day, I got ready to head into the office, donning a crisp white blouse, a tailored rose-colored skirt, and pearls. I was scheduled to meet with a senior member of the board, I'll call "Guy" to review a draft of a strategic plan I'd developed for the upcoming board meeting. Guy was a friend of Ric's who retired after a successful career as a real estate developer. I'd met with Guy the previous week at his impressive home in the hills surrounding the Bay. He was an imposing man with the stature of wrestler, and I found him intimidating. He reminded me of a kid who bullied me in middle school, but that probably says more about me than him. But that fear motivated me. I showed up that day thoroughly prepared because I was still trying to prove myself. I even thought I might be able to convince Guy that opening an office in New York was not a good next move.

When I walked into the office, Guy was already there clad in running shorts and a t-shirt. I immediately felt overdressed. I greeted him and we both walked into the conference room.

I sat down and nervously smoothed my skirt. I started to pull my presentation deck out of my bag, as he said, "I wasn't sure at first if you were smart enough to do this job. But I'm not concerned about that anymore." While I considered his veiled compliment, he went on and said something like, "but this isn't going to work out. There is a style conflict here between you and Ric. It's Ric's organization, so we are terminating your employment effective immediately."

I was stunned.

While I turned this news over in my mind, I realized I had no recourse. They held all the cards. I'd written my own offer letter lifting language from my Network for Good offer letter that stated I could be terminated "without cause, without notice." It's called "at will" employment because it gives the employer power to fire you at will.

Then he added, "You can't put the tape back in the machine, Kate."

What does that mean? I wondered.

"You are still on the board, and I'd suggest that you just keep all this to yourself, or we can play our own tape about you."

Huh?

I walked out to the parking lot and got back into my Honda. I'd been in Ric's office such a short period of time that the air was still cool inside the car, even though it was a warm fall day. Driving home, I started to panic. My divorce was final. I had custody of four-year-old Bobby and had bought my small house with a big backyard the year before. I'd put every penny I had into a huge down payment. So now I had a mortgage and needed health insurance for me and Bobby. That meant I needed a new job. Now.

When I got home, an epic headache was making my temples throb. I downed a couple of Advil. Then I took off the pearls, the skirt, and not-so-crisp-anymore white blouse, threw on sweats, and jumped online to look for a new job. Within a month I had one as a program director at a local organization, The Health Trust. The organization's tag line was "Serving the Underserved"—though not in Africa, right there in Silicon Valley.

A new Fistula Foundation board member, Deborah Harris, called me to introduce herself. I didn't know much about her, except that she was responsible for getting Dr. Hamlin on the Oprah show through what I'd heard was her charming tenacity and personal connections. She had a lilting Southern accent and her voice felt like a cashmere sweater—warm and embracing. We shared stories of our respective visits to the Addis hospital and our reverence for Dr. Hamlin. She asked what had happened with Ric, and I said that we simply didn't work well together. Deborah urged me to stay on the Foundation's board.

In the coming months Ric opened the office in New York staffed by two people. He also hired a consulting firm to help him manage the organization.

A couple of newer board members had reached out to me. They had joined the board after Oprah and were not friends of Ric's. One was a Wall Street hedge fund leader, Kassy Kebede; another was a successful litigator, Rob Tessler. They shared concerns about how opaque the decision-making was. The upcoming spring board meeting would give us a chance to get greater clarity.

10. HOLLYWOOD ENDING

A wise woman wishes to be no one's enemy;
a wise woman refuses to be anyone's victim.

—Maya Angelou

I sprinted from the parking lot toward the towering redwood trees that lined the playground at Appleseed Montessori School. A large red helium balloon was trapped in the branches swaying in the gentle breeze like a flag. In front of me was a small stage with a solitary podium and a dozen tiny empty chairs in two rows facing the forty or so empty seats that would have comprised the audience. Looking at the stage, sadness and regret hit me. Where were all the kids? Where was Bobby? How had I missed my only child's graduation from preschool, his first educational milestone? I had failed as a mom.

Then the alarm clock blasted me back to reality. I was so glad to be awake. Do all parents have these kinds of nightmares, or is it only working moms? And the particularly stressed out and guilt-ridden variety: working single moms. Today was Fistula Foundation's board meeting and Bobby's graduation from Appleseed.

That morning Kassy, Rob, Deborah and I met for breakfast and agreed that one of us would get finance and staffing added to the agenda. Our group took the elevators to the penthouse and the members-only Silicon Valley Capital Club. As we stepped into the lobby, the place felt like a boutique hotel, oozing calm luxury. We were escorted into an expansive conference room with a massive table and floor-to-ceiling windows on one end that flooded the room with morning light.

The meeting was supposed to end at 3 o'clock. Bobby's graduation was at 4. I thought that even with this new agenda item there'd be time for me to get to the graduation. But, as the day dragged on with sessions running over, I feared I'd either turn my nightmare into reality and miss graduation, or I'd miss the discussion. So, at about 2:30, I raised my hand and asked what was necessary to add a topic to the agenda. The Foundation's attorney Cynthia Rowland said I'd need to make a motion and then it would need to be seconded and voted on. So, I made the motion to have the next order of business be finance and staffing. I got a second and then a vote yes to amend the agenda. At this point, Ric left the room, so we could talk openly.

It is important to underscore that no one thought Ric was doing anything underhanded or unethical. Quite the opposite: people knew he had started the Foundation and put his own funds into getting it started. But some also felt that he was not good at considering the views of others if they disagreed with his own.

A tense discussion ensued that took longer than I would have liked. Not that it was not necessary, but I had my eyes on the clock. I needed to get out of there, ideally not later than 3:30 to make the twenty-minute drive to Appleseed. Finally, there was a vote to undo a few decisions Ric had made about staffing and related expenditures. We adjourned for a coffee break and one of the other board members went to give Ric the news.

I got to the graduation a tad late but felt lucky that the ceremony was just starting. I plopped myself down next to my parents and gazed at twelve cherubic faces clad in yellow caps and gowns seated on the stage. When they gave Bobby his diploma, he smiled broadly in his little mortar board and looked like he'd won a trip to Disneyland. I felt relieved joy.

After the ceremony, we went back to our house for a little party with my parents and a couple of friends. We were just settling into dinner of cheese pizza when my phone started buzzing. Within about fifteen minutes I got calls from several board members, some leaving messages because I was talking to someone else. I learned that after the coffee break the conference room had exploded with angry accusations flying in every direction. Bitter things were said between board members to each other. At one point both Ric and Guy resigned. Later both rescinded their resignations. It got ugly.

What was said couldn't ever be unsaid.

The tape couldn't be put back in the machine.

A week later Ric resigned, this time for real, along with Guy. This was astounding. I'd thought Ric would be with the Foundation forever. Now he was gone.

The board had a new challenge: leadership. We voted to appoint Kassy Kebede as the Foundation's new board chair. Kassy was born in Ethiopia and came to the US for college, got an MBA at Wharton, and never left. With his analytical mind and unassuming integrity, he had earned the respect of the rest of the board, me included. We also voted to close the office in New York.

But the Foundation needed someone to run it day to day. We explored hiring a headhunter to fill the role of chief executive. The cost for that was considerable, so the board decided to hire me to take over. I resigned from the Foundation board and my job at the Health Trust.

Was it a Hollywood ending?

Not quite, or at least, not yet.

11. CHARITY 101

In the nonprofit world the pressure to
perform is internal, not external.

—HARVARD BUSINESS SCHOOL LECTURE

I was buying a few ripe heirloom tomatoes at our local farmers' market when I spotted a FOR LEASE sign in the window of an adjacent office building. The Foundation needed a new home, and I hoped I had found it. It was a two-story, L-shaped structure with a Subway sandwich shop on the ground floor. The place for rent was in the inside corner of the L facing a two-story concrete parking lot, arguably the most undesirable unit in the building. The next week, after some haggling with the owner over the price and with permission from the board, I signed a five-year lease on the tiny office.

Starting any new job is a challenge, but with this one, I was flying blind. There was no briefing memo, no boss to guide me. I reported to a board of twelve, but they met only twice a year. I'd worked for two nonprofits, the Rockefeller Foundation and the Health Trust. But those were large, established outfits, and I'd had mid-level jobs with each. While I'd managed big groups of people in my advertising life, there I was accountable to both a demanding boss and to clients, with punishing deadlines that forced us to get things done on time. Here, it became clear on day one, that the drive would have to start with me. Neither the women that would benefit from our work nor the donors would be pressuring us. I had to get used to making it up as I went along. The problem was, I wasn't sure exactly where to start.

When I took over, the Foundation had three employees that Ric had hired to process donations, send out thank you letters, and answer phones. I would let one person go when it became clear we had more people than we had work. The other two, Terry Rodriquez and Anne Ferguson, continued to do what they had done before I arrived. We also had one indefatigable volunteer; a retired teacher named Jerry Goldstein who came in every week to stuff envelopes with those thank you letters.

Terry was sharp and hard working. She'd had children young and had earned her high school GED. Anne had followed her husband to the US from Edinburgh a few years earlier. While she'd worked as a skilled admin, her multiple degrees were in English literature. She was soft-spoken and listened with care when other people talked, a strength I didn't have and one I appreciated immediately. Anne had deep integrity, keen attention to detail, and soon became my own Radar O'Reilly.

At that point, both Anne and Terry worked hourly with no benefits. That had to change. I reached out to a labor lawyer at Cynthia's firm, Gina Roccanova, and got a draft copy of an HR manual, and found a Northern California Nonprofit compensation survey so that I could norm our benefits against an objective standard. I ran the revised manual by the board for approval so we would all get the same benefits. Excellent lawyers like Cynthia and Gina were worth every penny since I had no experience setting up a nonprofit and wanted to avoid unforced errors.

I also looked to the Better Business Bureau for guidance. Turned out, they have twenty standards for charity accountability "to help donors verify the trustworthiness of soliciting organizations and to strengthen charity practices." That sounded good to me, so I set out to earn their seal by meeting all their standards for things like board oversight and fundraising ethics. I also checked out Charity Navigator that rates charities by analyzing how they spend money. Donors used

Charity Navigator as a kind of *Consumer Reports* for charities; as a small upstart, we'd be foolish not to try to earn their four-star rating.

Anne and I got vital guidance from our auditors, Tanya Slesnick and Ted Mitchell. We also had a terrific CPA, Seble Gateneh, who balanced our books every month and is still working with us. Anne's husband Kevin Cameron generously gave us free tech support. During those first few months, I often went to bed thinking about what lay ahead the next day. There was so much to learn and do.

———————————————

I hate asking people for money. With fundraisers for my son's school or cub scouts, I'd buy the raffle tickets or overpriced popcorn myself, rather than asking friends or family to buy the stuff. I was going to have to get over that reserve, and fast.

A big opportunity was almost upon us: Christmas. Most charities, even secular ones like ours, raise a good portion of their money in December. I wanted to create a connection between our donors' kindness and courageous women like Hanna whose life could be transformed with surgery. If I'd learned anything in advertising, it is that we are "feeling creatures who think," and not the other way around. So, I wrote a letter about how surgery had given a woman named Desta a new life after years of misery. I showed donors they had the opportunity to gain the simple satisfaction of knowing they'd helped women like her get their lives back.

Thanks to Oprah we had thousands of names of good people. Terry, Anne, and I hand-signed all the letters—more than ten thousand of them. I know. This sounds bananas and I have to believe that's what Anne and Terry thought. But I wanted a letter from us to feel special, not like more junk mail.

We closed out 2005 raising more than $1.8 million. This was enough to fund more than a year of operating expenses for Dr. Hamlin's hospital in Addis. Each donor received a hand-signed thank you letter from us, no matter the size of their gift. I wanted even modest donors to know how much we appreciated their support. Their kindness and generosity were sacred. So, in January we were a thank you letter factory. Jerry was particularly busy.

That February, Anne and I, along with one of our board members, Dr. Larry William, and our chair, Kassy Kebede, headed off to Ethiopia for the biannual PIM—Partners International Meeting. Dr. Hamlin held these sessions once every two years, bringing together the trusts that supported the hospital from the UK, Australia, Germany, Japan, the Netherlands, Sweden, and New Zealand to inspire us to continue the critical work of raising funds.

The morning we arrived at the Fistula Hospital for the PIM, bright sunlight and memories from my first visit a decade before came flooding in. I was delighted that the place still felt tranquil, with patients sitting on the green lawns and the flower garden surrounding it as lush as ever. We headed down the hill from the hospital toward an octagon shaped building called the tukul that served as both a large meeting room and a church. When we walked in, Dr. Hamlin greeted us with a warm smile and a hearty hello. The day went by quickly. It was inspiring to meet her staff and supporters from around the world and be part of this international team focused on helping women.

Ruth Kennedy, Dr. Hamlin's right-hand, whom we'd met the previous fall on a visit she made to the US, offered to take Anne and me on a tour of the hospital. We jumped at the chance. Ruth was a second-generation missionary and a midwife that served as the hospital's Liaison Officer. She looked a bit like British actress Emma Thompson in *Love Actually*, with short salt-and-pepper hair, a wide smile, and infectious energy.

We walked through the hospital's ward drenched in afternoon light with pale blue curtains and bedcovers creating a peaceful energy. Ruth occasionally stopped to greet patients, speaking to them in Amharic. After each, she'd briefly relay their stories.

"Lelo thinks she is about thirty and had her fistula for twelve years; she was told her surgery was successful. . ."

"Sarah was brought here by her husband. She has both a rectal and vaginal fistula, so her cure is not guaranteed, but she said Dr. Hamlin is hopeful. . ."

"Nigest has two children. Her surgery took place last week and was successful. She can't wait to get home. . ."

"Fana came with her sister. She is excited to be cured and will be returning home in a few days. . ."

Ruth reiterated what I'd remembered hearing from Dr. Hamlin, that 90 percent of the patients were clinically depressed when they were admitted because they were often rejected and ostracized by their family and community. She explained that too often they are blamed for their injury; told they are cursed or deserved it. Their profound pain was both invisible and tenacious. The women in the ward carried a deep hurt. I could see it on their faces. Yet they also smiled. Surgery gave them a hopeful future.

When we got back to the hotel, Anne and I decided to go for a walk. We headed out onto the street, to the strains of Bob Marley's "No Woman No Cry" from a boom box perched on the window ledge of a small shop. Once we got a few blocks away from the hotel, many of the people we passed looked gaunt and hungry. It was easy to see that if your family didn't have enough to eat, fistula surgery, and even simple things like tampons or Depend pads were unaffordable luxuries.

Poverty was a wily thief. It stole futures and robbed the poor of opportunities. Poverty meant you couldn't get help when your labor was obstructed. It meant no C-section, days of labor, and a stillborn child. Poverty meant living a life of needless suffering from fistula because you didn't have access to curative surgery or couldn't afford it.

But thanks to Dr. Hamlin and her team, that injury didn't have to be a life sentence of misery. And if we were helping her, we were helping them. I came back home energized and wrote our quarterly newsletter to share my experience with our supporters.

I flew to New York on a Friday and stayed in the cheapest Midtown hotel I could find. The bed touched three out of four of the walls, but it was quiet, which was all I needed. My first board meeting since taking the job was the next day. I was anxious because I suspected a few of the inaugural board members were wary of me. To them, I was not only an upstart but an interloper.

One of our board members arranged for us to use a friend's law firm conference room. The next morning, I got off the elevator with armloads of pastries and coffee jugs I'd picked up at Starbucks. The place was dark, quiet, and felt like a large vault. It was a far cry from our last meeting at the posh Silicon Valley Club. But this was free. I sat in the conference room and popped a couple of Tic Tacs to kill my coffee breath. I unclenched my white knuckles and drummed my fingers on the table as I tried in vain to relax.

For CEOs of nonprofits, our boards are not only our bosses, but they also have legal responsibility to ensure a charity raises money ethically and spends it effectively. The board meetings were a kind of "command performance" and we'd mailed out a binder full of background materials to each board member the week before the meeting. I needed to prove to them and myself that I could do the job.

The first few minutes were where the most attention would be paid to me, and I wanted to nail it. When I opened my mouth to speak, my voice cracked. But, as we slogged through the lengthy agenda and as we finished each topic, I could feel my tension easing. It was almost over without any hiccups. Cynthia had suggested we add a standing item to every board meeting, something titled Executive Session. This meant that I left the room and the board could talk freely about me.

I sat in the lobby, but then started pacing to burn off my stress. Finally, Kassy came out and escorted me back into the conference room. He said they were pleased with my performance, thanked me for the work, and even gave me a small bonus as a vote of confidence.

As I said goodbyes and cleaned up the conference room, I realized my anxiety had been replaced with the warmth of gratitude. The hazy dream I'd had when I left Madison Avenue more than a decade earlier to try to make a small dent in global poverty had finally started to come into focus.

12. TALE OF TWO MOTHERS

*I think empathy is important, and I think only
when our clever brain and our human heart work together
in harmony can we achieve our full potential.*

—JANE GOODALL

I woke to the sound of rain like a drum beat on the tin roof of the guest quarters of the Addis Ababa Fistula Hospital. Dr. Hamlin had invited me to visit and I was excited that I'd get to see the hospital's work up close. My chaperone, teacher, and tour guide that week was Ruth Kennedy. First stop would be Bahir Dar in northern Ethiopia to see one of the smaller hospitals that Dr. Hamlin had opened a few years earlier. On the drive through rural Ethiopia, we saw few cars. Most people were walking. Carts were powered by donkeys. Roads the color of pumpkin pie were littered with giant potholes that frequently made it hard to go much faster than ten miles an hour. Ruth was a seasoned midwife, so I got the chance to learn more about the perils of childbirth in rural Africa.

"You know there's an African proverb you may want to memorize: the sun should not set twice on a laboring woman," Ruth said.

"I've never heard that before. Where does that idea come from?"

"Well, after more than a day or so in labor, the baby often dies in the woman's uterus due to lack of oxygenated blood."

"What about the laboring woman? Why is a long labor dangerous to her too?"

"Good question. The delay may lead to her developing a fistula, as the baby's head cuts off the supply of blood to her pelvic floor."

"Yeah, I remember Dr. Hamlin talking about that the first time I met her."

"Of course, there are worse outcomes than fistula when a woman doesn't get timely help with an obstructed birth. For instance, she can die from blood loss due to a ruptured uterus or from infection, and her baby can die too."

"Well, with the condition of the roads and so few cars, I could see how hard it would be for a woman to get to a hospital for a timely C-section."

"Even then," Ruth said, "in my experience, frequently a poor woman would arrive too late for us to save her baby and sometimes even herself."

<hr>

I was charmed by Bahir Dar, a sleepy town on the edge of Lake Tana, where the Blue Nile River begins. The next morning, we headed over to the Bahir Dar Hamlin Fistula Center that was right next to a larger maternity ward for the regional hospital run by the government. I was shocked to learn that the hospital served a population of seven million and had only twenty maternity beds. As we walked through the ward, I heard more from Ruth about the women it served.

"Most of the patients have never been to school. Many do not even have shoes. For a lot of these women, it's the first time they've been in rooms lit with electricity or slept in a bed with sheets and a blanket."

"Wow. I guess that makes sense. But I've never looked at it quite that way."

"They often arrive anemic and malnourished."

As I let that sink in, we walked over to the bed of a young patient. Ruth spoke to her in Amharic then translated her response.

"Her name is Shira. She said she was so glad to be here because the staff had been very kind to her. She said at home people told her she was cursed. She added that she would rather be blind than have a fistula, because at least people would sit with the blind, when they shunned her."

Shira had smiled as she talked. Now I understood why. She finally got not only treatment, but compassion and support.

When we got back to Addis, I asked Ruth if I could watch the surgeons work, to spend a day in the operating room with Dr. Hamlin. The closest I had come to observing surgery were episodes of *Grey's Anatomy*. Would watching surgery produce anxiety, nausea, or discomfort from knowing I was a voyeur? I would soon find out.

———————— ∗ ————————

The next day, I walked into the hospital and was greeted by Mamitu, who took me back to a set of small benches. She asked that I take off my shoes and socks and put on a sterile pair of plastic sandals and a green operating gown. She then guided me over to a long sink and showed me how to scrub my hands, nails, and forearms, before giving me surgical gloves and a mask. The smell of soap and disinfectant filled the air.

"You don't have to put on the mask until you are in the OR but try not to touch anything," she advised.

Dr. Hamlin was still conferring with one of the Ethiopian surgeons, Dr. Ambaye, so Mamitu asked if I wanted to meet one of the women who was scheduled for surgery that morning. I jumped at the chance. Outside the OR, a young woman in a hospital gown sat looking pensive. With an unlined face and her hair pulled back in a ponytail, she looked decades younger than me.

"I'd like you to meet Hawi. Her name means hope," Mamitu said.

With a tentative look in her luminous eyes, Hawi smiled, revealing a small gap between her front teeth that reminded me of what mine looked like in middle school before I got braces.

Mamitu asked her to tell us how she ended up at the hospital and translated her answer.

"She got married to a young man from her village. Very soon after, she knew she was going to have a baby. She said she was excited, and so was her family." I waited for Mamitu to translate more of what Hawi was saying and thought that her experience sounded familiar. I too became pregnant within months of my wedding.

Mamitu continued, "Hawi said the pains started in the morning. They'd come and go and at first, they weren't so bad. But after the sun went down, they grew horrible. She had never felt that kind of pain."

As I waited for more of Hawi's words to be translated, I remembered my own labor. I'd taken pregnancy yoga. I was ready. I started off so cocky. I breathed through the contractions. No sweat. But about twelve hours in when a contraction would start with a tortuous wave, a ten out of ten on the pain scale, I remember screaming and abandoning my hope for a drug-free delivery. So much for the childbirth classes, where they had us hold an ice cube to replicate labor agony, which is about as helpful as preparing for a marathon by racing to catch a cab. I was giving birth at a big New York hospital, so when I pleaded to get something for the pain, I was asked to sit on the corner of the bed. A doctor approached with a needle as long as a pool cue that he inserted into my spine. The pain ceased immediately.

Mamitu continued translating Hawi's story: "She says she stayed in labor for three days. She wanted to sleep but couldn't. Then she felt the need to push, and when she did, her baby finally came out. It was a little girl. But she was dead."

While my labor had started out like Hawi's, our birth experiences were so different. After twenty-four hours of labor, with the last three hours pushing with all the energy I had left, my big baby was lodged in my small frame, not going anywhere. Tests indicated that Bobby had developed a fever—not a good sign—so they needed to do a C-section. Now. I whimpered with worry about my son and felt defeated. With my epidural starting to wear off, they knocked me out.

As for Hawi, Mamitu said, "Things got worse after that. She was exhausted and fell back asleep. When she woke up, the bed was wet. But it wasn't blood, it was pee and it wouldn't stop. She said she hoped it would go away, but it didn't. Her husband said she stunk and was an embarrassment to him. He kicked her out, and she went to live with her parents. Finally, her neighbor heard about treatment, and her family all contributed money for the bus fare. But outside of Addis, she said she got kicked off the bus because she was leaking. So she walked the last five kilometers."

Trying to be hopeful, I said something like, "I am so glad you are here now. You are in such good hands with Dr. Hamlin."

"I heard my name." I saw Dr. Hamlin approaching us.

"Good morning!" I said. "I was telling Hawi that she's lucky to have you helping her."

"I'll do my best," said Dr. Hamlin. " It's time we start."

Mamitu escorted Hawi into the large operating room, and I followed. Natural light streamed in from large windows lining the side wall that gave the room an airy, cheerful feeling. There were four operating tables so that multiple surgeries could go on simultaneously. Above the tables were bright overhead lights. Mamitu helped Hawi onto the first table where she would soon get an epidural to deaden sensation in the lower half of her body. The place was quiet. There were no rock tunes blaring like on *Grey's Anatomy*.

Dr. Hamlin said, "Kate, dear, please come stand next to me, so you can watch."

I went to stand to her left, next to Mamitu who was there to assist. To the right was a small table with instruments and a nurse. Dr. Hamlin began by using a tool familiar to any woman who has had a pelvic exam, a speculum.

From there, Dr. Hamlin explained that she would locate the holes in Hawi's bladder and vagina that produced her incontinence and close them with sutures. "If we do this right, we'll end poor Hawi's nightmare."

I noticed that the operating table was tilted downward so that Hawi's face was below ours. I wondered what we looked like to her. I kept looking at Hawi. This must be scary for her. If I were her, I'd want someone to hold my hand. But was that what Hawi wanted? I wasn't sure, so I asked, Dr. Hamlin.

"I think that's a lovely idea, darling."

"Mamitu, can you ask Hawi if it is okay if I come hold her hand?" Hawi nodded yes.

I moved a chair from the corner so I could sit next to Hawi and stay out of Dr. Hamlin's way. My hand clad in the surgical glove, which wasn't ideal. As I took Hawi's hand, she gripped mine tightly, at which point I put my other hand around hers to cradle it. At various points, Dr. Hamlin signaled to Mamitu what she needed, and instruments passed between them in a seamless choreography practiced over decades. I'd been told that at nearly eighty-two, Dr. Hamlin was slowing down, but in the OR that morning she seemed energized and younger than her years.

After about forty-five minutes, Dr. Hamlin said, "It's time to see if we were successful." I don't know what she meant exactly, but I saw the nurse injecting purple liquid into Hawi's catheter. Dr. Hamlin explained, "You see, Kate, if we've cured Hawi and the holes have been closed, the bladder will hold the liquid. If we haven't, we'll see purple." After a minute, she said, "Good news, Hawi. We are done, and I think we have fixed your problem. You should be able to go home to your parents in a couple of weeks."

Mamitu translated Dr. Hamlin's words, and a smile spread across Hawi's face. I squeezed her hand one more time and wished her good luck. They took Hawi's legs out of the stirrups and rolled her out of the OR to a recovery room. By then, the other three beds held patients. I spent the rest of the day rotating among the tables, observing Dr. Hamlin, Dr. Ambaye, and another Ethiopian surgeon, Dr. Haile. The women were stoic as needles deadened their lower halves and quiet as surgery went on above them. I could feel their anxious hope.

That day, I learned that fistula isn't like a birth defect, say a cleft palate, where there is a similarity to each patient's injury. I'd heard one of the surgeons joke, "You've seen one fistula, you've seen one fistula." In other words, each woman's injury was different. After one day in the OR, I could see why. Some women, like Hawi, were there for less than hour, others far longer. I was told there are a variety of factors that determine the complexity of the surgery: the number and size of holes, scar tissue—a surgeon's enemy—because it makes repair much harder. The easiest fistulas to repair were small holes near the vaginal opening without any scar tissue. The tougher cases were the opposite of that, larger holes with scar tissue closer to the cervix.

Some women also have collateral damage to other organs like their urethra that can make a complete cure hard to achieve. I had read that renowned fistula surgeon Dr. Kees Waaldijk described fistula surgery as like operating at the toe inside a boot. I could now see why. I left with increased respect for the surgeons and understood why fistula surgery is a skill learned over a lifetime, not over a weekend.

⎯⎯⎯⎯⎯⎯⎯⎯ ⸸ ⎯⎯⎯⎯⎯⎯⎯⎯

I went to take off the scrubs and put my street clothes back on. I rubbed my neck, exhausted from standing most of the day peering at each operation. I was amazed by the stamina of the surgeons.

When I walked out of the hospital, I could see the sun was just setting in the distance and a glowing band of gold hugged the horizon. I went to the tukul. It was empty, as peaceful as a cathedral, and seemed like a good place to reflect on everything I'd seen. In all, that day, more than a dozen women had received life-transforming care.

Hearing Hawi's story of being abandoned in her time of need brought back memories of Bobby's birth. I came to in a recovery room after my C-section staring at the ceiling. I was all alone. It was around 10 p.m. and I was still somewhat numb from the waist down from the earlier epidural. I had no idea what happened with my baby.

I cried out for the nurse, who came in with tired eyes. In a tone of voice that suggested I had interrupted her coffee break she said my baby was okay but still had a fever so was under observation. I asked if I could see him, and she said, "not right now." I asked about my husband, and she said she didn't know but she'd check. She came back a short while later.

"I was told your husband left."

"What?"

"That's all I know."

"When may I see my baby?"

"I can wheel you by him on the way to your room."

My first view of Bobby was of him crying alone in a clear plastic basinet. I was unable to hold or even touch him. My husband wouldn't be back until the next afternoon, later telling me he was exhausted after Bobby's birth. The abandonment by a husband at a moment of need which Hawi had experienced was a heartbreak I could identify with.

And like Hawi, I was blessed to have parents that supported me when I needed it most. From my hospital room, I called Mom and Dad to tell them they had a new grandchild. When they asked about my husband and I said he'd gone home before I came to, they were on a plane the next day. The old wounds all of us had from my teenage years started to heal as they bonded with Bobby the day after he came into the world. They stayed with us in New York for several weeks helping after my C-section.

When we moved to Silicon Valley and I was close to starting my job at Yahoo and hiring a nanny to take care of Bobby, I asked Mom to interview her. About a half an hour after the interview, I got a call from Mom. She said she didn't want a stranger taking care of her grandson and that she would look after Bobby. And she did. For a whole year. Yes, the person I'd slammed relentlessly when I was a teenager for being "just" a housewife stepped in to help me and care for my infant son. There are some debts that can never truly be repaid. When my marriage ended and my heart was crushed, Bobby and I moved in with Mom and Dad for a time. The love I needed was there and it got me through the unrelenting gloom of my divorce.

I took a deep breath, closed my eyes and tried to think of Hawi, and her days of agonizing labor, then a stillborn girl, and the grief she must have felt. Stillborn. There's a euphemism if ever there was one. Sounds gentle, serene, and almost divine; so much better than dead baby or gray lifeless body, a child who would never take a breath. Hawi shouldn't have lost her baby girl. Then she endured years of isolation and stigma when what she needed was love and an hour of surgery to cure her.

I'd told my son's birth story so many times. I'd thought twenty-four hours of labor, a forced C-section, a baby with a fever and a low Apgar score, and an AWOL husband, meant I'd really gone through something. I sure had. I'd gone through a safe childbirth experience. What would have happened to me if I'd given birth in Hawi's village? How long would I have stayed in horrendous pain? Would Bobby's fate have been like Hawi's stillborn baby girl? The answer was very likely yes.

I may have left the hospital with a bruised heart and C-section stitches, but my baby was healthy and so was I.

I was lucky.

So lucky.

Tears streamed out of my eyes.

I was so so lucky.

There were at least a million women like Hawi all over Africa and Asia. They were forgotten, their suffering ignored, too often told they were cursed and blamed for their own misery. I wiped my tears on my sleeve. There was so much more to do.

———————⚓———————

We closed out 2006 raising more than $2.3 million; 25 percent more money than the year before. We'd gained support from a dedicated group of Ethiopian American women and had raised enough money to fund a new hospital in the Ethiopian city of Harar. Our team was delivering.

Could we continue to grow at this rate every year so we could help more and more women?

13. HEARTS AND MINDS

*Living a minimally acceptable ethical life
involves using a substantial part of our spare
resources to make the world a better place.*

—Peter Singer

Pulitzer Prize-winning columnist Nicholas Kristof of *The New York Times* is one of the best friends any woman with fistula ever had. One of his articles launched a chain of events that did more to raise visibility of their plight than anything since Oprah. That started with two guys both named Steve.

The first Steve read one of Kristof's columns and was so moved his thought was *Somebody should make a movie about this*. His second thought: *It should be my friend, Steve Engel, of Engel Entertainment*. The first Steve gave the second Steve a seed grant of $50,000 to get the ball rolling. You have to love people who put their own money behind their ideas.

Steve Engel's team traveled to Ethiopia and documented the journey of five women with fistula. Each had a different story, but all had suffered lives of isolation and misery for want of life-transforming surgery. They began filming in stark rural villages and followed each woman to the Addis Ababa Fistula Hospital where they were treated by Dr. Hamlin and her surgeons.

Steve Engel invited me to visit their office in New York to meet his team. The director, Mary Olive Smith, and her co-producers, Amy Bucher and Alison Shigo, had contagious energy as they described the five women whose stories of hope and healing that they told in their film. I was inspired by their passion for Dr. Hamlin, the women they featured, and their movie. Alison was so moved by the experience she went on to found an amazing organization called Healing Hands of Joy in Ethiopia. She empowers former fistula patients to become safe motherhood ambassadors, providing education and access to safe delivery options for pregnant women.

We decided to hold two receptions for donors and screen the full-length movie. One was in the Bay Area to coincide with its showing at the San Francisco Film Festival. The second was in New York, where both Nick Kristof and the Steve who provided the seed funding spoke. Thanks to Steve Engel and his wife Heidi Reavis, *A Walk to Beautiful* premiered at a variety of film festivals around the country, giving it extra visibility.

The film would go on to win best feature-length documentary from the International Documentary Association. The PBS show, NOVA, bought the rights to a fifty-two-minute version that would air on public television stations. The next year it would win an Emmy. While we didn't receive a flood of donations like we did after Oprah, because the PBS audience was far smaller, the film was powerful and it introduced many people to fistula.

One Sunday morning around the time the film premiered, I was skimming *The New York Times* before Bobby got up and I turned into a pancake chef. I came across an article in the magazine with a title that caught my eye: "What Should a Billionaire Give—and What Should You?" It was written by philosopher Peter Singer. This paragraph intrigued me:

For more than thirty years, I've been reading, writing, and teaching about the ethical issue posed by the juxtaposition, on our planet, of great abundance and life-threatening poverty. Yet it was not until, in preparing this article, I calculated how much America's Top 10 percent of income earners actually make that I fully understood how easy it would be for the world's rich to eliminate, or virtually eliminate, global poverty.

I did some Googling and discovered that Singer had been making the moral argument for addressing global poverty since 1971. At the same time George Harrison and Indian musician Ravi Shankar were holding their benefit "Concert for Bangladesh" in Madison Square Garden, Singer wrote the seminal *Famine, Affluence and Morality*. In it, he urged action to stop the starvation of millions:

"It makes no difference whether the person I can help is a neighbor's child ten yards away from me or a Bengali whose name I shall never know, ten thousand miles away . . . The moral point of view requires us to look beyond the interests of our own society."

Tragically, neither Singer nor George Harrison and Ravi Shankar were very successful. By December 1974, an estimated 1.5 million Bangladeshis had died from preventable starvation and disease in what became known as the Bangladesh Famine. Seems like something I should have known even if I was a kid when it happened. Singer's call for action to help the poor across divides of race, borders, citizenship, and time zones made him someone I wanted to meet.

Then, like the hand of God, as my missionary friends would say, I got an email indicating that Singer would be in San Francisco giving a lecture sponsored by Princeton University where he was a tenured professor.

The event was being held at a white shoe law firm. When I got off the elevator into the lobby, its walls of glass and a sparkling view of the San Francisco Bay screamed power and influence. A wave of intimidation flowed through me. I assumed the event would be packed, but I was wrong. There were only about thirty people in the expansive room.

As Singer started his talk, his calm voice and measured tone made me relax. He seemed more like a good friend who wanted to help us understand something he found important than an intimidating globally renowned ethicist. Over the next hour, he led us on a guided tour of the core arguments of a book he said he was writing. His key message, as with the famine piece, was that the lives of all people everywhere are of equal fundamental worth. And, as citizens of a rich country, we were immoral if we did not act to end suffering in developing countries. I was hooked.

After he finished, he took a few questions then the event wrapped up and the audience trickled out. A few people lingered to talk with him. I held back, biding my time, and when no one was left, I approached Singer. I droned on about how his arguments resonated with me and how much I loved his talk. He listened with patience, then asked what I did. After I gave him my elevator pitch on fistula and the Foundation that I could do in my sleep, he asked a host of perceptive questions. I pillaged through my messy purse looking for a business card, a bit overwhelmed by his interest in our work. We exchanged a few emails over the next several months.

A while later, I got an email from a friend saying Singer's new book was coming out titled *The Life You Can Save*. I immediately preordered it.

One night I got home from work to find the lean book on my doorstep. When I checked the index, I was delighted to find he'd written about fistula and the Foundation. Turned out this brilliant man thought fistula was a great example of the kind of tragic suffering that too often gets ignored because it impacts the poorest people. He used us to demonstrate how outside support can alleviate needless misery. The book was a tour de force. It was impossible to put down and I finished it late that night. My praise doesn't do it justice. Here's what *The New York Times* reviewer said:

This book is part rational argument, part stinging manifesto, part handbook. It's a volume that suggests, given that 18 million people are dying unnecessarily each year in develop-ing countries, that there is a 'moral stain on a world as rich as this one.' We are not doing enough to help our fellow mortals.

This captivating masterpiece introduced the Foundation to people who would turn out to be some of our most ardent supporters. Singer would hate to think of himself as a salesperson, but he's done an exceptional job opening hearts, minds, and wallets, too. If it was possible to have a platonic crush on someone's mind, I had one on his.

14. WOMEN DELIVER

A woman with a voice is, by definition,
a strong woman.

—Melinda Gates

The alarm blared, jarring me out of a dreamless sleep in a tiny hotel room a few blocks from The British Museum. Several weeks earlier, Ruth Kennedy had reached out to tell me that she and Dr. Hamlin would be traveling to London to attend the Women Deliver Conference, and she wanted to see if I could join them. Truth be known, I was on the fence. While I get that conferences enable people to meet face to face and can be fun, too, often the payoff for the time and money spent to attend seems low. But this was the first-ever global conference focused only on maternal health. Plus, there was going to be a panel devoted to fistula.

I got to the conference center and found the session on fistula. The room was drab and windowless with not more than fifty people in the audience. As I downed a double latte, trying to jump-start my jet-lagged brain, a speaker from the UN wrapped up her remarks. Then a young Kenyan woman named Sarah Omega took to the podium. She gazed across the room, standing poised as a ballet dancer in a tailored suit with her chocolate-brown eyes focused straight ahead.

"I was orphaned at fifteen," she began. "Then raped by a man at my church at nineteen. I became pregnant as a result." Her words were devastating. But it was her voice that grabbed me. It resonated with resolve.

"I was anxious about the delivery and was hoping to have my baby at home. But after more than eighteen hours, I was still in labor, so we went to the local hospital. Then I was wheeled into the operating theater and a C-Section was performed. But it was too late. My baby boy was delivered stillborn."

I heard audible sighs as she continued telling us about her journey. "I was discharged, but I was leaking urine. I didn't know it at the time, but what I had was a fistula. I tried to get treatment but was turned away from our local hospital who said they couldn't fix my problem. I was isolated and ostracized because of my smell. I wanted to kill myself many times. Then, ten years later, through my church, I met the man who would change my life forever, Dr. Hillary Mabeya. He said he could cure me and, at first, I didn't believe him. But he operated on me and healed me. Dr. Mabeya gave me something priceless: my health and my future."

She said all this to an audience of strangers without even a hint of nervousness or embarrassment. Sarah had let nothing destroy her.

Not being orphaned.

Not the violence of rape.

Not delivering her stillborn boy.

Not the social isolation resulting from her fistula.

I was in the presence of an extraordinary person.

I noticed the room was emptying. If I wanted to meet this inspiring woman, I needed to get up now or I'd miss the chance.

I walked over, smiled, and introduced myself saying, "I don't have a daughter but if I were your mother, I'd be very proud of the woman you've become. I am so moved by you—by your courage, your strength, and your resolve." *Where on earth did that come from? Who did I think I was to mention her late mother? I was an idiot.*

Sarah smiled. She seemed touched by my awkward blathering. "You are too kind," she said. "I am glad you liked what I said. This is my first trip out of Kenya. I guess I'll be doing more talks like this before I head home."

"That's great because you are such a compelling speaker," I said.

"You can help people understand why fistula is so devastating, and how life-transforming surgery can be."

We exchanged email addresses, and I wished her good luck. She said she hoped we'd meet again and her smile lingered, which put me at ease. The next year, I'd invite Sarah to join our board to share her powerful perspective with us.

As I walked out of the room, I realized something vital. Women like Sarah have certainly been victimized by an unjust world, one indifferent to their need for care when they are most vulnerable: delivering babies. But this does not mean that the women are defeated or that they must remain victims. Far from it. They are often the most resilient souls on the planet—unbroken by profound suffering.

I found Ruth and Dr. Hamlin sitting outside the room, and we decided to visit the giant conference hall before going back to the hotel to get lunch. The hall was bustling with hundreds of booths and thousands of people. I watched as Ruth guided Dr. Hamlin through the chaos with gentle patience. When we arrived at the hotel, Ruth helped Dr. Hamlin to her seat in the crowded restaurant, getting her tea to relieve the chill from the cool London day. The memory that is clearest from our time together was Ruth's care of Dr. Hamlin, tending to her like a loving daughter. It was easy to see why Ruth had become indispensable to her. Dr. Hamlin was as warm as she'd been toward me on my trips to Addis. It was soothing to be with them both.

About a month later, I opened my email and found a short letter from the hospital's CEO saying Ruth had resigned. I was shocked. For years she had been not only Dr. Hamlin's deputy, but also a critical link between the hospital and organizations supporting their work, like ours. It was hard to imagine Dr. Hamlin without Ruth by her side. Ruth had decades of useful work experience in sub-Saharan Africa and she had earned the respect of seemingly everyone around her.

This was a huge loss to the hospital, to the women it served, and most of all to Dr. Hamlin.

I contacted Ruth to find out more. She said she had taken a job with a fellow missionary at a children's home in northern Ethiopia. Ruth was her normal cheerful self but didn't offer additional information. I sensed there was more to the story, but I just didn't know what was not being said.

15. THE HILTON ACCORD

Almost as color defines vision itself, race shapes the cultural eye—what we do and do not notice, the reach of empathy and alignment of response.

—TAYLOR BRANCH

Bright morning sunlight was streaming through my kitchen window when I dialed the twelve-digit number and listened to the ancient ring tone. It was nearly 7 p.m. in Addis, but I suspected Dr. Ambaye Woldemichael would still be at the hospital since she was tireless.

I'd met Dr. Ambaye on my visit to the hospital the previous fall, and had watched her operate. Dr. Hamlin had said she and another Ethiopian woman, Dr. Mulu Muleta, both had graduated near the top of their classes in medical school. They'd trained at Fistula Hospital, fallen in love with the work, and never left. Dr. Hamlin also told me they had more experience treating fistula than virtually anyone in the world. Both had what the best surgeons always do: an ability to focus for hours if needed on the patient in front of them, with what my dad would call "do it right or don't do it at all" precision. I also heard that Dr. Ambaye spent her weekends in rural villages diagnosing otherwise forgotten women, treating them herself in far flung provincial hospitals. She was the real thing: a deeply dedicated doctor.

When Dr. Ambaye came on the line, I asked her what had happened with Ruth. She paused and said that she wasn't sure. Her voice sounded wary, perhaps of me, and of whatever was unfolding in Addis. My Spidey sense said she knew more but was going to keep her thoughts to herself. I held my pushy self at bay, for once.

Meanwhile, a couple of Ethiopians on our board who had ties to the hospital told me they'd heard rumors that Ruth had left because of tensions with the new CEO and several trustees.

For decades, the hospital had been run like a family business without the systems needed to accommodate their plans for expansion. We understood the CEO was trying to change this situation, an extremely difficult evolution to achieve for even the most seasoned leader. At the same time, we had our own challenges with the hospital's management. For months, we had been seeking basic financial documents, such as an annual audit and a strategic plan, but hadn't been able to get them. To be clear, we were not worried about fraud. But our requests for more information seemed to fray the relationship, as they implied a lack of confidence in the hospital's team.

Over the next couple months, more signs of alarming human resource problems emerged. Those same Ethiopian board members had heard that all the hospital's Ethiopian surgeons, including Dr. Ambaye, were near revolt. They felt they were being mistreated by the hospital's management. This was the core surgical staff doing most of the fistula surgeries. Their departure would be a body blow to the hospital.

Meanwhile, I'd gotten a call from an expat hospital trustee. He wanted me to meet with one of the other Ethiopian surgeons who was in the US on leave, and to chastise the surgeon for some inexplicit act of insubordination. The same surgeon had reached out to me in a panic because he felt intimidated. What was driving this mayhem? It was hard to know for sure, but it seemed that their relatively new CEO was struggling.

He was an Australian missionary whose last position was running a refugee program in Syria. No doubt, he had been doing useful work there to help vulnerable people. He had a loving wife, four beautiful kids, and was hard working and dedicated. On one hand, this was a kind thing to do, placing a good man in a job that needed to be filled. On the other hand, he had no training in medicine or public health and had never run a large surgical hospital or lived in sub-Saharan Africa. In fairness, it would be challenging for anyone, even a very experienced leader, to fill Dr. Hamlin's big shoes while introducing new management systems to the hospital.

The Australian Trust and Australian government were the biggest funders of the hospital and it seemed their man got the job. I'd met representatives from the Australian Trust during the last PIM. Without exception they were polite and friendly. Many seemed to be members of the same Anglican Church in a prosperous suburb of Sydney. They were successful in their chosen fields, the kind of people you'd see on boards of schools and arts institutions in the US.

The ones I spoke to were dedicated to the hospital, and all but one served as volunteers. That said, their involvement with Africa and Ethiopians seemed to go not much farther than the perimeter of Dr. Hamlin's hospital, kind of like the Americans I met at the American Club in Tanzania. Their natural loyalty appeared to be to fellow Australian, Dr. Hamlin, and now to their Australian CEO. Perhaps I'm being unfair, but that's what it felt like. The upcoming PIM in Addis that May gave us an opportunity to talk with the hospital's trustees and try to do what we could to help.

I arrived in Addis the afternoon ahead of the PIM. We'd scheduled a meeting with me, a few members of our board, Dr. Hamlin, and a few of the hospital's trustees that night. After some small talk, we elaborated on the concerns we'd shared earlier about the lack of audited financial statements and a strategic plan and tiptoed around the problems between the CEO and the Ethiopian medical staff. We suggested mediation to resolve the conflict with the doctors. Dr. Hamlin, as I recall, said very little. She seemed to defer to the men, much the same way growing up I'd seen my mom defer to my father. I thought this must be a generational thing, where capable women are used to turning power over to men who are accustomed to taking the lead. After a couple hours of polite, circular discussion, we got nowhere.

The next morning I met Anne in the lobby and we headed over to the Hospital. The PIM was held again in the large tukul. The room was drenched with yellow morning light. About twenty representatives from support organizations from Japan, Germany, the UK, and Australia, hospital trustees, Dr. Hamlin, along with a couple of members of our board, including our chair, Kassy Kebede, were slowly entering and sitting down in rows of chairs.

After a series of bland presentations from each support organization, Dr. Ambaye came in to make a brief prepared statement to the assembled group. She was accompanied by Dr. Haile, whom I'd met on my last visit. Dr. Ambaye was petite, with cropped black hair and delicate wire-rimmed glasses. She was easy to underestimate because of her small, slender frame and her gentle voice. Her hand trembled as she looked down at the paper she grasped. She said that what she was going to say was very hard. As her voice cracked and her eyes welled with tears, she said that she loved Dr. Hamlin and her work at the hospital.

The weight of her words fell on the silent room as she continued. She said the CEO and trustees had made work intolerable for the Ethiopian doctors. At this point, a member of the Australian Trust shouted from the back of the room, "You should be quiet."

"Please let her finish," I said. I tried to speak in a calm tone, but it's likely I was more domineering than I want to remember.

Dr. Ambaye continued to explain that the work environment had become so bad that she and her fellow Ethiopian surgeons were ready to leave if things didn't change. This broke her heart because she was dedicated to the women with fistula and to Dr. Hamlin.

Dr. Ambaye added that the CEO and the board made them feel that their work wasn't valued, and they weren't wanted.

At this point, a hospital trustee came bounding out of his chair. He lunged toward her with the physical anger that you'd expect in a drunken bar brawl and shouted, "You're a liar!" Before he could hurt her, the CEO restrained him.

Dr. Ambaye and Dr. Haile stood and walked out quickly through the back door.

Kassy spoke up. "Fistula Foundation is very concerned about the situation. We are going to withhold funding until the dispute with the doctors can be resolved."

At this point, a member of the Australian Trust directed his anger squarely at Kassy, yelling, "How dare you!"

Another was telling Kassy, "You can't do that."

It felt as if a grenade filled with angry words had exploded at Kassy's feet. He tried to explain our concerns, but he wasn't getting through. Kassy remained calm, even as he was attacked. I was amazed by his reserve.

Dr. Hamlin sat there stunned and silent, as did the delegates from the other countries. It was dreadful, like watching a family fight. In all my crazy years in advertising and politics, I'd never seen anything quite like this. Here were people screaming at our mild-mannered Ethiopian board chair, with a threat of physical violence against a slight female Ethiopian surgeon.

A hospital trustee, a lean man with thinning grey hair and bifocals, walked to the front of the room and said, "We are going to close the session and take a tour of the new midwifery school."

I stepped out of the now stuffy tukul onto the lawn surrounding it. The Executive Director of the Australian Trust walked toward me. His face was the color of a tomato as he screamed at me, "What do you think you are doing?" Before I could answer, he added, "The whole PIM is against you."

I took a deep breath and bit my lip. I didn't want to say something I'd regret. What I wanted to do was find Dr. Ambaye, not absorb his rage. So, I said, "I'm sorry you feel that way. Maybe we can talk later."

I walked toward Anne and Kassy who were standing near the door of the tukul. Two other Foundation board members had lost the plot and gone off on the tour. The three of us headed to the surgeons' offices at the back of the hospital. There we found Dr. Ambaye and Dr. Haile.

We asked how they were doing after that brutal interchange. They expressed heartbreak that Dr. Hamlin didn't step in to help them. This was what seemed to bother them the most: that the person that they revered and had worked with for years, in Dr. Ambaye's case decades, had not intervened on their behalf. Their pain was palpable. I sat there, overcome by deep sadness. I felt powerless. I hate that feeling.

Then one of the Australian Trust members, the head of a big hospital in Sydney, I'll call Dr. Goodman, walked in. His manner was reserved; not warm, but also not hostile. Like us, he mostly listened. This seemed like a good sign; his instinct was to get the doctors' side of the story.

"How can someone with no training in medicine or hospital management, be given authority to tell us how to do our jobs?" Dr. Haile asked while Dr. Ambaye nodded in agreement.

It was unclear what Dr. Goodman thought of the situation. But when he suggested getting representatives of the Australian Trust together with me, Kassy, and other Fistula Foundation board members to try to chart a path forward, I thought the odds of resolving the conflict improved dramatically.

The next day, I was trying to remain optimistic about our ability to work with the Australians to avoid the train wreck of the Ethiopian doctors resigning. I joined the three members of our board in the lobby—Kassy, a woman also from Ethiopia, and an American man. We walked down to a veranda by the pool. There, we met five members of the Australian Trust—all male, all middle aged and older, all Australian, and all but one white, the other Asian. One of the Australians waved to a group of middle-aged white women, as one of them said, "The wives are going shopping."

The Australians shared a draft agreement that they had written. It focused on better communications among the hospital's CEO, trustees, and support organizations like ours. We added points about our concern that the doctors were being mistreated. And we reiterated that we needed an audit and a strategic plan and agreed on the need to hire additional staff to strengthen accounting practices. But we believed the most important action item was the immediate engagement of a professional mediator to resolve the labor dispute between the CEO, trustees, and the Ethiopian surgeons.

We all shook hands at the end of the meeting. The Australians were a likable lot. They had understandable pride in the hospital, since they'd been its largest supporter for years. Any tension about what had happened with Dr. Ambaye in the tukul seemed to have faded. We jokingly referred to our agreement as the "Hilton Accord." I headed off to the business center at the hotel with a member of the Australian Trust so we could amend the document to include the new actions we'd agreed upon. Then, we would share it with the hospital CEO and trustees.

———————————————

Later that afternoon, Anne and I grabbed a cab to the airport for our flight home. In the gate area, we ran into Dr. Goodman who was boarding the same flight we were to Dubai. I said we would need to stay in close touch with both sides, and likely have weekly check-ins to ensure that what we'd agreed upon was implemented. He said that he didn't see the need and was confident the hospital's trustees and the CEO would work it out. My heart sank. I said the rage we saw in the tukul made that unlikely without us staying involved. He didn't argue with me. Nor did he agree.

16. LABOR OF LOVE

Don't be color blind, be color brave.
Embrace diversity as a competitive advantage.

—Mellody Hobson

Over the coming weeks, Kassy and I talked a few times with several of the Ethiopian doctors, told them about the Hilton Accord, and tried to be supportive. Since at that point both of us were PNG (persona non grata) with the hospital trustees, other members of our board reached out to them. But it was becoming clear that nothing was happening.

I emailed Dr. Goodman in Australia to see if we could have a call to discuss the situation. When we finally got on the phone, after a few pleasantries, Dr. Goodman cut to the heart of the matter. He said he was troubled that the head of the Australian Trust—the guy who had screamed at me in front of the tukul—had forwarded the Hilton Accord to the CEO and hospital trustees with the "track changes" clear.

As his words sank in, I realized this meant that it would be obvious what actions and issues Fistula Foundation had added to the draft written by the Australians. Concerns about the pending resignation of the Ethiopian surgeons due to mistreatment, our involvement in professional mediation efforts to ensure it moved forward; those were all actions we thought were critical. The Australians, not so much.

I blurted, "What? You're kidding, right?"

"I'm sorry . . . I agree, it's unfortunate," he said.

As a volcano of fury enveloped me, I screamed, "Unfortunate? It's a betrayal! No wonder none of the things we wanted done are happening."

"It isn't my job or yours to fix the situation. We need to leave it to the CEO and trustees."

I clenched my teeth and squeaked out, "I have to go," and hung up.

———————

The Hilton Accord had been a naive waste of time. I felt like we'd been played. Maybe that's not entirely fair. What was true was that the Australians had a very different view of the damage to the hospital that would result if all the Ethiopian doctors resigned.

The next week, our board received a letter from the chair of the Australian Trust that reiterated what Dr. Goodman had said; that it was not our role or theirs to intervene. He elaborated that the action steps in the Hilton Accord we thought we'd agreed were necessary, were not actually required. They were only suggestions. For good measure, he also chastised Kassy and me for "siding" with the traitorous doctors. He said we owed the trustees and Dr. Hamlin an apology. I would have rather drunk bleach. While I had no desire to hurt Dr. Hamlin, I was saddened that she had not defended Dr. Ambaye and the other doctors.

It looked like we had no ability to fix the situation. That power resided with the same group that had been responsible for the choice in successor to Dr. Hamlin: the Australian Trust and the hospital trustees.

———————

Then one morning, I opened my email to find a copy of a letter from the Ethiopian doctors sent to Dr. Hamlin. The first line was from the Bible, Hebrews 6:10:

For God is not unjust to forget your work and labor of love which you have shown towards his name.

It was their resignation. The doctors described their love for Dr. Hamlin, the hospital, and their work to heal needy women. But they explained that the CEO and several trustees had made the work environment intolerable. Most damning, they asserted that, "It is obvious that the CEO is deliberately worsening the condition to achieve his ambition of a hospital free of Ethiopian doctors by disregarding the doctors' effort to reconcile."

The Ethiopian Society of Obstetricians and Gynecologists (ESOG) responded in writing with a searing indictment of the hospital's treatment of the surgeons. They said that the resignations produced "profound shock, regret, and great concern," and urged that the matter be revisited:

> The senior gynecologists who recently resigned have more than five decades of service and experience among themselves. ESOG believes that the loss of their experience and service to the AAFH and Ethiopia will have a long lasting and perhaps permanent damage to this important public service rendered to the poor and unfortunate fistula victims. . . . ESOG is extremely concerned about the message the sudden termination of services of these colleagues who have dedicated their lives to public service will give young doctors and providers, especially at a time when the government and all partners are making enormous efforts to break the cycle of brain drain from our country. Is this the culmination that nearly five decades of dedicated service deserves? What message does a young doctor who is eager to serve this country get from these developments?

I could not understand Dr. Hamlin's actions. Why had she let the CEO, the Australian Trust, the hospital's trustees hurt the hospital she'd dedicated her life to building? Why did she trust them so completely? Why didn't she instead listen to the voices of her Ethiopian doctors? This was an unholy end to a disastrous chapter in the hospital's history.

Like most failures, this one was instructive. One obvious conclusion was that an organization built and led for decades by one person needs to think hard about a leadership transition. A clear don't: hire someone with sparse relevant experience simply because they are a "good person." A clear do: develop a succession plan that's tough-minded and involves experienced outsiders to help guide the transition so you don't make wishful mistakes. This lesson was an easier one to process since the blame wasn't ours. The decision to place the CEO at the hospital was the Australian's and the hospital's trustees.

The other lesson learned was more painful. We had no meaningful impact on what happened ten thousand miles away—to convince the doctors to stay or the hospital to change its management practices. It's quite possible we even made the situation worse. It was hard to tell. But our failure was sobering. We realized that even as a major funder, our power to influence how a hospital was run was limited. This lesson would influence everything we did going forward. We needed to be humble and realistic about our role.

The word *diversity* is thrown around a lot lately. In some quarters it's looked at as simply a politically correct buzzword for a fuzzy aspiration. I came away from the disastrous ending to the hospital's labor dispute to see true diversity as a force for better collective thinking and decision-making, if diverse voices are heard and respected.

Looking back to the meeting where we drafted the Hilton Accord, there were four of us representing Fistula Foundation.

Two men. Two women. Two of us white, born in the US. Two of us black, born in Africa. Two of us with international development experience. By contrast, the Australian Trust members were all men. All Anglican. All but one white, the other Asian. All older than me. None had perceptible international development experience. Would the Australian Trust have acted the differently if their board contained Africans, women, and people with international development experience? I must believe the answer is yes. If the women with fistula were their "true north," I think they would have treated the Ethiopian surgeons—those doing the bulk of the surgeries to heal those injured women—as if they were irreplaceable. Because they were.

I reached out to Dr. Ambaye and some of the other doctors who left to offer whatever words of support I could muster. But my solace didn't pay their bills or give them a place to practice fistula surgery.

I wanted the Foundation to provide bridge funding to the surgeons so they could form their own organization to practice fistula surgery at other hospitals in Ethiopia. They had expertise that was rare, precious, and truly invaluable to women with fistula. At the next Fistula Foundation board meeting, I tried to make that happen.

Ahead of the meeting I coached myself: Do not get excited. Do not become emotional. Just make the case. At the meeting, I went to the mat, meaning I completely ignored my own advice. I was so zealous and stubborn that I lost. Big time. I did not convince a single board member that it was a good idea. All I got was one limp abstention from a guy who said he was 100 percent behind the idea, and then sat mute when the discussion grew heated as I tried the board's patience with my impassioned pleas. The board passed a motion to prohibit us from funding anyone in Ethiopia other than Dr. Hamlin's hospital for at least a year.

In retrospect, what I wanted may have been reckless. Had the Foundation shifted direction to support the Ethiopian doctors, the situation may have devolved into bitter acrimony and a public fight. This could have tarnished the Foundation's reputation and inadvertently hurt the very women we all wanted to help. However, the ESOG prediction about the loss to Ethiopia's medical capacity was accurate. Two of the fistula surgeons with decades of experience now live in the US, where they do exactly zero fistula surgeries.

Since I'd joined the Foundation three years earlier, we'd had a singular focus: supporting the Addis Ababa Fistula Hospital and Dr. Hamlin. But those days were now over. We knew that Ethiopia was not alone. Women with untreated fistula existed anywhere women lacked access to emergency obstetric care, namely C-sections. So, we adopted a new mission:

> The Mission of the Fistula Foundation is to raise awareness of and resources for fistula repair, prevention, and education programs worldwide.

We also set aside the money we'd raised to date for use by Dr. Hamlin's hospital that we'd disburse once we had solid financial information from them. The new money we'd raise would go toward our global mission that could include funding Dr. Hamlin.

During this trying time, I was deeply grateful to our board for sticking by me and Kassy. They had our backs and gave us the confidence to plow forward.

PART THREE:

A MILLION
REASONS

17. THE REAL DEAL

*Someone who helps you in a time
of need becomes a part of you.*

—SOMALI PROVERB

I stared up at the stage as a technician wearing all black adjusted the microphone for the guest of honor, Dr. Denis Mukwege. I was in search of new partners and Mukwege, who had built a hospital called Panzi in the Democratic Republic of Congo (DRC), was at the top of my list. The country had a notorious reputation as "the worst place in the world to be a woman" because there, as is often the case with armed conflict, rape was a tool of war. In the darkness, there are heroes who light candles, and in Congo that was Mukwege. While I had looked into flights to DRC, I learned he was coming to San Francisco for this talk. I reached out to organizers and after a bunch of unreturned calls, finally got a meeting set up with him the morning after their event.

Eve Ensler, the pathbreaking playwright of *The Vagina Monologues*, who now used the name "V," kicked the discussion off introducing her friend Denis, pronounced in French as "Denny." She explained that Panzi Hospital sat in Bukavu near the shores of Lake Kivu and was what human rights champion Stephen Lewis called the "epicenter of resistance." She said Mukwege had treated more than twenty thousand women.

Mukwege said that he had started out to be a pediatrician. But he saw that women were dying needlessly in childbirth and changed direction to focus his energies on what he saw as a maternal health crisis. He described the long-run problems faced in his home country. First, there was exploitative colonialism at the hands of the Belgians, followed by rapacious rulers and murderous battles that had spilled over from neighboring Rwanda and infected his country. He said the current conflict in DRC was more deadly than anything since the Second World War. The threat of violence was perpetual, shattering the quiet security that made the daily pleasures of life possible.

The most savagely injured were the women. They had been raped and maimed. The perpetrators were striving to inflict the most suffering possible not just on the women, but on their families and communities. Mukwege was reserved, yet there was an unwavering intensity as he described the wrenching challenges he faced. He said it was these brave women who motivated him to persevere against extraordinary odds.

Lest we think that Congo is unique, he added that rape is a staple of war. The rape of Chinese women by Japanese in Nanjing or Muslim women in Serbia underscore that these crimes are not new or unique to DRC. Mukwege asserted that the root cause of this violence is deep-seated inequality. It starts in the home with girls being fed less, given less schooling, and being expected to perform all household chores and disproportionate manual labor. This devaluation lays the foundation for the same disregard for the rights of women and leads to weak maternal health care. He added that the poorer the country, generally, the stronger men's hold on power over women. Mukwege asserted that men throughout the world still have more economic, political, and social power than women. It is men that are critical to long-term solutions.

After the session ended, a small crowd swarmed the stage. I was thinking I could introduce myself quickly. But Mukwege darted out a side door, avoiding the people like me who found him so inspiring.

The next morning, I drove up to San Francisco with board member, Dr. Larry William. When we got to the lobby of Mukwege's hotel, we huddled in a quiet corner. When the elevator door opened, I spotted Mukwege with a lone woman by his side. I walked toward him, since I figured he'd have no idea what I looked like and introduced myself and Larry. He smiled and shook our outstretched hands.

"Your talk last night was so moving," I said.

"It was exceptional," Larry added.

Mukwege smiled again but seemed uncomfortable with our praise. He quickly changed the subject to talking about Panzi Hospital as we all sat down in the corner.

My French is poor, and Mukwege speaks English, but was more comfortable in French and asked if we'd mind using his translator to help us. Of course, we were okay with that.

He said, "The women we see have often been victims of rape. And not just by one man, but often by many men. They come to us with their bodies and their spirits broken. We try to heal both."

I said, "I don't know how you do what you do, how your soul stays whole when confronting such agony and pain."

He said, "My father was a minister. I try to do with my hands what he did with his words: make the world a better place. I feel blessed to do the work I do." He radiated a gentle, confident calm. I realized we only had a short bit of time with him, so I tried to summarize why we were there to meet him.

"Dr. Mukwege, our organization, Fistula Foundation, expanded our mission from focusing on only supporting Dr. Hamlin's hospital in Ethiopia so that we can help doctors like you treat women with fistula. We want to know if more funding would enable you to help more women."

As the translator changed my words to French, a bright smile spread across his face as he shook his head yes. He then said in English,

"I can use money. Now. One of our largest funders cut back their support without notice because of the global recession. I had to lay off twenty of my staff. This has meant we are not able to treat as many women. It's been a very hard time."

My expectation when we sat down was that this would be the beginning of a "get to know you" process, and that down the road we might be able to support some of his work. But in front of us was a man so dedicated to the women he served, and yet in dire need of funds.

I looked at Larry, with a "stop me if you think I am wrong" look, and got back what felt like a "go for it" look, so I said, "Would $50,000 be adequate to hire your staff back?" That seemed like a big, but not-too-big number. I was winging it.

Then Mukwege said, "Of course, I could hire my staff back with that. It would not be enough to keep them forever, but it would enable me to get them back in their jobs. This would help me, and, of course, them too."

"Can you send us a proposal for that amount?" I asked. "We'll also need audited financial statements if you have them. We will need to get approval from our board."

"No problem," Mukwege said. "I can have my team at Panzi email that to you."

At that point, a more unguarded Denis emerged. "Do you mind if I ask you for one more thing?"

"Not at all," I said, "What do you need?"

In a tentative tone, he asked, "Can you get me urethral plugs?"

(Wondering what those are? Well, the plugs help a woman whose urethra has been destroyed by rape or childbirth keep from leaking urine. She will pull the plug out to empty her bladder. I know, yuck. But think of what it would be like to have no urethra, that little muscle that lets us control urine. I never think of mine, any more than I think about my pancreas or my aorta but can't live without them either.)

At that point, the words were racing out of my mouth. "Yes, I'm sure we can do that. We've got a good relationship with the supplier and have ordered them for use at Dr. Hamlin's hospital. You're here for another week, right? We can likely get a shipment to you to take back to DRC."

As the translator communicated this in French, Mukwege's face lit up like the skyline on a Fourth of July evening. He said, "That's fabulous. I'm so happy. You see, for women that I've tried to help but who remain incontinent, the plugs are the difference between wet and dry. They can be in public again. It can give them back their lives." The exuberant words were unnecessary; his bright smile and sparkling eyes said it all. He's the *real deal,* the kind of person I dreamed we'd be able to support with our new mission.

Dr. Hamlin was a very tough act to follow, but in Mukwege, we'd found another compassionate and dedicated person who could use our help. (The next year I'd meet him again at a hotel in New York like a drug runner but with a suitcase filled with more urethral plugs, but I am getting ahead of myself here . . .)

———————⚹———————

Three days later, in my email I had the proposal for the $50,000, Panzi's audited financials, references—all from a team in a war zone, and with Mukwege still in the US. It was solid. I sent it on to the executive committee, a committee of the board whose approval I needed to send the money. Within hours, all responded with unanimous and enthusiastic support. I sent out an email to the entire Fistula Foundation board to share the good news.

The same day I got a call from a board member who was not at all happy. This person had volunteered to go with a few other members, including Larry, in a couple weeks to tell the Fistula Hospital trustees that we had gone global and would be funding other hospitals. He felt I had undercut him. I said something like, "I can understand your perspective, but I don't think this will be a problem. We are not making a public announcement about the support for Mukwege." This was not what this board member wanted to hear. My guess is what he wanted to hear was that I was wrong and very sorry. The problem was, I didn't feel that way. At all.

So, without contrition on my part, what I got back was more anger that felt like rage. Like, YOU CAN'T DO THIS! Problem was, yes, I could, and I had.

I get it. In a perfect world, we'd tell the hospital in Addis we were going to fund other organizations before we did so. That order of operation makes sense. Except this wasn't a perfect world. If it was, the women in DR Congo that Denis Mukwege was treating wouldn't be getting raped. They wouldn't be delivering babies without help, left with holes in their vaginas, bladders, and sometimes rectums, too. Also, I was so appalled by how the Ethiopian surgeons had been treated by those in power at Hamlin's hospital, that I didn't care what they thought of us, or me. If they couldn't see that funding a hospital in a war zone was the right thing to do, that was their problem. I was arguably pig-headed. The board member had a good point, but I couldn't see it that way at the time.

Mukwege told us our support enabled him to rehire the people he had had to lay off and they could provide care to more patients. I was thrilled by this. I loved that we could move fast and get funds where they needed to go; the opposite of the way I'd seen the US government move. I'd hoped our small organization could be nimble—like a speedboat with an ATM on the back, rather than the Queen Mary. But this was fast, even for us.

We were heading in a new direction while the worst recession in eighty years was imperiling the global economy. But as it turned out, maybe it wasn't a bad time to launch our new mission after all. The cutbacks in support for people like Mukwege made what money we could raise even more useful.

18. SMILE TRAIN OF VAGINAS

*What you do is more important than how
you do everything else, and doing something
well does not make it important.*

—TIM FERRISS

The US is populated with more than 1.5 million nonprofits: most raising less than $500,000 a year and growing at a rate not much greater than inflation. The reality is that nonprofits don't generally face the threat of being pushed out of business by a superior competitor. Nor do they face the pressure that politicians do, of being thrown out of office by a more capable challenger. This means that nonprofits can continue operating with limited results and modest growth. As one Harvard Business School professor put it bluntly, "in the nonprofit sector, mediocrity is not only sustainable, it's normative."

In 2009, the World Health Organization estimated that at least a million women suffered with untreated fistula. If we stayed small and ran in place, the opportunity cost for our sluggish growth would be measured in all those women we wouldn't be able to help. But they were not pounding on our door. The pressure to help more women would have to start and end with us.

We had a new mission statement, but it was really broad. It enabled us to treat fistula, prevent fistula, provide medical training, and create public awareness. You could drive a truck through that thing. I joked, we could spend all our money on Super Bowl ads to build awareness and comply with our mission without actually helping any women. Where should we go from here?

In some ways, this was a business question, and my long-ago-set-aside marketing thinking returned to the front of my mind. What was our product, and how would we sell it? As I type that, I wonder if it seems cold to think of helping women with fistula as a "product." But looking at our enterprise that way helped me see through a fog of myriad options. It seemed like we needed to ask two basic questions and find out where there was an intersection.

1. Why do women suffer from untreated fistula?
2. What will donors pay Fistula Foundation to do?

Why do women suffer from untreated fistula? Numerous factors contribute to a woman getting a fistula, besides a lack of doctors to perform C-sections. Child marriage can mean girls may give birth before their bodies are developed. A lack of contraception can lead to unwanted pregnancies and inability to space deliveries. Inadequate prenatal care means problems ahead of delivery aren't spotted. It can get complicated, but the through-line was clear: poverty and gender discrimination. Women got fistula because they were poor, and their poverty made treatment unaffordable or inaccessible.

What will donors pay us to do? This question was at least as important as the first one. No money, no mission. I'd learned one important thing from our existing donors: they were shocked that women were suffering needlessly. They wanted to help, whether that was paying for a single surgery, multiple surgeries, or contributing to fund part of one.

A clear sweet spot emerged. Women with fistula usually can't afford surgery, and donors would like to pay for said surgery. I told Anne we could be the "Smile Train of Vaginas," funding fistula surgery the way Smile Train treated cleft palates! We'd leave prevention and awareness building to others. And this outcome was measurable. We could track the number of surgeries we funded. More money had to equal more women getting helped, or we weren't doing our jobs.

To demonstrate "I've got this," and to prove to the board I could lead, I developed a plan based on this commonsense approach to share with the board committee formed to guide our strategy. I added a cover that quoted Gandhi. "The future depends on what we do in the present." I sent it to the committee chair, Dr. Jerry Shefren, with ample time to review before the first committee meeting.

———————⊥———————

The next week, Jerry came to our office to discuss the committee's work ahead of the meeting. He was an accomplished man with quiet confidence and steely integrity whom I respected. He was an Ob/Gyn and always showed up for board meetings well prepared and asked insightful questions. I was anxious to hear what he had to say about my strategy and hoped he'd like it.

After some small talk, I asked him for his reaction to it as I pulled out two copies, I assumed we'd review. He said, "I haven't read it." Before I could ask why, he said "I want to green-field our approach." He went on to explain that the committee would have a wide-open process for considering all options.

My plan sat in front of him untouched.

When he left, he didn't take it with him.

I was crushed.

On the surface, a green field approach may have been a good idea, exploring all possible paths. But to me, it seemed like a waste of time.

One of the members thought we should aim to be a center of excellence for fistula knowledge and information. But we'd be starting from a very weak base. At that point Fistula Foundation was me, Anne, Terry, and the board. None were surgeons let alone fistula surgeons or public health experts. Another person thought we should consider pursuing fistula prevention. The problem was one of scale and ability to prove impact. To prevent fistula, we would need to provide what we have in the US: availability of emergency obstetric care for any laboring woman. About half of the more than forty million births a year in sub-Saharan Africa happened outside of hospitals, meaning roughly twenty million babies were born at home. Prevention was out.

Through all these rabbit-hole conversations, I subtly tried to sell what seemed like a sound strategy. In the end, we reached a consensus: we would focus on providing treatment to women with fistula. Jerry had been right to approach the process the way he had. The committee owned the strategy. This was the best result possible. It wasn't my plan. It was our plan.

There was no debate that we would have a rigorous approval process to ensure we were effective in deploying donor money to fund surgeries. But we had a major disagreement about how we would go about selecting the hospital partners doing those surgeries.

Some members of the committee thought we should use a model common with US charities and the US government and do an RFP (request for proposal). This meant we would put out a general notice about what we wanted to fund, communicate the parameters—how much, for what, where, and a due date—and then wait for the proposals to roll in. Review, pick winners, and then fund. Sounded good.

But not to me.

I believed it was critical that we get out to the field, talk with expert fistula surgeons, find out who was really getting things done. Our goal was to select true winners from those who could simply write a good proposal. Also, money can warp relationships. We had money, and the potential hospital partner was looking for it. From the beginning, this created a power imbalance and could be an incentive to withhold tough truths.

I'd seen the USAID model, where we'd cynically joke that the

US government spent $8 out of $10 to ensure that the other $2 wasn't stolen or wasted. That was the opposite of what I wanted for us. We needed to recognize that the hospitals and doctors we were funding would always know more about what would work in their community than we would. Jacqueline Novogratz, founder of Acumen, said it best: "There is no currency like trust." I wanted the hospitals we funded to not be just beneficiaries of our largesse, but to be true trusted partners.

The stakes for getting it right, funding dedicated and capable people, were high. We'd be funding vaginal surgery in far-flung corners of Africa and Asia. There were formidable obstacles for even the best-intentioned doctors. We knew from research that an overconfident surgeon who views themself as the "best chance" for a woman, but who has inadequate training, can permanently injure a woman who might have been cured by a surgeon with the right training. I pounded on about this and in the end, we agreed that our "verify, trust" strategy was the way to go.

A few weeks later we presented the whole plan to the full board who approved it with overwhelming support. We now had a road map to chart our way forward. With the global economy still in the throes of the Great Recession, we had the wind in our face, but at least we knew where we were headed.

A while after the board meeting, I got a call from Jerry. He said he was concerned about how the Foundation was investing the money we'd set aside for the Fistula Hospital when we went global. At that point, a committee of three men on the board was investing the money in a handful of individual stocks and a couple mutual funds. Even I knew this was not the best way to go, since it was a risky approach that over time was unlikely to pay off. I should have said something but I didn't want to rock the boat—pick your battles and all that. Yes, I was chicken. But when Jerry called, I saw an opening. I agreed completely that we should hire a firm to manage the money based upon board-approved goals rather than debate which stocks to buy.

There was one obstacle: the head of the board finance committee responsible for investing the money was a retired businessman who took great pride in his investment prowess. I suspected he'd not be happy with this idea since it implied he wasn't getting the job done. When I called to talk to him, I tried to let him down easy.

I said, "You can help select the firm, and they'd of course report to you . . ."

What came back at me, in a matter-of-fact tone, was something like this: "Well, Kate, we all know that children raised by single mothers don't turn out as well as other kids. So, who are you to ask me to step aside?"

Huh?

I sat there shocked and wounded, like I'd been punched in the stomach. If the guy was searching for the most hurtful thing he could say, he'd surely found it. Anger surged through me like an emotional rip tide. While I wasn't ready for that lacerating comment, I was ready for push back, so I said, "I think this will be for the best," and I hung up before I exploded.

In my mind I was biting back with something closer to, *if you got your entitled self out of our way, we'd make more money. And were you mean to me just now because you know you're wrong?*

I walked right to Anne's desk and unloaded a rant laced with enough salty language to make a nun's ears melt. Then, with Jerry's help, we called the other members of the board committee and started getting references for a firm to invest our funds. The one we chose and still use, Sand Hill Global Advisors, was founded by a woman.

19. TWO WORDS

I want to give women a space to feel their own
strength and tell their stories. That is power.

—Beyoncé Knowles Carter

I lifted the Sunday *New York Times* off my front porch and then sat down on the couch. I grabbed the four-color one-hundred-page magazine out of the paper and flipped through the pages. There it was, our full-page ad with the headline:

16-year-old Nsimire endured hours of
agonizing labor . . . the baby died . . .
but her nightmare wasn't over.

My heart sank. It wasn't the headline I wanted.

———————————

A few weeks earlier, I picked up the ringing phone and found myself talking to an energetic ad sales rep from *The New York Times*. I was ready to tell him "No thanks," since we don't advertise. But he got my attention when he said they'd be running an entire Sunday magazine featuring themes from a new book by Nicholas Kristof and his wife, Sheryl WuDunn. The book, *Half the Sky: Turning Oppression into*

Opportunity for Women Worldwide, was scheduled to go on sale the following month. Many of our most loyal supporters had first learned about fistula through Kristof's masterful columns. A book co-authored by him and focused on women, was likely to be a hit with our supporters.

This seemed like an ideal opportunity to create much-needed awareness about our new mission and interest in supporting it with *Times* readers. I asked the rep two questions: How much will it cost for a full page? (Go big or go home.) And can we be the first ad in the magazine if we commit soon? The amount was both big and small—$34,000. Big, because we had zero money budgeted for advertising. Small because the audience seeing the ad was likely our tribe, and on Sunday about two million people got *The New York Times*. The upfront positioning was key to me. I didn't want our ad to be in the back with the tail ends of long articles and ads for chia pets.

I emailed the exec committee of the board to get approval. One member asked a good question: who will create it? I said, "I will." I called the rep back, locked in the rate and the positioning, and got to work on the ad.

At that point, our only partner outside of Ethiopia was Denis Mukwege's Panzi Hospital in DRC. I thought that the best way to engage people in what we did, and why, would be to tell the story of an individual woman with fistula. I reached out to the team at Panzi, who provided me with a heartbreaking story about Nsimire. With only one page, a powerful headline that was critical. Here's what I came up with:

16-year-old Nsimire was raped, became
pregnant, endured hours of agonizing labor...
the baby died...but her nightmare wasn't over.

Do you notice the difference between that version and the one that ran?

Hint, it's just two words.

The body copy filled in the details:

Nsimire went into labor without medical help. The labor left her incontinent with an obstetric fistula—a common injury for women with unrelieved obstructed labor. The good news: Nsimire got the curative surgery she desperately needed at the Panzi Hospital in Democratic Republic of Congo, by the dedicated team headed by Dr. Denis Mukwege, and funded by the Fistula Foundation. Tragically, the World Health Organization estimates two to three million women suffer with untreated fistulas, for want of surgery that would transform their lives. We're working hard to help women like Nsimire. Learn how you can sponsor a life-transforming surgery for only $450.

I was pleased with how the ad had turned out and was excited to move forward. I decided that I should share it with the exec committee. I was not seeking their approval but hoping for their praise.

Instead, one of the exec committee members reached out to me and said that I had to take "was raped" out of the headline. Why? Well, because one of the other exec committee members thought it reflected negatively on African men, that it reinforced a stereotype about violent black men. While I am sensitive to negative stereotypes, this concern seemed misplaced, at best. This was Nsimire's story. She was raped. By an African man. I tried to explain that in DRC, rape was used to destroy not only women, but families and communities. It was not an isolated incident; it was a brutal, horrifying fact of life for women there. I got nowhere.

I need to add, though our board was roughly half men/half women, all the members of our exec committee who could act on behalf of the full board were men. None had international development or public health degrees or much advertising experience.

I decided to call one of the committee members and make my case again, thinking perhaps that he could win over his colleagues. I try to assume good intentions, so I asked a few "help me understand" questions. Then I pleaded with an intensity on the verge of anger. This got me a few sympathetic words, but not a change of direction.

I hung up and took a deep breath. That's because the voice inside my head was saying, *"Are you frigging kidding me? You can't do that. It's her story!!"* That voice was yelling.

I went for a walk and tried to burn off my anger. Was my view being ignored by the exec committee because I didn't inspire confidence? Or was it that they were all men, all but one older than me, and most of their lives they'd been in positions of authority over women, so bossing me around came naturally? Maybe both were true.

Ads were my jam. I liked the ad. It worked. And I didn't want to change it based on one person's whims—unless that person was me. But there was more at stake here than my ego. The ad was about Nsimire and the women like her. I was being told to whitewash her story to make it less horrific, to assuage the feelings of one man.

This came on the heels of the wounding comment about being a single mom, the blow-up about funding Denis Mukwege, the initial indifference to the strategy I'd developed, and the long running disagreement about our invitation-only partner selection. I wasn't sure I wanted to have to battle for everything against men who I thought had less relevant experience than I did.

———————

I stopped by my parents' house that evening for dinner and shared what had happened. I told them something like, "I'm going run the ad my way and let them fire me. That should be interesting!"

My mom, trying to be supportive, said, "They can't do that, can they?"

"Sure, they can. I am an 'at will' employee. They can let me go without cause, without warning, without notice. In this case they'd have cause."

My dad, always the more stoic of the two, just listened. I'm sure the idea of me losing my job unnerved him. Also, I don't think I've ever heard him use the word rape or come to think of it, vagina, or fistula either. I left with Bobby and went home to stew.

———————————•———————————

The next morning before I'd finished my coffee, the door to our office opened. The worldwide headquarters of Fistula Foundation was still that tiny office in the back of the L-shaped building. I'd guess that even the least famous Kardashian had a shoe closet larger than where we worked at that point. And through that door walked my dad. I was shocked since I didn't think he even knew where our office was. He sat down in front of my desk.

"How are you doing?" His voice was calm, but the situation felt strained and awkward. Dad was not a big talker, and had strong boundaries, like the Great Wall of China, around himself and others. This could be a strength but could also make him seem detached. He added something like, "I want to talk about last night and what you told your mom and me."

This set me off again, and I riffed on my "how dare they" rant. He remained placid.

Then he asked, "Are you really going to run the ad the way you want and risk getting fired?" Without missing a breath so I had no time to get defensive, he added, "I can see why you'd want to do that." Then he paused, and added, "but are you sure you really want to?"

The air was still. He was looking at me, waiting for my reaction. I was overcome by his focus on me. I didn't know what to say. My dad was not the kind of guy to give me or anyone else advice about anything. His love language was action. His humility was one of his strengths. But because he'd phrased his advice as a question, it felt more like a supportive statement.

He added, "You seem to enjoy your work a lot." He paused again, then continued, "I'm struck when you talk about this place, by how much energy there is in your voice."

I gazed at him sitting in the cheap wooden chair I'd bought on Craigslist, still amazed that he'd found our little hole-in-the-wall office. In that moment what surged through me was my dad's love. I was quiet because I was pretty sure if I opened my mouth I was going to cry, and I didn't want to do that in front of Dad and Terry and Anne.

As his words sank in, I realized he was right. I did like this job. A lot. I got to get up every day and help women too often treated like lepers regain their lives without an unwieldy bureaucracy getting in our way. I had a lot of freedom and could be creative. I more than liked this job. It was my dream job.

With his question hanging in the air, he stood up. "Looks like you've got a lot of work to do," as he glanced at my desk. It was cluttered with piles of paper, newsletter articles that needed to be proofed, donor thank you letters yet to be signed, and UN reports I would likely never get around to reading.

As the door closed behind him, I knew I wouldn't risk getting fired. I'd take Nsimire's rape out of the headline.

And a big part of me knew I'd been a coward.

Within a week, we'd raised close to $100,000 that we could attribute directly to the ad. Much of that money was from new donors who would very likely continue giving.

The next year, the same rep reached out to me about a new NYT magazine focused on "do it yourself" foreign aid, that he thought we'd be a fit for it. I agreed, and developed a new ad. This time, rather than getting upset, I talked to individual board members about what I wanted to do: tell Wabiwa's story, unvarnished. Here was that headline:

WABIWA WAS SEVEN MONTHS PREGNANT.
SHE WAS GANG RAPED BY FIVE MEN.
HER BABY DIED.
BUT HER NIGHTMARE WASN'T OVER.

20. TALENT SCOUT

*With rare exceptions, all of your most
important achievements on this planet will come from
working with others—or, in a word, partnership.*

—Paul Farmer

I am not a doctor. I have never run a hospital. There was so much I didn't know. The charity world can be unforgiving of mistakes. One misstep, such as funding a fraudulent hospital, could prove devastating to our new venture. That kept me humble. I spent a lot of time talking to experts in maternal health and became obsessed with learning everything I could about fistula treatment. The more I learned, the less scared I was of screwing up. I wanted to find local health champions—people like Denis Mukwege—because they knew best how to work within their communities. Our goal was to empower people as close to the women who needed help as possible.

I reached out to a trusted source for ideas, Direct Relief. Founded after World War II, Direct Relief had grown into one of the largest charities in the world. They provided medical equipment and supplies to hospitals in developing countries. Luckily, their headquarters was in neighboring Santa Barbara, so I flew down to get their ideas for strong potential hospital partners for us. I was greeted at the airport by one of their program managers, a young woman named Lindsey Pollaczek. Only a few years out of college, she was tall, engaging, and clearly sharp.

The team at Direct Relief mentioned a hospital that could use immediate help. It was in Somaliland, the Edna Adan Hospital, named for its founder. Her hospital had only one operating room which was inadequate to deal with her patient volume. She needed another one, in part to have a place to treat fistula patients. This sounded like a good project to me. I asked for and received a detailed budget and plan for construction which was solid, so we agreed to co-fund it with Direct Relief.

I contacted another colleague who worked in Afghanistan. We had a lengthy call and she said she knew of a terrific hospital in Kabul called CURE. She put me in touch with their medical director, who turned out to be a retired US surgeon. A lot of people choose to spend their retirement in leisure activities. The retired doctor on a golf course is cliché but often not far from the truth. But that's not how Dr. Rick Manning was spending his retirement.

I flew out to Pennsylvania when Rick was home to visit his family, to meet him and learn more about their program. He had built a team in Kabul composed of Afghans and was training Afghan women surgeons to treat fistula. Because of the wars—first against the Russians, and then against the US—many women were unable to get to health facilities when they needed emergency obstetric care. He was seeing many fistula patients and could use our help.

I reached out to one of our most dedicated board members, Linda Tripp, who had strong ties with surgeon Dr. Steven Foster in Angola. Linda was a seasoned professional with deep knowledge about international development gained in her thirty years working with international powerhouse World Vision. Her recommendation was rock-solid. Foster was a second-generation missionary and had trained with Dr. Hamlin.

We now had four new partners, and I had four inspiring reasons to go to work every day.

———————— · ————————

With our new mission, I thought we needed expert advice about our fundraising. Since I took over, I'd been winging it, relying on books for information. Many were by Mal Warwick, a globally recognized expert. I found out his firm's office was about an hour from us. They offered a service they called a "development audit." I was astounded when we got Mal himself to do our audit.

Mal arrived at our dinky office with a flustered look on his face. I guess our website made us seem bigger than only the three of us with our view of the parking lot. He spent three days reviewing all our fundraising materials and donor database, and weeks later produced a report. The good news: we were doing the basics right. That said, Mal encouraged us to invest more money in direct mail. I did what he advised and opened the purse strings on fundraising and mailing costs. While Mal didn't put it this way, I think he thought I was being "penny foolish"—in other words, my miserliness was inhibiting our growth. This would be an issue I would continue to struggle with. When is it wise to spend more money? When is the ROI, the return on investment, enough to justify the cost?

"Life is suffering, but some do really suffer more than others. Therefore, I decided a long time ago to do something about it and will continue to lessen the suffering of others as long as I am able to do so. Together we are strong," proclaimed Dr. Kees Waaldjik, the president of the newly formed The International Society of Obstetric Fistula Surgeons (ISOFS). I was sitting in the audience as Waaldjik delivered the keynote for their meeting in Nairobi. I'd been invited to attend, but wasn't sure what to expect.

There's a joke about surgeons: What's the difference between God and a surgeon? God doesn't think he's a surgeon. Surgeons rule an operating room, and often lives are literally in their hands. I was thinking that fistula surgeons could project that sort of superiority. But that's not what I found. These docs could have chosen to treat well-heeled patients rather than incontinent, often destitute, women. They were a uniquely selfless and compelling breed.

In addition to Waaldjik, I met other amazing doctors including Tom Raassen and Brian Hancock. Each had immense experience and was leading the way for the next generation of fistula surgeons. Waaldjik had treated tens of thousands of Nigerian women and published decades of his work to help guide new surgeons. Raassen was flying to far-flung corners of Africa and Asia to treat otherwise-forgotten women, including in war zones and refugee camps. Meanwhile Hancock, living in the UK, remained an expert advisor to many younger surgeons.

The best contact I made was with another surgeon, Dr. Sinan Khaddaj, who had worked with Doctors Without Borders. He radiated intense energy, and ran an organization called WAHA (Women and Health Alliance) that supported maternal health programs in multiple countries. I took an immediate liking to him. This was in part because he had hired two of my favorite surgeons, Dr. Ambaye and Dr. Mulu, who spent two decades with Dr. Hamlin. It was clear that Sinan was someone who made things happen—make dust or eat dust—in other words, our kind of guy and a very promising future partner.

The week after I returned from that whirlwind trip, an editor from *Huffington Post* contacted me and asked if I'd like to contribute pieces. They were trying to build their reader base, and we were trying to gain more awareness of our work. I was thrilled. I had heard Adriana Huffington's goal with *Huffington Post* was to make it the "cultural bloodstream in real time." I wrote my first piece where I shared my birth experience and contrasted it with one of the patients from Angola. I spent what felt like days producing a couple pages that may have been worth five minutes of someone's time to read. The whole exercise gave me more appreciation for those who write for a living. Over the coming years, I'd write more than thirty articles to help create awareness of our work and motivate readers to support us.

Two days before Christmas, we got one of the best presents any non-profit could wish for: a compelling recommendation from Nick Kristof in *The New York Times*. We were one of only nine organizations he recommended with a column titled "A Most Meaningful Gift Idea."

A couple months later, Kristof would write another column about our biggest partner, Denis Mukwege and Panzi Hospital. It gave me goosebumps when I read it. Two heroic men: one treating traumatized and injured women, the other traveling to a war zone like Congo to report on it. Here's another part that left me feeling a quiet joy. In his column, Kristof described Panzi Hospital as being "supported by the European Union and private groups like the Fistula Foundation." Yep, the European Union with its 450 million people, and Fistula Foundation, at that point, me, Anne, Terry, our volunteer, Jerry, our board, and a mighty band of compassionate donors getting equal billing in the Sunday *New York Times*! Mukwege was doing heroic work and our team was providing fuel for his operations.

And when it felt like we couldn't get luckier, a friend sent me a new book I'll never forget, *Cutting for Stone*, by Abraham Verghese. It's a sweeping, masterful novel about twin brothers growing up in Ethiopia. One of them becomes a surgeon, the other a fistula warrior. The book would stay on *The New York Times* Bestseller list for over a year, be translated into sixteen languages, and introduce millions of readers to life in Ethiopia and to fistula.

Coming up on our first-year anniversary of officially going global, we now had four new hospital partners and the potential for more at Sinan's partner facilities in Zimbabwe, Ethiopia, and Chad. We closed out 2009 raising over $2.6 million, up more than 20 percent after the downturn with the recession in 2008. We earned our fourth consecutive four-star rating from Charity Navigator. The first year with our new mission had gone better than I could have dreamed. We weren't doing enough, but we were off to a good start.

21. MUSLIM MOTHER TERESA

Feminism isn't about making women stronger.
Women are already strong. It's about changing the
way the world perceives that strength.

—G. D. ANDERSON

I felt like I was in a sauna. My back was sweating against the plane's
seat. With the engines off, the cabin smelled of jet fuel. We were
sitting on the tarmac in Jijiga in Eastern Ethiopia. Out the window,
I could see the ground crew loading tattered cardboard boxes of who
knows what onto the plane. Our milk run flight was hopscotching
across Ethiopia on its way to Somaliland, where I was headed to
visit Edna Adan and the hospital named for her. Finally, I heard
the plane engines rumble as cool air started flowing from the vent
above. We lumbered down the bumpy runway and took off. Next
stop: Berbera, Somaliland.

I'd had the chance to meet Edna in New York a few months
earlier and came away smitten. She was beautiful like Tina Turner—if
Tina wore burqas. At seventy-five she had the energy of someone
decades younger. She was a woman of many firsts: the first woman
in Somalia to drive a car, the First Lady of Somalia, and the country's
first qualified female midwife. The plan was that I'd spend the
week with Edna and see for myself not only the new OR that the
Foundation funded, but her whole operation.

Somalia brought to my mind an array of distressing images. Who
could forget the horrendous famine years back and the heartbreaking

images of families starving, or US marines dying at the hands of a warlord in the movie *Black Hawk Down*? But the first time I'd heard the word "Somaliland" I drew a blank. It sounded a bit like one of those made-up countries from an episode of *The West Wing*. I needed a stronger reference point than an action film and learned that Somaliland isn't a "real country," meaning it's not recognized by the UN. It's a self-declared republic that emerged from a civil war with neighboring Somalia in the 1990s.

It wasn't until the 1970s that Somalis developed a written language. Ninety-nine percent of Somaliland's population is Muslim and is tucked into the northeast corner of the African continent known as the horn of Africa. It's also very poor, with an average income of less than $700 a year per person. Most alarming, there are only about two-hundred doctors to serve its 3.5 million people. With so much poverty and so few docs, it has one of the highest maternal mortality rates in the world, with a lifetime risk of death of 1 in 18. Edna was on a mission to change that brutal reality.

After about an hour, the plane descended toward Berbera, and I could see the shimmering blue waters of the Gulf of Aden out the window. As the plane banked left, turning toward the airport, the city came into view. It was comprised mostly of small buildings and single-lane roads against a backdrop of tan earth. I didn't know what to expect when we landed.

I descended the stairs to the tarmac. Bright sunlight hit my face and as I looked around, I noticed that ours was the only plane. Several men in green uniforms with automatic weapons slung casually over their shoulders were standing nearby. I could see what I assumed was the terminal. It was a single story, and not much bigger than your average Walgreens. It had what appeared to be bullet holes in the sides, resembling an abandoned building in, say, inner city Detroit. There was litter in the dirt surrounding it, like you might see on the side of a freeway off ramp in the US. It was hard to believe the airport was functional, but we'd arrived safe and sound, so the team had gotten the job done.

As I was getting my bearings, I could see Edna walking briskly toward me. She radiated the same determined confidence I'd seen when we met in New York. As a Muslim, her attire was modest, but she was the opposite of dour. Her dress that day was a floral pattern in vibrant green, and her hair covering was a fitted cap, not the more common headscarf that would have descended to her shoulders. She greeted me with the warmth of a long-lost friend. I noticed that everyone at the airport from the pilots to the ground crew, referred to her as "Edna." They treated her like royalty—with respect, deference, and amazing familiarity.

I exchanged some dollars into schilling for pocket change and tips. I'd been warned that since the country doesn't officially exist, the Somaliland shilling is about as useful as monopoly money outside the country.

The plan was for me to stay in the doctors' quarters at her hospital. I loved this idea. Not only would I save money on a hotel, but I'd also get the chance to observe Edna in action, since she lived in an apartment in the hospital and I'd see how the institution she built ran day in and day out.

We walked together toward an SUV covered in fine dust in a small parking lot. When we reached the car, Edna introduced me to a man named Hassan who took my bag to put in the back. Edna got in the driver's seat, and I got on the passenger's side. Hassan closed the hatchback door and then got in the back seat. I turned around to thank him for his help and noticed a large gun next to him. I don't know much about weapons, but this was a lot bigger than the ones my cousins in Montana use for hunting deer. Was it an assault rifle? I guess Edna sensed my anxiety and said, "Don't worry, this is only a safety precaution."

I tried to act like this was no big deal. "Sure. Thanks," I muttered. Going through my mind was: what if we come across a car with two guys with two guns? Then what?

We were on our way to Edna's hospital in Hargeisa, at least an hour away. Once we got out of Berbera, the simple modest houses seemed to evaporate. They were replaced by parched valleys the color of khaki. We passed herders with camels, and off in the distance I could see small settlements of colorful tents shaped like gumdrops, dwarfed by the vast plain. Beautiful and stark, it reminded me of the American Southwest with wind occasionally launching sand into swirls. There were only a few other vehicles on the two-lane road, and the occasional bus driving in the opposite direction. The ride gave me a chance to get to know more about Edna.

"Can you tell me a bit about how you built your hospital?" I asked.

"Sure. After the war with Somalia ended in 1991, our country was in ruins. It was horrible. People were starving."

"It sounds like a nightmare. What was left standing?"

"Not much. Most of the bigger buildings were destroyed or significantly damaged."

"With so many needs, where did you get your inspiration to build a hospital?"

"I thought of what my dad would do if he were still alive. He was always my role model. I idolized him. He was a prominent doctor and I knew this is what he would have done."

"Where'd you get the money to build it?"

"Well, I had some savings, but I also cashed in my UN pension, sold my Mercedes, and my jewelry."

"That's amazing. Then you got to work building it?"

"Yes, but I didn't have all the money I needed, so I built it over four years. I lived on the site to save money. That also gave me the opportunity to oversee every phase of the construction."

"Wow. You know, most people would not do what you did. I don't think I would have."

"Some people thought I was crazy. They didn't get why I didn't just retire to London where I have friends."

"So, why didn't you?"

"Honestly, I thought about it, but I didn't want to spend my so-called golden years in what would have been luxurious boredom."

"Instead, you opted for decades of toil! What portions did you finish first?"

"My first love is delivering babies so that was a priority. We've done more than twenty-thousand deliveries. Of course, fistula prevention and treatment are part of what we do."

When we approached Hargeisa, a town that looked like Berbera but a lot bigger, the Edna Adan Hospital, with its three stories, stood out. It was white too, but massive—one of the largest buildings in the city. When we arrived, Edna took me up to where I'd stay that week. It was a dorm-like suite on the top of the building, with a handful of small bedrooms and a seating area in the middle. It was designed for visiting doctors, of which I was told there were many over the course of a year. They did everything from advanced gynecological surgeries to cleft palates and club foot repairs, and, of course, fistula surgeries.

The next day we left early for what Edna warned would be a long drive. Our destination was a rural outpost where nomadic women could get healthcare. It was on the border with Ethiopia in the West. Edna was driving, and Hassan was in the back with the gun. I'd almost gotten used to it. As we left the city behind, we started out on a simple two-lane paved road but after a few minutes veered onto a dirt road. At least I assumed it was a road. It felt like we were driving across a never-ending dry field with small clouds of dust rising in our wake. The few bony trees looked dead. We saw no one, except the occasional herder.

After several hours, in the distance, I could see a flagpole and a few small mud-colored buildings. Sure enough, this was Edna's clinic. The expression "in the middle of nowhere" was designed for this place. And yet, here, health workers were screening pregnant women, the kind of prenatal visits that could be lifesaving for both mother and baby. They also had a basic OR for emergency operations like C-sections. On the walls there were large charts to track the procedures and outcomes. It was Edna that made it possible for women living at the end of the earth to receive life-saving care.

We drove back across the empty plain chasing the setting sun. A shadow fell across the open desert and soon seemed to devour us in darkness. When we arrived back in Hargeisa, I was exhausted, not over my jet lag, so I headed up to the doctor's quarters. Edna went back into the hospital ward, telling me she was going to check on a few patients that she was concerned about.

The next day, I was able to observe Edna in action again. From early morning until late in the evenings, I followed her around like a shadow she didn't need. I can still hear the click-clack of her low heels against the linoleum floors, moving always with speed and purpose. It was hard to keep up with her. She made sure those around her embraced her high standards. With kindness, I saw her chastise a nurse for a less-than-clean counter and an orderly for an unemptied waste basket. Edna modeled the standards of care she expected kept by everyone who worked there. No excuses.

Besides treating patients, it was clear Edna was committed to building the human infrastructure to provide healthcare to her people, long after she was gone. She'd arranged for her doctors to get training in critical specialties like anesthesiology that the Foundation funded. She'd also had trained lab techs, pharmacists, and an army of more than one thousand midwives to help enable women to have safe deliveries, so both they and their babies would survive.

On my last full day, we drove out to Boroma, a town of about forty thousand in the north of Somaliland, three hours from Hargeisa. We were on our way to visit one of our other partners, National Boroma Fistula Hospital, and meet more fistula patients. An American named Walter Stewart, who'd served in the Peace Corps in Somalia in the 1960s, was using his retirement years to "give back," and had been the matchmaker on this partnership. He had kindly organized a group of fistula patients for me to interview.

The women were gathered under a massive white tent outside the hospital. Walter was going to videotape those interviews for me to share with our donors. With the camera rolling, I interviewed several women who had horrendous stories about their deliveries and about their years of isolation. But these women's journeys ended with successful treatment and happy anticipation of returning to their homes dry and healed.

The next woman up looked very young, with pore-less skin. She had on a headscarf the color of eggplant that fell to her shoulders and framed her narrow face and large, dark eyes. She seemed withdrawn and was glancing down at her hands clasped tightly in her lap. I tried to smile and speak in a gentle tone to help put her at ease. I assumed that she was anxious because of the camera and talking to me, a stranger. So, I started with a few basic questions that the translator translated:

"My name is Kate, what's your name?"

"Abay." Her voice sounded as though there was lead in it.

"How old are you, Abay?"

"I'm eighteen." (That was young to have already had a baby but not unusual for Somaliland.)

"Where are you from?"

"Mogadishu."

"What is Mogadishu like?"

"It's a big city."

"Can you tell me about how you came to need treatment here?" I was trying to make this seem like not a big deal with my tone, to make her as comfortable as I could. She was the age of a high schooler and seemed uncomfortable talking with me.

Abay looked down again at her hands then glanced up, but her eyes didn't want to meet mine. Compared to her other answers, this one was much longer and seemed more tortured, as she said a few words. Stopped. Then continued. I assumed that she was mainly embarrassed.

The translator summarized what Abay said. "She was living in a refugee camp with her family and went to get water. A man grabbed her and took her behind the building where they stored food. He ripped off her clothes. She was so scared; she screamed for help. But the man started to rape her. Her brother heard her cries and came to try to save her. But the man then pulled out a knife and stabbed her brother. She watched him die. Then she said she became pregnant. Her baby died and she was left leaking all day every day. That was a year ago, but then she came here for treatment."

I felt a familiar eruption of sadness and fury. I took Abay's hand and said, "I am so sorry." I paused then asked her, "How are you doing now?"

She said, "I'm okay. I've been treated well here."

I wanted to hug Abay, but I quickly realized that this was to comfort myself, and that the last thing she needed was a stranger clinging to her. I tried to put the images of that rape and murder out of my head. What if I'd had to watch my brother Eric be murdered before my eyes while trying to save me? The trauma Abay had lived through was hard to fathom. I could feel tears in my eyes and quickly wiped my face with my sleeve.

I gave Abay a wan smile, said I was grateful for her time, and repeated how sorry I was about the loss of her brother. She thanked me for the treatment she was receiving at the hospital, and I did what I always did, directed that gratitude to her doctors and caregivers. I interviewed a couple more women. Each had difficult stories, but I was finding it impossible to focus on them.

Once the filming was done, Walter could tell how upset I was and tried to reassure me by saying, "Without you and your donors' help we'd have to turn Abay and women like her away." That should have left me with quiet satisfaction but at that moment it didn't.

Walter and I talked with the lead doctor at the hospital about Abay, to find out about her treatment plan. The good news was that her fistula had been closed. So, at least she would be continent again. We were told that she was getting counseling but was reluctant to return immediately to Mogadishu. She wanted to stay in Boroma so she could learn English. I was impressed by her courage to further her education and stay in this place where she knew no one. Walter and I teamed up to provide modest support of roughly $1,000 of our own money to fund Abay's stay in Boroma. We got reports that she was doing well and was a fast learner, but eventually she returned to Mogadishu. I wished we could have stayed in touch with her, but once she left Boroma we got no further word about her. More than a decade later, I can still see Abay's face and the heartbreak and sorrow in her eyes.

The next day it was time to drive back to Berbera to catch a flight to Addis then home. On our ride, I wanted to take this last opportunity to learn more about Edna. She'd been campaigning against FGM (female genital mutilation) and I wanted to know about her experience. I'd written a paper on FGM in grad school when it was euphemistically called "female circumcision," but I'd never talked to someone who'd undergone it. She explained that her father was opposed to it. It was done to her against his express wishes while he was traveling. "My mother and grandmother felt that if I didn't have the procedure, I'd never marry. They thought they were doing the right thing. I was only seven. I had complications, which is not unusual."

Edna pulled over to the side of the road and said she wanted to show me something. We got out and walked toward a scruffy-looking skeleton of a tree. She pulled off a few spikey bone-white thorns that were about an inch long. Then she told me that thorns like these were used to tie tissue together after a clitoris and sometimes labia too were sliced off. I shuddered, trying to imagine what that would feel like. "It was more painful than you can imagine. It's why I became an advocate for the abolition of FGM. I want no girl to go through what I went through. It must end."

As our drive continued, I also learned that Edna had divorced a physically abusive husband. She'd also faced down warlords and lived through two disastrous wars, the second of which killed 250,000 people in a country of 3.5 million. That old expression that which doesn't kill you makes you stronger could be Edna's motto. She's turned horrendous loss and adversity into power and resolve.

When we got to the terminal, we were told my flight to Addis had been cancelled. Edna asked about other flights that day and was told there was one going to Dubai on a no-name airline that only took cash. Edna then told the guy behind the desk that she'd pay him back later if he could get me on the flight. Edna's word was like a verbal Amex because he then issued me a ticket.

I got stuck in Dubai for thirty-six hours because all the flights out were full, at least in economy. While there, I drafted a piece for *Huffington Post* titled "The Muslim Mother Teresa." It started with this: "I hope I live to see the day where a humanitarian hero is referred to as the Christian Edna Adan. Seeing Edna in action reinforced what I think most of us already know: no religion has a monopoly on compassion. I see the same caring in the eyes of Muslims like Edna as I do in Christians. They are people doing what good people everywhere do—look after their brothers and sisters." I ended with: "I don't know any Norwegians on the Nobel Prize Committee, but if I did, I would humbly suggest they honor Edna, one of the finest human beings God has created, with their glorious Peace Prize. In doing so perhaps they'd also help more people see that the world is full of humanitarians of all faiths—even if there's only one incomparable Edna Adan."

Today, at eighty-seven, Edna still has more energy than people decades younger. She won the prestigious Templeton Prize in 2023. It was first awarded to Mother Teresa in 1973. More than ever, I believe that Edna deserves that Nobel Prize.

22. DIGNITY

Dignity is as essential to human life as water,
food, and oxygen. The stubborn retention of it, even
in the face of extreme physical hardship, can hold a
man's soul in his body long past the point at which
the body should have surrendered it.

—LAURA HILLENBRAND

The driver of the van instructed me to keep the curtains closed. Out the windshield, I could catch only glimpses of the crowded streets of Karachi. As we came to a stop, I spotted the Marriott sign. Two tanks were poised at each end of the driveway in front of the hotel. A man put a large pole with a device on the end under our vehicle, presumably to check for bombs. I could see snipers on the roof of a small building across from the main entrance that was part of the hotel complex. Foreigners had been targets of random violence, and I guess they weren't taking any chances.

The next morning, I met up with Sinan Khaddaj who'd flown in the previous night. We shared a much-needed espresso as we waited for Shershah Syed, the visionary Pakistani surgeon we were there to meet. Shershah was the president of the Society of Obstetricians and Gynecologists in Pakistan and was widely respected. Pakistan has one of the highest maternal mortality rates in the world and has a corresponding problem with fistula. In Shershah they had the champion they needed.

As he strode forward to introduce himself, though in his sixties, he moved with the vitality of a college student. He was lean, which made sense, since I heard he ran marathons, was confidently bald, and wore glasses. He talked with visible passion as he escorted us out of the lobby toward the parking lot so we could drive to one of his hospitals, Koohi Goth.

He'd created an organization serving vast numbers of women called Pakistan National Forum on Women's Health (PNFWH), that was the country's only provider of free fistula treatment to all women in need. They operated nine regional centers across the country, with the hub at Koohi Goth Hospital where roughly one thousand women with fistula were treated each year. His teams not only treated patients but also provided training to rural healthcare providers to identify fistula patients for referral.

We got in Shershah's dusty sedan, and pulled away, leaving the tanks behind. As we drove, we heard more from Shershah about his background and the work he'd done to found PNFWH back in 2003. He told us his parents had migrated to Pakistan from India with nothing. They raised their eight children in a Karachi slum. His dad was a teacher, and education was of paramount importance in his family. He told us that all his siblings were now doctors, as was his mom, who trained in middle age after her children were grown.

He'd gone to Ireland to do post-graduate training, spending eight years largely focused on infertility. He figured when he got back, he'd set up a practice to cater to Pakistan's wealthy. But soon after returning, he abandoned his dream of a prosperous future when he witnessed numerous women dying in labor from preventable injuries. By contrast, during his time in Ireland, he said he'd seen zero deaths of women in childbirth.

"My country has some of the most advanced weapons in the world," he said, his voice growing fervent. "F-16 jets cost tens of millions of dollars each. But we can't provide help so that women don't die giving life to children."

With the feeling of *I hear you brother*, I said something, like, "America spends more than $900 billion dollars a year on our military, more than the next five countries combined, yet we have the highest rate of maternal mortality amongst wealthy countries."

"It's maddening," he said.

———————————·———————————

Sinan asked if I could do him a favor and meet the person who'd launched WAHA in the UAE (United Arab Emirates). My flight and Sinan's were connecting through Dubai, so I said I'd be happy to. Then I found out the person he wanted me to meet was Her Highness Sheikha Salama bint Hamdan Al Nahyan of Abu Dhabi, in effect the equivalent of the queen of the most powerful of the Emirates.

Sheikha Salama had offered to send a car for us, and thus we were met at the airport in Dubai by a helpful young man in a sparkling SUV. We drove ninety miles to Abu Dhabi at what felt like one-hundred miles an hour through the desert on the largely empty freeway. Being a rube, I was impressed by the car and driver, but Sinan told me the palace has about three hundred of those vehicles. As we neared the city the glimmering glass towers of the skyline came into view. Soon we were pulling up to the entrance of one of them. The Sheikha was picking up my hotel costs, and I had a suite, so I decided to give my puritan thrift a rest and enjoy the stay.

When I got settled in my room, I walked into the expansive bathroom. It was nearly as big as my bedroom back home and sparkled with huge mirrors on two walls. As I gazed at my reflection, I realized I had a weird bump in the hair on the back of my head the size of a taco where I'd slept on it wet our last night in Karachi. I glanced down at my ragged nails and decided I needed a manicure and a blowout. After all, I was meeting royalty. Nothing about this situation was typical for me.

I put on a long black dress that hit a few inches above my ankles, a conservative jacket, and a scarf over my head. I looked like a Greek widow, but with nice nails. The same car picked me up to take me to the palace. The car stopped at the imposing gate of an immense walled compound that was at least a city block long. A security gate opened into what felt like a massive public park. I was dropped at the entrance of a large single-story building that could have been a Four Seasons Resort in Palm Springs, with expansive lawns but no trees. Then I was escorted into the sprawling entryway and into another large room that felt like a giant living room with large sofas and small seating areas.

Sheikha Salama walked toward me smiling and dropped her head scarf. I was thankful for that because my head was starting to sweat, likely ruining my blowout. So I dropped mine as well.

Her warmth put me at ease, and I was surprised to feel comfortable in a palace. A small group of women was assembled on two long sofas. I assumed this was her staff as all had on the traditional black burqa. I wasn't sure how old Sheikha Salama was, I'd guess forty-something, with high cheekbones, no trace of makeup, only glowing skin, and sparkling eyes. In the US, she would have been voted best looking in her class. I had heard she'd been educated abroad, and her English was perfect.

We started off talking about the Foundation, something I could do on autopilot, like talking about a family member. At one point, a plate of some kind of fruit I had never seen was passed. Without thinking, I took a gold oblong thing about the size of baby carrot. But as I did, I realized I had no idea what it was or how to eat the thing. It sat in my hand. *What was I doing?* Thankfully, the conversation felt relaxed as we talked about the struggles women faced across continents and cultures. Where possible, I shared my glowing opinion of Sinan.

At one point her youngest of nine children, a six-year-old boy, joined us with his nanny. He looked like a miniature Omar Sharif, with dark almond shaped eyes. It was International Women's Day, and he handed his mom a card he had made for her. Sheikha Salama opened it smiling, thanked her young son and then handed it to me.

It said Happy International Women's Day in English. But below were words in Arabic, and below that, what I presumed was the same message in Mandarin. Mandarin! This six-year-old was learning three languages, all with very different alphabets.

When I expressed what I was feeling, near awe, she asked if I had children. I told her about Bobby and perhaps my face lit up, because she said something like, "You seem to enjoy being a mother."

I said, "Yes. It's the thing in life I am most grateful for."

I glanced down at my watch and realized I had been there over an hour. I finally admitted to her that I had no idea what to do with the piece of fruit in my hand. This led to giggles from her court and a warm smile from the Sheikha. A waitress came out of nowhere and I dutifully dropped the fruit and the napkin on the tray. It turned out it was a date, but an undried one, something I'd never seen before. She walked me to the door, and said she hoped I would visit again.

Sinan picked me up for dinner and soon we were planted at an inviting outdoor restaurant nestled on the harbor. As we noshed on delicious hummus, tahini, and olives, and sipped chilled Heinekens, the cloudy sky turned a rosy pink when the sun set.

I wanted to learn more about Sinan and what had led to his work with WAHA. With his usual intensity, he told me about his time working as a surgeon with Doctors Without Borders in Central America. He talked about bodies being brought to the hospital by truck and having to search for the living among the dead.

He'd also been on the scene within a day of the deadly tsunami in Indonesia in 2004 and described the injuries of people ravaged by the menacing wave that had moved like a wall of concrete through villages.

As I had learned from young Joseph with polio in Tanzania, I didn't have the emotional toughness to have confronted the suffering that Sinan did, day in and day out, for years. I sat there with deepening admiration for this amazing man who had left a prosperous life as a surgeon in Paris to heal wounded bodies from bloody wars and natural disasters, and now was proving to be one of our best partners.

As we kept talking, he said tentatively, "May I ask you a question?"

"Sure," I said.

"What's the thinking behind your tag line from despair to dignity?"

"Well, you know that fistula too often leaves women not only disabled, but also can make them social outcasts. Surgery restores not only their physical health, but also their sense of well-being and place in their community."

I paused, expecting Sinan to say something, but he was quiet. So, I continued. "We put the tagline on everything—our website, our stationery, our business cards, our brochures. We even added it as a kind of signature on the border of silk scarves we had custom made as gifts for donors. We love it."

Sinan didn't say a word, but his silence spoke volumes.

He obviously didn't agree with me.

So, I asked him: "What do you think of it?"

"Honestly, I don't like it."

"Really? Why?"

"Well, the despair part makes sense. Most fistula patients are very depressed, having often been ostracized. But dignity, that doesn't work for me."

As he took a sip of his beer, I said, "Tell me more."

"I don't think you can give someone dignity. I think you can act in ways that doesn't respect someone's dignity, but that's different than saying you are giving them dignity." He paused and for once I shut up. He continued, "Who are you to say that a woman with fistula doesn't already have dignity?"

I sat there. Stunned.

As Sinan's words sunk in, I realized he was right.

And I hated that he was right.

I hated that I had missed this. That somehow, I had smugly taken the halo for me and our donors to wear—donned because we were giving poor women not only their surgery, but their dignity too. We had not only been taking more credit than we deserved, but at the same time we implied fistula patients didn't have something they were entitled to, with or without surgery: dignity.

I'd like to think I thanked Sinan for his candor and insight. But maybe I didn't. Maybe my pride wouldn't let me.

But, when I got back to San Jose, I took the line off our website, and with each new order of stationery and other supplies, we lost the line. I changed it to *help give a woman a new life*. It doesn't have the alliterative ring of the old line, but it is more accurate, humble, and expresses what our donors enable us to do.

I stood at the podium, looking into the bright lights of a local news crew. I could feel my hands trembling and grabbed the edge of the lectern. I hate public speaking and with this big crowd, I was more nervous than usual. I was in northern Ethiopia for the opening of a new fistula ward at Gondar University Hospital, built in partnership with WAHA using Fistula Foundation funds. I reminded myself, it didn't matter what I said because the ward behind me where women would get life-transforming care was the main event. Besides, a good portion of the audience didn't speak English so wouldn't know what I said anyway.

One of the people in attendance was the CEO of FIGO, the Federation International of Gynecology and Obstetrics, the only global organization representing national societies of ob-gyns, with 1.5 million members. His name was Dr. Hamid Rushwan. He hailed from Sudan and had the warmth and grace of Nelson Mandela. He told me he and the chair of FIGO's Fistula Committee, another august figure, Lord Naren Patel—yes, as in "House of Lords"—wanted FIGO to train the next generation of fistula surgeons. He got my attention, since this would help remove one of the obstacles to getting more women treated: a lack of trained surgeons.

Rushwan and Patel had worked with expert fistula surgeons, like Andrew Browning, Tom Raassen, and Sayeba Akhter, to develop a detailed three-stage approach to training that would be competency-based. This meant that a surgeon would have to demonstrate in an operating room that they'd mastered one stage of fistula surgery before they advanced to the next. By certifying new surgeons by skill level, FIGO would help ensure that women with more significant injuries would only be treated by those with advanced skills. The program would give us something invaluable: a pipeline of new African and Asian surgeons.

I loved that their program used what is referred to as "south to south" training. That meant that rather than having surgeon trainers come from the north—US or Europe—here the program would be built around Africans and Asians. FIGO had a group of master trainers, surgeons already practicing in Africa and Asia, and new trainee surgeons traveled to those locations to apprentice. This also was cost-efficient, requiring only modest stipends for the surgeons and trainers.

For the better part of the last decade, the program has been led by one of my heroes in the fistula world, an amazing British midwife named Gillian Slinger. She previously ran the UN's Campaign to End Fistula. In that role she'd led the way to establishing the UN's International Day to End Obstetric Fistula. She has dedicated her life to serving women in the poorest corners of the world including working with Doctors Without Borders for years in Chad. I twisted her arm to join the Foundation's board so that we can take advantage of her deep knowledge to help guide our expansion efforts.

23. HALF THE SKY

The most common commodity that life in a wealthy country
can provide you is also the most insidious: complacency.

—MICHAEL SCHUR

Bright morning light streamed in through the massive bank of windows lining the spacious entrance of the New Jersey headquarters of Johnson & Johnson. As I waited for my J & J counterpart to come down to meet me, I gazed up at the wall in front of me. It had "Our Credo" carved into stone. It was their mission statement, four paragraphs long and roughly fifteen feet high. It began with this line: *We believe our first responsibility is to the doctors, nurses, and patients, to mothers and fathers and all others who use our products and services.* Only in the last paragraph is there any mention of shareholders. The statement was written in 1943, long before most of us were born. What Johnson & Johnson stood for was not going to be edited by branding mavens to meet the challenges of a given day. It was designed to stand the test of time, markets, and Wall Street.

Most companies want their brand name slapped all over their good deeds, not J & J. Over the last decade, they had emerged as the largest corporate funder of fistula treatment and one of our biggest donors yet wanted little public credit for their philanthropy. I was there to pitch an idea I hoped they'd like—sponsoring a video game to create awareness of fistula through a contest that would live on Facebook.

You may be wondering what a video game has to do with fistula. I'm not a big video game player, but a lot of people under the age of thirty are. So, video games can be a way to open new minds to new issues. That's what authors Nick Kristof and Sheryl WuDunn had in mind when they reached out to a pioneering group in New York called Games for Change. As their name suggests, their mission is to empower game creators and social innovators to use games and technology to drive real world change. In this case, the goal was to extend the reach of the key message in Kristof and WuDunn's best-selling book *Half the Sky*: that the central moral challenge of the twenty-first century was the full emancipation of the world's women.

The idea with the game was that it would provide an opportunity for players to learn more about problems impacting women in developing countries, like lack of access to education or fistula treatment. Players would progress through a series of quests and stories related to these real-world challenges that women and girls face. When a player won, they'd unlock money that would be donated to the charities whose causes were reflected in the game. This would motivate players and provide funding to organizations like ours.

My first thought when I heard about the game was that I wanted Fistula Foundation to be a part of it. It would be such a great way to build awareness for the Foundation and our mission. The catch: we needed to get someone with deep pockets to provide the funds that would be unlocked and donated when players were successful playing the game. My second thought: J & J seemed like the perfect sponsor. The team at J & J loved Kristof and WuDunn's book and immediately grasped the potential power of the game, agreeing to donate the amount we proposed: $250,000.

That fall, one Friday night, the office was closed and quiet when Anne came to my door and told me that a donor was on the phone and wanted to talk to me. At that point we had about sixty-thousand names in our donor database, so my initial instinct was to ask her to take a message. But that little voice I try to not ignore told me to take the call.

I picked up the line, and Lisa Queeney-Vadney introduced herself. She told me she was calling to thank me for a thank-you letter I had sent her for her recent donation. Classic. Lisa, so giving and humble wanted to thank me for thanking her. Her voice was warm, bright, and engaging. She said she lived in a rural area, where "bears outnumbered people." The population of her county and the next, bears included, was about fifty thousand. Though she'd lost her husband, her children and grandchildren brought her joy. With an infectious laugh, she said she was "only a working stiff." I liked her. She reminded me of my Montana cousins Russ, Liz, Marina, Yvonne, and Jody—grounded, unpretentious, salt-of-the-earth stock.

When I asked how she'd found us, she explained that her brother-in-law had given her a copy of Peter Singer's book *The Life You Can Save*. She found the theme—that any of us can and should act to help end world poverty—motivating and wanted to help. She started by buying a case of the book and giving copies to her family and friends.

But she wanted to do more and found fistula particularly compelling. She added that she thought her gift would enable at least seventy women to get treatment. This took me back. Seventy women! At that point, fistula surgery cost as little as $450, so that meant she'd given us over $30,000. Our average gift was under one-hundred bucks. This made Lisa one of our biggest donors. I was kicking myself for not recognizing her name.

As my mind raced, Lisa's story got even better. She said she was not a rich woman, but she'd had a windfall recently. A lawsuit she thought would never go anywhere was finally resolved, and she'd gotten a settlement. The case was for gender discrimination. She said her co-worker had used her share of the settlement to buy a new car. But Lisa wanted to do something else: use her money to help heal women also injured in an unjust world. After some research she decided she wanted to help women with fistula.

I was speechless.

Then I blabbered about how moved I was by what she had done, and how fortunate her kids and grandkids were to have someone as generous as her in their lives.

When I finally hung up the phone, I knew I'd just talked to an exceptional woman, one I'd never forget.

I've found I can be in New Delhi or New York; no one wants to talk about women with holes in their vaginas, bladders, rectums. It's hard to work fistula seamlessly into cocktail party conversations. We don't host glamorous fundraising galas, nor do we put donor names on buildings. We offer little of that. So, Lisa, and people like her are motivated by something that to me is truly selfless, the simple knowledge that they've helped a woman half a world away regain her continence, her health, and her life. Without people like Lisa, we'd be out of business, and the tens of thousands of women we've helped would still be suffering.

The Half the Sky game launched on Facebook with great fanfare and media attention. We'd hired a terrific communications pro, Jessica Love, who proved to be just the person we needed to help get our message out. She connected dots others didn't see and seized every opportunity she could for us to garner press attention, helping make the launch a success. Fistula Foundation was in good company. Heifer International, United Nations Foundation, Room to Read, and World Vision, all powerhouse charities, also benefited from the game. We were definitely punching above our weight.

Another name drop alert: I was invited to the LA launch event hosted by Maria Shriver, Kristof, and WuDunn. Shriver was easy to envy—beautiful, smart, successful, a Kennedy by birth, with four amazing kids. I was expecting to feel intimidated, but she couldn't have been warmer or more welcoming.

All the media attention around the game meant that not long after it launched, video players unlocked the total amount donated by J & J. We used the $250,000 to treat women. It provided an online opportunity to effect real world change offline. It helped players understand that poverty and gender discrimination are its root causes, but that curative surgery could give a woman back her life. Who knew video games could be a force for enlightenment?

24. MOTHERS OF SONS

*I have learned to look when I want to look away. I have
chosen to stay when I'd prefer to run out of the room and cry.
The prelude to compassion is the willingness to see.*

—Dr. Sunita Puri

I slapped on mosquito repellant and sunscreen and went down to the hotel lobby. Out the window I could see a steady stream of lean people on the narrow road heading to work on foot, in buses, on bikes, and motorcycles. I walked out into the driveway and warm, sticky air hit my face. I was in Cox's Bazar, Bangladesh, in the far east of the country, about thirty miles as the crow flies from the border with neighboring Myanmar to meet one of our newest partners, Dr. Iftikher Mahmood.

Word was getting out to talented doctors in corners of Asia and sub-Saharan Africa that we were looking for dedicated fistula surgeons to support. Iftikher had come to the United States for medical school and decided to stay, starting both a family and a pediatrics practice. But his mother and nine siblings still lived in Cox's Bazar, so he was back often and had opened a small hospital there, Hope Hospital for Women and Children. With no services in the area for women with fistula, he was determined to remedy that situation.

Iftikher greeted me with his wide smile, and we drove to the hospital—a modest single-story building. He took me on a quick tour to see the simple operating room, lab, and ward packed with about forty beds. It felt a bit like a massive school cafeteria, linoleum tiled, but with the now-familiar smell of disinfectant rather than, say, mac and cheese.

The most impressive part of the hospital was not the physical structure, it was the team running the place. Last year I had reached out to two respected fistula surgeons, Dr. Mulu Muleta, who had left the Addis Fistula Hospital, and was working with Sinan, and Dr. Steve Arrowsmith. Both had made trips to Hope to treat patients and help train their dedicated on-site Bangladeshi surgeon, Dr. Nrinmoy Biswas. One of the counselors, Nokima Begum, had personal experience that she brought with her every day. She was a former fistula patient who had been left by her husband and disowned by her mother and sister. Her case was complex, but she was finally cured after several surgeries. She knew better than any of us what fistula patients endured. Hope had also recruited doctors hailing from Russia and Saudi Arabia, and a nurse all the way from Scotland. They were paid little but received invaluable experience working with Hope's seasoned local doctors.

The hospital was the center of the wheel for a set of smaller clinics that provided primary healthcare. These clinics were also a referral network for more serious problems such as fistula. One of the clinics was on an island off the coast, and Iftikher suggested we visit.

We took a short drive to the port where we boarded a small boat that could hold only a handful of us. As we pulled away from the dock and moved slowly into the harbor, we passed massive wooden fishing boats that looked like pirates could have used them centuries ago. We glided over the briny water into the Bay of Bengal, finally getting far enough out of the port that I could see Cox Bazar's famous beach. Iftikher said it was the longest natural beach in the world—ninety-six miles. I could not see an end to it. After about forty minutes, we arrived at the island and docked at a short wooden pier. The place reminded me of something out of Treasure Island because I didn't see any people or structures.

We walked down a long path from the dock, and a small village became visible. As we got closer, I could see a smattering of kids playing in a clearing. They stopped and gazed at us with wide-eyed curiosity. Two brave boys came over to shake my hand. I imagined that they didn't get too many middle-aged white ladies there for a tour. We continued walking through rice fields and finally arrived at the clinic. There, women could receive contraceptives, children could get vaccinations, sick kids and adults could get basic care. In addition, women with fistula could be referred for treatment. Lives could be extended and improved by strong primary healthcare like this.

Iftikher had big plans. The current hospital was at best rudimentary, with air that on a hot day could feel stifling and stale. He wanted to build a new hospital, complete with air-conditioned operating rooms, so all women in need could access curative fistula surgery and C-sections to prevent fistula and maternal and child deaths. Iftikher was the kind of person who made things happen. He wanted our help, and I promised he would get it.

———————✦———————

The next day, Iftikher had arranged for a local TV news crew to join us for a visit to the hospital. I always enjoy talking with patients, but the bright floodlights and cameras made me anxious. I tried to smile and pretend that this was just a normal day for me. While most of the patients were from Cox's Bazar, the hospital also treated refugees from neighboring Myanmar, where the military junta had persecuted the largely Muslim Rohingyas.

As we were walking by a bed in the corner of the vast room, a patient grabbed my hand tightly, not letting go. I crouched by her bed and noticed a young boy standing next to her who was about the same age as my son, roughly ten. I looked into her pleading eyes and her face etched with worry. She was imploring me in words I did not understand. Her voice was loaded with desperation. I asked one of Iftikher's doctors to translate. I so wanted for her frantic tone to be misplaced.

"She was saying, 'Please help me.'"

I said, "Can you tell me more about her?"

"She is from Myanmar. She went into labor after they fled the country. She didn't have access to care, and so the baby was stillborn. She came here because she was leaking urine. They said they couldn't do anything for her in the refugee camp."

"Can you cure her?"

"Unfortunately, there is not much we can do. Because her labor was so long, her bladder has been nearly destroyed."

When his words sank in, I looked up at her son with his large, sorrowful eyes gazing back at me—the American lady with the cameras on her. He was now in a country not his own, living in a refugee camp with his wounded mom. Her fear and his beamed brighter than the floodlights. I looked into her eyes and cupped her hand in both of mine. I said, "Your son is beautiful. How old is he?" The young doctor translated, and I forced a smile. I didn't know what else to do or to say.

Sorrow welled up inside me, threatening to break through my professional facade. I so wanted to help her. But there was nothing I could do. My heart ached for her and her precious son. Why was the world so horribly cruel sometimes? Why was it so often women and poor women in particular who suffered needlessly?

We talk about the 90 percent of women with fistula whose surgeries are successful, the happy endings. But the tragic reality is about 10 percent of fistula patients are incurable, meaning their incontinence can't be fixed. For these women, the baby's head pressed down on their pelvis so long that it cut off the supply of oxygenated blood to organs like the urethra, bladder, rectum, and other pelvic muscles. Without oxygen, vital tissue dies. It is still maddening and shocking to me that the devastating injury that has ruined this woman's life likely could have been prevented with a timely C-section.

The young doctor said something comforting to the distraught woman. She let go of my hand, and he escorted me to the next row of patients on the other side of a low wall. I didn't have much cash with me but gave the cash I did have to Iftikher and asked him to give it to the woman after we left. It would not do much for her.

I could not get her pleading voice and the terror on her son's face out of my head.

I walked outside to get back in the car as rain pummeled the windshield. It felt like the heavens were opening with tears.

I was glad that this was my last day in Cox's Bazar. I wanted more than anything to be home, hugging my own young son. That would be a few days off since Iftikher had set up more press, including a *60 Minutes*–type TV show in the capital, Dhaka. So, we went to a television studio where Steve Arrowsmith and I were interviewed by a supportive journalist under more bright lights for the hour-long show. We also went to the US embassy and met with the deputy chief of mission to get support for Iftikher and his inspiring hospital. It's unclear that any of that did much to help Iftikher. As one Bangladeshi health leader had said, "Fistula is not just a hole in the birth canal of a woman, but also a hole in the public health system of the country."

We raised almost $5.2 million that year, more than twice what we had a few years earlier. This enabled us to dramatically increase the number of surgeries we'd funded to more than 2,500. This was a five-fold increase in just three years since we went global. We received our seventh consecutive four-star rating from Charity Navigator. I'd been pestering the CEO of Charity Watch, that only evaluated about six hundred of the biggest charities, to put us through the paces. *The New York Times* had called Charity Watch the "pit bull of watchdogs." Finally, we got what overachiever me wanted: an *A*. My hope was that all these stellar ratings would translate into trust and more money being donated to support treatment for more women.

25. WONDER WOMAN OF WESTCHESTER

It is the heart that does the giving; the fingers only let go.

—NIGERIAN PROVERB

I had just finished my microwaved burrito when I opened an email I wasn't expecting. It was from a financial management firm in St. Louis I'd never heard of. The sender, the head of the firm named Kathy Strong, wanted to have a phone call to learn more about our work on behalf of one of her clients. We did some Google sleuthing and it turned out the firm had close to $1 billion under management.

A few days later, Anne and I were on a conference call with Kathy. Her tone was reserved as she asked us a series of detailed questions about our plans and finances. It felt like an intense job interview. We got off the phone hoping for the best, but I had no idea what Kathy thought of us. Several weeks later we received a $10,000 donation from her client, who at that point was anonymous. We sent back a gracious thank-you. The next month Kathy asked me to have dinner during her upcoming visit to the Bay Area.

I dropped Bobby off at my parents' and headed up to San Francisco, meeting Kathy at a lovely restaurant in a posh hotel downtown. After some pleasantries, I asked her to tell me about herself. I wanted to know how she'd built her organization. She said she'd cut her teeth at a large investment firm, and then left to start her own shop with only a few clients. She said it was scary at first to not have the support of a large organization behind her, but over time she grew her client base and expanded her team. As I took it all in, she used it as an opportunity to shift the discussion and give me advice she thought I needed.

"Kate, our client likes what you are doing. She had heard about fistula from another fistula organization associated with Washington University. But when she had us investigate the other organization, I found your website and then reviewed your annual reports and tax returns. That's why I called you last month, to get more information. I thought you were a better choice for our client."

I said something like, "I had no idea. I appreciate you doing that."

All business, she said, "I'm only doing my job. That's part of what she pays us for. This donor has the capacity to give a lot more to you than she has. But I am not going to advise her to do that until you expand your team."

I must have looked ashen because she added, "Listen, I know from our call last month that you are trying to build your organization and put your money into the surgeries."

"Help me understand why you think my existing team isn't enough."

"Not to take anything away from your crew, but you are the only one traveling to meet partners, right?"

"Yes, that's true, but the people I have are exceptional. They are hardworking, smart, and dedicated."

"I want to recommend bigger gifts from our client. But you need to grow your team first."

Her tone was so grave, I decided to pivot to talking about the work we were doing. Before we parted, I said something like, "While I would rather have heard that your client was going to be sending us more big donations, I appreciate your candor and advice. You've given me a lot to think about, I'll get back to you."

I spent the drive back home mulling over what Kathy had said. We were stretched thin, but I was very hesitant to add new people unless I could prove that they were needed and would add value. One more person paid in San Jose was less money to fund hospitals and surgeries in Africa and Asia. But maybe I was being too thrifty, and Kathy was right.

The next day, my first stop was Anne's office. I plopped myself down and explained what Kathy had said. Anne was at least as much of a miser as I was, but we both were too often triaging opportunities. Could we raise more money and thus help more women if we hired a few key people—a fundraising person and more administrative help?

So, over the next few months, we added two full-time people. I sent Kathy an update and a new org chart, and got back a simple acknowledgment, which, honestly, was disappointing. I was hoping for positive feedback and another big donation.

———————✦———————

Fast-forward a few months: Kathy emailed to tell me she was again going to be in San Francisco and asked me to come up and have lunch with her. We met at Il Fornaio, the Italian restaurant in Levi Plaza where I'd bided my time, passive aggressively drinking coffee and reading the paper to escape my old boss. This time I was there to meet someone who had the power to help us provide surgeries for scores of women.

I described the growth of our team and our expanding network of partner hospitals, outlining our increased capacity to help more women, and asked if she had any questions. Kathy wanted to know our biggest constraint to growth. This time, the answer was simple: lack of money, even though our revenue was up by 50 percent in the last three years. Kathy could be a great poker player because she was inscrutable.

The next week, Kathy emailed and asked us to submit a proposal for more options for her client to consider. She did not, however, give us a budget, so we put together a robust, wide-ranging proposal. It was a detailed menu of just about everything we could think of that could use funding. The price points went from $450 for a single surgery, all the way up to $150,000 to fund the yearly expenses for one of our newest partners in Chad. We didn't know how big was big. I pushed send on the email and waited.

About two weeks later, I got a call from Kathy. She finally gave me a bit of background about her client. Her name was Paula Weil. She had retired after a career teaching in New York City public schools. It was almost like she could read my mind when Kathy added that Paula's parents were wealthy and had bequeathed her a sizable fortune, since most teachers work tirelessly for a comparative pittance and don't have a lot of money to give away. I then thought, what kind of person chooses to teach in New York City public schools? I guessed a selfless one.

She told me that Paula had selected our three biggest projects, including the program in Chad, for a grand total of a bit over $300,000.

I yelled something clearly unprofessional at Kathy like, "You're kidding!"

This was the biggest single donation we'd ever received.

───────────────⊥───────────────

About that time, I got an email from a woman named Eva Hausman. She explained that along with a small group of her friends, they had started an organization called Mothers' Day Movement. Their tag line was "Make Mother's Day Meaningful." After learning how much was spent annually in the United States on Mother's Day for things like flowers, cards, and meals out, they were astonished. So, they founded Mothers' Day Movement to encourage all of us to rethink our giving priorities each Mother's Day. They moved the apostrophe to make the day a Mothers' Day, which honors all mothers. She said that every year they select a different organization to be featured and to be the recipient of that year's charitable giving campaign. I was overjoyed when Eva told me Fistula Foundation would was selected as their featured charity of 2013. This was a terrific way to head into the new year.

26. SOUVENIR FROM CHAD

We need to slow down to the speed of wisdom.

—VICKI ROBIN

It was 3 a.m. in the Dubai airport and the place was bustling like a shopping mall on December 24, though it was March. Anne and I had flown in earlier that night from San Francisco. We were killing time browsing through airport stores filled largely with luxury goods we didn't need or really want before our flight to Addis. I had twisted her arm to go with me so we could visit a couple hospitals that Paula Weil was now funding. Anne would be my videographer. We would stop in Addis to meet up with Sinan Khaddaj. Then we'd fly together to Chad in central Africa, smack dab in the middle of the Sahara Desert, before going to Gondar in northern Ethiopia. The day we left I had run out of time and not gotten my Ambien prescription filled. Big mistake.

When we finally landed in Addis, the sun was coming up, but my watch said it was 8 p.m. in San Jose. According to my body clock, I was about to miss a second night of sleep in a row. The air in the terminal was stale with the faint smell of smoke, but I was glad to be off the plane. I got a cup of strong Ethiopian coffee before we met up with Sinan for the packed four-hour flight to Chad.

Most of Chad's population is nomadic, with fewer than one in six women having any skilled help when delivering babies. This resulted in one of the world's highest maternal mortality rates; women faced a lifetime risk of 1 in 15 of dying due to maternity or childbirth, a rate even greater than Pakistan's and like Somaliland's. The center's location, near the borders with Cameroon, Nigeria, and Niger, meant that women throughout the region benefited from it.

As the plane descended toward the capital city of N'Djamena, out the window was desert the color of gravy in all directions. In the distance I could see a small oasis—Lake Chad, for which the country was named. Soon we were flying over single-story dwellings that were made of mud and dirt roads that turned to asphalt only as we got nearer the airport. When we descended the steps to the tarmac, the air felt like it was coming out of a furnace. I could see heat radiating in waves off the pavement.

We headed over to the Center for Reproductive Health and Fistula Repair where Sinan's team was providing fistula surgeries. As we drove, the roads, the spindly trees, even a few skinny dogs all seemed bleached by the bright Saharan sun. While I was dead tired, it wasn't like I was walking into the OR and doing surgeries, a Paul Farmer–like hero, so on we went. The hospital was a single story, U-shaped building with a large courtyard. The team greeted us in a receiving line, brimming with enthusiasm as they said "Bienvenue"—*Welcome* in French. Their smiles energized me in the one-hundred-degree heat.

We met with the doctors to hear more about their work and the challenges of dealing with a largely nomadic population. But it was one of the nurses' aides who most moved me. Her name was Micheline and she shook my hand with a shy smile. She couldn't have been more than five feet tall and had her hair pulled back behind a pale pink scarf. As we walked through the ward, she showed palpable kindness toward the patients, stopping to gently grasp a hand or stroke a brow. I asked about how she'd come to work at the hospital, and she shared her own story.

When she was fourteen, she went into labor with her first child. She was excited, but after two days enduring excruciating pain, she said her family took her to the nearest health facility. By the time she delivered her baby the next day, it was stillborn and she awoke in a urine-soaked bed, a sure sign of fistula. Her young husband abandoned her, and her friends shunned her, so she went to live with her mother. Then she heard about treatment and came to this center where she was healed. She wanted to stay and help other women like her. Her dedication was so clear that they offered her a job. When I asked her if she enjoyed her work, her face lit up with a smile that brightened the room.

Before we left, Anne filmed me with a row of nurses, all women wearing rose-colored uniforms and sitting on a long bench outside the main ward. I got them each to say "Merci, Paula," one after another like a chorus of gratitude. The nurses thought it was funny, so we got them on tape laughing, too. I also interviewed patients talking about the life-transforming impact of their surgery. We replayed part of it. The picture was crisp, but the audio made me sound like I was buried under a mound of blankets. But the emotion of the patients was what counted, and we got that, right?

By early evening, I only wanted to get back to the hotel and go to bed. As the sun had sunk into the horizon turning the sky a sullen gold, I was glad that it seemed to take the scorching heat with it.

We got out of the car at the hotel. I smelled roasting meat and French fries at a makeshift café on the corner of the parking lot where loud music I didn't recognize blared from a giant boom box. The place felt like a very run-down Holiday Inn. And it was $300 a night, cash only please. I asked Sinan, "What's with the cost?" and he replied that the hotel knew that all these guys are being funded by their governments, so they can price gouge. As Sinan gestured to the dining room which had the charm of the DMV, I could see it was filled with men in military uniforms.

The languages that emanated from the crowded dining room were all over the map. I heard French, which made sense given Chad had been a French colony, but I also heard Arabic and German too. I wanted to ask what they were doing there, but I was too tired to strike up a conversation, and besides my French would get me laughed out of the place.

I got up to my room and opened the door. It smelled of mildew and came complete with well-worn indoor/outdoor carpet and beat up Ikea-like furniture. I took a shower with water that never got warm. I didn't care. I only wanted sleep and was relieved that the wheezy air conditioner seemed to work. I fell asleep fast.

But too soon I was awakened by earsplitting noise. It sounded like there was a helicopter taking off in the bathroom. I opened the door to my room and saw a bunch of other people in the open-air causeway.

"What is that noise?" I shouted at an older white man with a resigned look who had emerged from the room next to mine.

"It's the military planes leaving."

"Where are they going?"

"Oh, to Mali, to bomb those Islamic terrorists that have turned that place into a hellscape." He said this with a lilting French accent that can make "I'm going to the bathroom" sound elegant. Nothing to worry about, just your average defensive bombing. I walked out into the courtyard and gazed up at the black velvet sky sprinkled with stars. I didn't see any planes.

I got back to my room with cortisol running through my veins. I fell asleep, but a couple hours later I was awake again. I stared at stained ceiling tiles, damning myself for not getting the Ambien prescription filled. Exhaustion coupled with insomnia is a special kind of misery. I'd been mugged by jet lag.

Trying to avoid the afternoon heat, we went back to the hospital the next morning to film more patients. But as the sun rose the light that streamed in the windows became harsher and the heat more intense. It was finally time to head back to Addis. As we drove to the airport, a wind was coating everything in fine red dust reminding us that the Sahara, the world's largest and hottest desert, still ruled.

After takeoff, the black top roads thinned to sand, and all I could see was the khaki-colored desert in every direction. After a couple hours, the gaunt peaks and the deep ravines of the Ethiopian mountain highlands came into view. As we got closer to Addis, I could see small villages perched on ridges with no roads visible. What would you do if you had a medical emergency like an obstructed labor so far from help?

———————————⊥———————————

From Addis, Sinan, Anne, and I grabbed another flight up to Gondar in northern Ethiopia. The ancient city, and former capital, contained an immense stone castle that had housed 17th century emperors. We welcomed the misty air, cool at seven-thousand feet, and met up with a crew financed by Johnson & Johnson there to film fistula treatment at the Gondar Hospital that we'd helped finance. It was a husband-and-wife team, Elisa Gambino and Neal Broffman, clearly pros who shot amazing footage of patients and doctors. They wanted to do an interview with me, too. I hated being on camera; it seemed like it took them about an hour to get twenty usable seconds of me. Neal and Elisa were so patient, I wanted to hug them.

After another night of not-good sleep, we returned to the hospital to get more interviews and shoot surgery. I caught sight of myself in a mirror and had raccoon circles under my eyes. At this point I was running on caffeine, adrenaline, and fumes.

We flew back to Addis and from there to Dubai, crammed into packed coach sections and I started to feel crummy. My throat hurt, my head throbbed, and knew I had a fever. Over the coming week, the sore throat persisted and my head still ached. The fever would come and go but my exhaustion remained. I was supposed to be going to London the next week to meet with fistula treatment partners at FIGO, several donors, and a potential board member. I told myself I had to go. I had already arranged for Bobby and Dad to come too, renting an apartment from VRBO at a great price. (London is not exactly a tourist hot spot in winter.) Dad was going to look after Bobby, and we could spend evenings together.

But when we got to London, I was even more exhausted than I'd been at home. I was getting worse not better. Each meeting I went to felt more draining. I sat at a breakfast with a potential new board member, picking at my soggy eggs. I downed coffee after coffee trying to jump-start my body. But I could barely hear what she was saying because I only wanted to go back to bed.

Thursday was the last full day and since all I had to do was get dressed, grab a cab, sit in a conference room, and listen to people talk, I could do this. I downed a couple of Advil trying to kill the headache. The meeting was at FIGO, meaning I was surrounded by doctors. I didn't want to seem melodramatic or, God forbid, weak so I made a few noises about a lingering flu and kept quieter than my normal chatty self. By the end of the afternoon, all I wanted was to go back to the apartment and get in bed.

That night my body could not seem to get rest. I tossed and turned, thoroughly drained and yet unable to stay sleep. My arms and legs felt like sandbags and ached. My head throbbed. In the morning, something was wrong. My heart was racing. I didn't have chest pains so I didn't think it was heart attack, but I had never felt so unwell in my life. I was scared.

I called a doctor friend who seemed both concerned and sympathetic and told me to head over to her office. Bobby, Dad, and I were supposed to be getting on a plane in three hours. Our rental apartment was up that day. I didn't like the idea of sending my elderly dad and son home without me, but I also didn't want to get on a transatlantic flight feeling so unwell. I told them I'd catch another plane later that day.

27. BROKEN

*Difficult moments that started with defeat and
frustrations can become our most cherished souvenirs because,
looking back, they were the seeds for success.*

—DIANE VON FURSTENBERG.

I gazed at Bobby with bewilderment, fear, and tears in his eyes,
with my dad standing stoically by his side as the elevator door
closed. I wanted to go with them, but my body was not cooperating.
I dragged myself and my suitcase downstairs and grabbed a cab to
my friend's office.

While I was waiting in the exam room, I was short of breath,
dizzy, and lightheaded, like I was going to faint. My heart was still
racing. The doctor came in and told me to lie back, took my blood
pressure and pulse, and said something about tachycardia. Then she
called the UK equivalent of 911. Within what felt like seconds,
there was a team taking me by stretcher into a waiting ambulance.
They put oxygen on me and monitors on my chest. There was a lot of
commotion and people rushing around me. The tech looked at the
paper coming out of the machine, and said, "Good news, you are not
having a heart attack. But I am concerned about your shortness of
breath, your heart rate, and your blood pressure."

My doctor friend suggested a private hospital off Harley Street.
I got a private room, complete with a comfy white bathrobe. The

menu was in English and Arabic, though I had no appetite. I still felt dazed. A doctor came in and I described my extraordinary fatigue, body aches, joint pain, and the scary way my heart raced.

As a nurse came in to draw blood, my heart ached in a different way, thinking of Bobby and Dad on the plane without me. My dad was like a load-bearing wall; someone who you could count on to never let you down. He paid his bills on time, told the truth always, showed up when he said he would, but he wasn't, as therapists say, "emotionally available." An old boyfriend who'd grown up outside of DC had suspected that dad's NASA job was a cover and that he was in fact with the CIA. That's how tightly coiled he could seem. His coping strategy for life was to persevere. This worked well for him, but was not what my sensitive, sometimes anxious, thirteen-year-old son, likely consumed by worry about his sick mom, needed. My intrepid Mom was out of the country, traveling with her girlfriends in Croatia.

But the doctor said they wanted me to stay at least overnight and to keep me in the cardiac ward where I stayed for the next two days, hooked up to monitors. This was the first time in my life I'd felt utterly, frighteningly broken, and my first hospital stay, other than delivering Bobby.

I was finally discharged with instructions to see my cardiologist when I got home, and a car came to take me to Heathrow. I got taken by wheelchair to the plane and could feel eyes looking at me. A half hour before we landed, I stood up to get my passport and became very dizzy and felt like I would faint. The flight attendant who had been over several times to check on me, had seen me fall back into my seat.

"Are you okay?" she said with a worried look on her face.

I said, "I don't know." My mind raced. *How am I going to get out of the plane, get my bag and get home? I can't even walk.*

"We can have a medical team there when we land."

This seemed like too much drama, but I was a mess. Also, as a single parent, my biggest fear in life, other than Bobby dying, was that I would die when he was still growing up. So, two guys came on board and wheeled me off the plane.

Next thing I knew I was at the ER at Stanford. Twelve hours later with several different doctors and more tests, nothing came up to help them determine what exactly was wrong. I was told they could admit me, but at that point I'd had enough of hospitals and wanted to go home. God knows where my suitcase was; all I had was my purse. A car service took me to my parents' house. I made it from the car to the front door, then plopped into a large bed in the front room, my childhood bedroom, next to my sleeping son. Dad took Bobby to school the next morning. I slept, called my internist and cardiologist, and then slept some more.

I went to an infectious disease doctor who ran more tests. He said I had markers for dengue fever, which is unusual and could explain the headaches and relentless body aches. When he asked if I'd ever been sick like this before, I explained I'd had a bad case of mono in college. He said I likely had a post-viral fatigue syndrome and explained that people who've had other significant viruses, such as mono, can be more susceptible. He tried to be reassuring, saying that most patients got better over time. But when I pressed him for more information about when I'd feel better, his responses were vague, that there wasn't great data. I left his office feeling glad that at least I wasn't dying or nuts. But I was also troubled that he couldn't tell me how long I would feel so sick. It was like I stepped into a time machine and I'd gained decades of age and the infirmity to go with it. This may be how people diagnosed with long-Covid feel.

I took a few weeks off work and rested. My goal was to get enough energy to get myself to the office. Anne made sure I didn't drop any balls by carrying them herself. I was told some people with post viral fatigue have problems with brain fog. My problem wasn't fog; it was simple exhaustion. Sometimes my sleep was so heavy, I'd barely notice that my room was flooded with light or hear the neighbors' normally deafening lawn mower. When I wasn't sleeping, I'd be streaming things on Netflix, most of which I'd already seen, like whole seasons of *The West Wing* and every Nora Ephron film ever made. My neighbors Jane and Gabor, whom I carpooled with, generously took Bobby to and from school for months. We lived off Trader Joes premade dinners and take-out. My parents and several friends took Bobby on the weekends, and I slept.

I have a distinct memory of the first time I walked to the end of the street. Then I tried to walk a little bit farther every day. If I overdid it, I experienced a malaise that felt cellular—everything in my body hurt. I'd pop a couple of Advil that had little discernible impact. After three months, I was finally back to feeling almost normal.

Before getting sick my blood pressure had always been low. But now it remained stubbornly high. My cardiologist put me on a blood pressure medication, but also asked me "have you ever tried to meditate?"

I said, "It seems like a good idea, but who has the time?" What I was thinking was that it always sounded a little woo-woo to me.

Well, he said, "I've been meditating twice a day since medical school." Yes, but you have a wife to get dinner on the table and take your kids to school. Likely true, but not really relevant.

That's how I became a meditator, and my blood pressure went back to normal, without medication. Meditation gave me time to reflect on how I got so sick. I forgave my body for failing me, but I spent a lot of time interrogating my arrogant soul. Why had I ignored my body's signals, the flashing dashboard that said I was not okay when I came home from Chad and Ethiopia? Why was I such a jerk to myself? I had broken my body, and I had hurt Bobby and his emotional well-being. I would never take my health for granted again.

One thing we did get done in these muddled months was to ship off that video to Paula Weil, that Anne and I had gone all the way to Chad and Ethiopia to shoot. The thing was hopelessly amateurish, but it had heart. With Kathy's blessing, we also sent Paula another proposal. It covered eight of our biggest programs, with no price point under $100,000—a compelling menu. How could she not say yes to at least a couple of the programs? We didn't know how high up was, so we thought we'd swing for the fences.

That summer, I opted for a staycation to rest. Bobby had been bugging me to get rid of the Sponge Bob theme in his bedroom. One afternoon we were in Target looking at bedding when my phone rang. I saw it was Anne, so I picked up the call.

She said, "Are you sitting down?"

"No," I said, "Why?"

"Well, I guess Paula Weil liked our video and our proposal. I just got word from Kathy that Paula is sending us $1 million to fund more programs."

"Oh my God!!" I screamed at a volume to awaken the dead.

The woman in the aisle next to us quickly put down a throw pillow and scurried away. I must have appeared unhinged. And I kind of was. That call put more wind in my sails than a month's worth of bed rest.

Mom, Dad, me, siblings Shelley, Eric and Susie,
Sunday best, early 1970s

Linda and me in Nepal with our guide, Taran

First Lady Hillary Clinton who made "Women's Rights are Human Rights" the rallying cry for a generation, with me at the White House, 1995

Dad, Bobby and Mom, Appleseed Montessori School graduation, that fateful day in 2005

Board member, Deborah Harris, Dr. Catherine Hamlin, and me, 2006 at the Addis Ababa Fistula Hospital

Anne Ferguson, as usual, doing two things at once

Kassy Kebede, our stellar board chair,
me and board member, Rob Tessler, 2005

Jerry Goldstein, our indefatigable volunteer

Our youngest volunteer, Bobby

Ruth Kennedy, Dr. Catherine Hamlin, and me, Women Deliver, London, 2007

Board Members, Linda Tripp, Jerry Shefren, Larry William, and Steve Saunders

The inspiring, Sarah Omega

Dr. Ambaye Woldemichael,
courageous fistula surgeon

The incomparable Dr. Denis Mukwege with patients at Panzi Hospital, DRC

16 year old Nsimire endured hours of agonizing labor... the baby died...but her nightmare wasn't over.

Photo: John Paul Doguin

"Just about the worst thing that can happen to a teenage girl in this world is to develop an obstetric fistula that leaves her trickling bodily wastes, stinking and shunned by everyone around her."

— Nicholas D. Kristof
Pulitzer Prize Winner

Nsimire went into labor without medical help. That labor left her incontinent with an obstetric fistula – a common injury for women with unrelieved obstructed labor.

The good news: Nsimire got the curative surgery she desperately needed at the Panzi Hospital in the Democratic Republic of Congo by the dedicated team headed by Dr. Denis Mukwege, and funded by the Fistula Foundation.

Tragically, the World Health Organization estimates two to three million women suffer with untreated fistulas, for want of surgery that would transform their lives. We're working hard to help more women like Nsimire. Learn how you can sponsor a life-transforming surgery for only $450.

◆ The FISTULA
FOUNDATION
from despair to dignity
www.fistulafoundation.org
1171 Homestead Rd., Suite 265
Santa Clara, CA 95050
866-756-3700

New York Times Ad, 2009

Wabiwa was seven months pregnant.
She was gang raped by five men.
Her baby died.
But, her nightmare wasn't over.

"Just about the worst thing that can happen to a teenage girl in this world is to develop an obstetric fistula that leaves her trickling bodily wastes, stinking and shunned by everyone around her."

~ Nicholas D. Kristof
Pulitzer Prize Winner

After delivering her stillborn baby, Wabiwa was left continuously leaking urine, the sign of fistula. Fortunately, Wabiwa got the curative surgery she desperately needed at the Panzi Hospital in the Democratic Republic of Congo by the dedicated team headed by Dr. Denis Mukwege, and funded by the Fistula Foundation.

Tragically, the World Health Organization estimates two to three million women suffer with untreated fistulas, for want of surgery that could transform their lives. We're working hard to help more women like Wabiwa. Learn how you can sponsor a life-transforming surgery for only $450.

◆ The FISTULA
FOUNDATION
from despair to dignity

www.fistulafoundation.org
866-756-3700

New York Times Ad, 2010

179

Edna Adan Ismail and intrepid Nick Kristof in front of
the extraordinary Edna Adan Hospital, Somaliland

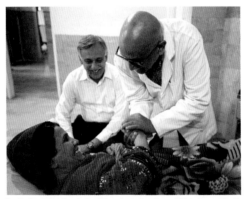

Dr. Sajjad Siddiqui, Dr. Shershah Syed, and fistula patient,
Naseema, at Koohi Goth Hospital in Pakistan

Dr. Nrinmoy Biswas and Dr. Iftikher Mahmood
at Hope Hospital in Bangladesh

Frances Alonzo interviews me for Voice of America

Half the Sky Game helps raise $250,000

Dr. Hamid Rushwan, Lord Naren Patel, Denis Robson, Dr. Thomas Raassen, Dr. Sinan Khaddaj, Dr. Kees Waaldijk, Patricia English, Dr. Sohier Elneil, and me at International Federation of Obstetrics and Gynecology's London office, to discuss their pioneering surgeon training program, which the Foundation was proud to sponsor.

Lindsey Pollaczek leading outreach effort in West Pokot, Kenya

The amazing Dr. Hillary Mabeya with blueprint for
his new hospital, Gynocare in Eldoret, Kenya

Peter Singer, me and Paul Simon at that unforgettable benefit concert in New York

Dr. Omboga with the exceptionally generous and humble Joe and
Sharon Kemper at Kisii Gynocare Fistula Centre, Kenya

Louis CK hosting Saturday Night Live and serving as a human billboard for us

Gynocare's welcoming patients

This was a joy filled day, the grand opening of Dr. Mabeya's Gynocare Hospital in Eldoret, Kenya, with Astellas executives, Foundation and Gynocare staff and dance troupe

Mwanantena gives me a chicken, as Habiba watches in Kenya.

Pam Lowney, our brilliant
Chief Operating Officer

My hero and our first partner when we went global,
Nobel Peace Prize winner, Dr. Denis Mukwege and me

Foundation dedicated Board members and staff in Kenya, left to right, Hannah Mann,
Bill Mann, Ling Lew, Rob Tessler, Teri Whitcraft, Kelly Brennan, Sean Brennan, me, Denis
Robson, Thomas Huntington, Mal Warwick and Lindsey Pollaczek

Fistula patients celebrating at CCBRT in Dar es Salaam, Tanzanian

Bobby and me at the opening of the new Hope Hospital in Cox's Bazar, Bangladesh that Iftikher built, just like he said he would.

Dad and Mom with Bobby at his high school graduation. They'd pass away before his college graduation.

NPR's always insightful Brooke Gladstone moderating a discussion
between Peter Singer and me at the 92 Street Y in New York

Our stellar board chair Cleo Kiros, vital board members Gillian Slinger
and Dr. Charlotte Polle, and me in our San Jose headquarters

My last visit with Mamitu and Dr. Hamlin, the woman who changed the course
of tens of thousands of women's lives including mine, in Addis Ababa

PART FOUR:

IN IT
TO END IT

28. GAME CHANGER

*Authentic hope requires clarity—seeing the troubles in this
world—and imagination, seeing what might lie beyond these
situations that are perhaps not inevitable and immutable.*

—Rebecca Solnit

That fall Anne and I got a call from a woman named Jane with a London PR agency that specialized in corporate social responsibility. This meant her firm likely helped for-profit companies project to their shareholders and customers that they tried to do good things in the world. Jane explained they had a client that wanted to invest philanthropically in fistula treatment. It was a large Japan-based pharmaceutical company neither of us had heard of: Astellas Pharma. Her firm's role was to help Astellas select which fistula charity to fund. Their budget was up to 1.5 million euros over three years, which at that point was close two million US dollars. They wanted a plan from us about what we could do with this size donation. She had our attention.

Jane said that they wanted to focus on Kenya. I asked if we could develop an alternative plan for another country, since Kenya is a middle-income country with several established fistula treatment programs. The need there was not as great as in many other poorer countries in sub-Saharan Africa. No, Jane told us we'd have to focus on Kenya. What I didn't add was that we'd done little work in Kenya. The proposals were due a week from Friday, only ten days away.

We'd be competing against several other organizations: Direct Relief, UNFPA, One by One, and Freedom from Fistula. Jane and her team had clearly done their homework. Direct Relief, the group we'd partnered with to build Edna Adan's operating room, was huge with a yearly budget of over $1 billion. Yes, a billion. They were the Amazon of international nonprofits. UNFPA (The United Nations Fund for Population Activities) is the UN agency that started the Campaign to End Obstetric Fistula a decade earlier, so another good choice. Both had better relationships with the Kenyan government and Kenyan hospitals than we did. One by One had a solid fistula treatment program in Western Kenya. Freedom from Fistula, founded by Scottish billionaire Ann Gloag, ran twice-yearly treatment "camps" at the main public hospital in the capital, Nairobi.

On the face of it, each of these four competitors was a better, more logical choice for Astellas than we were. They knew the Kenyan fistula treatment landscape well. Us, not so much. While I had traveled in Kenya several times and we had supported two treatment programs, our experience there was thin. We were clearly the "dark horse" in this race.

———————————⊹———————————

I went home that night and thought hard about what we could propose to win the funds from Astellas. Ideas bounced around my head like steel balls in a pinball machine. This was a huge amount of money, so we should be bold. I wanted us to dream big. What would it take to ensure that no woman would have to wait for treatment to truly end fistula in a generation in Kenya? We'd need to develop a network of hospitals, so that women would not have to travel too far from home to access treatment. These sites would collaborate so that women with more complex injuries would have the benefit of being treated by a surgeon with more advanced skills at a neighboring hospital. Surgery would be free.

We'd also need a robust outreach program. One thing we'd learned over the years was that a *Field of Dreams*—build-it-and-they'll-come approach—was not effective. Skilled outreach workers that could find too-often stigmatized women, help screen, and transport them to hospitals would be critical.

Finally, the most important variable to get a woman treated was a well-trained surgeon. We knew there were too few of them since doctors in many medical schools weren't trained to treat fistula. So, surgeon training would also be critical. An idea went off in my head, one in need of a highlighter. A three-prong strategy: treatment, outreach, and surgeon training at scale.

I came into work the next day and plopped down in Anne's office.

"What would you think of a country-wide treatment network? We would combine a network of hospitals spaced around the country, robust outreach, and surgeon training at a central 'center of excellence.'"

Anne said, "Sounds good."

Then I cut in and added: "That's the plan—a trinity, a triad, a three-legged stool—treatment, surgeon training, outreach?"

"OK, then what?"

"What if we hire a full-time country director to link all the pieces together, so that a woman anywhere in the country can access treatment?"

Anne cocked her head and listened with great patience, and then asked, "How much will that cost?"

"I have no idea, but I think we can ballpark it. We can do high-medium-low estimates of costs for each of the three main components based on our experience in other countries and see what we come up with."

———————————⊹———————————

Where to start to build a network of hospitals? One fabulous tool was the Global Fistula Map, an online resource that, as the name suggests, maps fistula treatment providers in more than forty countries. The map was something we'd partnered with Direct Relief and UNFPA on—small, incestuous community that we were. Here was a listing by country of hospitals doing fistula surgery—bingo! —we had the beginning of a plan.

We had been funding FIGO's surgeon training for two years. If we were able to launch the network in Kenya, it would offer an ideal opportunity to leverage our partnership with FIGO. We could set up a training center where Kenyan surgeons could be trained by FIGO trainers. It felt like the pieces were starting to fall into place, even if I didn't have a clue yet what it would cost.

———————

But there was no getting around the fact that "Team Fistula Foundation" was small, with no track record in Kenya. I figured it would be smart to partner with a big established organization on our pitch, so I reached out to Direct Relief.

I called the program manager we'd been working with for several years, Lindsey Pollaczek, and asked her if they'd like to combine forces with us on a proposal. She seemed hesitant to talk with me, and I was surprised by how awkward the conversation felt. At first, I thought it was because I was more than two decades older, and the decision to partner with us may have been above her pay grade. But my assumption about her reserve was way off. The truth was she'd already picked a partner and it wasn't us. Direct Relief was going to pitch their plan with One by One.

I got off the phone and went to tell Anne.

"We're screwed. Direct Relief is partnering with One by One. Direct Relief is massive, with decades of experience. One by One has a ton of local knowledge about Kenya."

I went back to my desk. Above my PC is a quote from Wayne Gretzky, the Canadian hockey great: "You miss all the shots you don't take."

So, on we went.

Later that week, a colleague called to tell me that the core plank in Direct Relief and One by One's plan was to hold a big meeting of all the local stakeholders in Kenya, then craft a strategy with the feedback from that vast array of people. Now, this might have turned out great. Or not. I started calling their plan "Feeding Frenzy." I know, I sound like I was in middle school, but I felt like a rejected teenager and was acting like one.

As the days slipped by, we made progress on our plan. We estimated first-year costs for surgeries, outreach, and surgeon training. Then we projected those over the full three years. We reached out to several of the individual hospitals via email and pulled descriptions and photos off websites to flesh out the proposal.

The Friday deadline loomed. By late afternoon Thursday, I still had work to do to finish our plan. But I needed to get home and feed Bobby dinner, so emailed the draft to myself from my PC at the office and after dinner, plugged away on my home PC and finished it around eleven. I was scheduled to leave for a weekend trip to LA with Bobby midday Friday, an adventure for my birthday. I went to bed relieved, and fell into a dead, dreamless sleep.

The next morning, I got to the office and opened my email on my desktop PC to retrieve the document that I had emailed myself the night before. Problem was, when I opened it, it was the draft from 5 p.m., not the version I'd saved at 11 p.m. I raced home, thinking I'd emailed the wrong version the night before, and the right one would be on my home PC. But as I looked through all the files, the 11 p.m. version was not there. The only document was the 5:00 p.m. version. In my exhaustion I had somehow saved the old version, not the new one.

I headed back into the office, grabbed Anne and Jessica, explained my complete stupidity and that I needed to recreate what I wrote last night over the next few hours. At 2 p.m., I punted the thirty-page draft to Jessica and Anne. Within fifteen minutes, both were in my office. There were some goofy spacing problems, brain-dead grammatical mistakes, and a chart with the wrong heading that Jessica said she could fix. Other than that, there were no big problems. By 3 p.m. it was ready to go. We loaded it into an email. Anne double-checked it, and I finally pushed send and the wait began.

I was more drained than elated. My adrenaline rush had been replaced by crushing exhaustion. Everything ached. I worried that the familiar dreaded fatigue was coming back from the virus I had picked up in Chad and Ethiopia that spring. I was scared of breaking myself again. While I was looking forward to the birthday weekend, I decided to cancel it. I couldn't face an airport and Friday lines at security and a rental car desk and LA traffic. Bobby seemed disappointed when I picked him up later than planned from school. But one of the great things about him is he is resilient, and he rolled with it. We hung out, watched Indiana Jones movies, and ordered pizza as I tried to make the weekend fun while also trying to recharge my battery.

At the end of the next week, we heard back from Astellas.

I was gob smacked: they picked Fistula Foundation over Direct Relief, UNFPA, One by One, and Freedom from Fistula.

The bad news: it wasn't a done deal. I'd need to go to London to present our plan to senior management at Astellas Europe.

Two weeks later, I walked through Heathrow after a red-eye flight from San Francisco. The place brought back a chilling memory of how horribly sick I had been only six months before.

The next morning, I headed to Astellas headquarters. It was a massive glass-walled building with a vast reception area where reportedly scenes from a recent James Bond movie had been shot. I was met by Jane, who took me into a large conference room and introduced me to two senior corporate communications people from Astellas.

The four of us would be planted there for the next eight hours, going through our proposal word by word.

The following day I'd be presenting it to their executive VP, Naoki Okamura, whom I was told had the power to say yes. Normally, presentations make me nervous, but this one surprisingly didn't. I knew the proposal inside and out, so describing it was easy. While the presentation itself was a blur, I walked out feeling like it had gone as well as it could.

29. ACTION ON FISTULA

If your dreams do not scare you,
they are not big enough.

—ELLEN JOHNSON SIRLEAF

The following week, I got a call I'll never forget.

It was from the team at Astellas.

We got the green light along with a promise of $1.5 million euros.

Now for the hard part: we had to build what we designed.

Next to giant Astellas Pharma, Fistula Foundation was a pygmy. Astellas had more than $10 billion in annual revenue, at least seventeen-thousand employees, and offices on five continents. At that point, Fistula Foundation's global workforce totaled six full-time and two part-time staff in one office in San Jose. Our annual revenue was about $6 million.

I needed to hire a program director to build what I'd outlined in the plan we presented to Astellas. I had someone in mind that would be ideal, Lindsey Pollaczek from Direct Relief. She had just finished getting her master's in public health, knew Fistula Foundation well, and was planning to move to Africa to gain field experience. I thought she had the energy and drive required to make our plan a reality. I offered her the job and she took it.

Our lean team got a lot done, but without much detailed documentation. We were like a culture with a strong oral tradition, but a weak written one. By contrast, Astellas seemed to document every step in thorough timelines, budgets, and spreadsheets. While we had a promise of funding from Astellas, by mid-April, we still hadn't seen a penny. This motivated me to continue to work with Lindsey to produce the mind-numbing planning documents they required.

Our goal over three years was to build a network of hospitals, engage community and women's groups, and train new surgeons in partnership with FIGO. This was the first time that the Foundation would work on this kind of scale. We wanted to end the wait for fistula treatment for all women in Kenya. The pressure was on us all to get the basic outline of the network built fast. Astellas wanted to officially launch the program on the UN's International Day to End Obstetric Fistula, May 23.

By mid-May, we were ready to host the CEO and other VIPs from Astellas to see the program in person in Kenya. Lindsey had put together a packed schedule where we would visit hospitals, interview outreach workers, and visit a fistula patient in her rural home. All this would culminate in a press conference in Nairobi to unveil our program. I arrived a couple days early, so I could meet with key hospital partners.

I could hear the crunch of the gravel driveway under the tires. As we came to a stop, I did a double take. I saw a single-story building painted a dusty yellow with a large, scruffy lawn surrounding it. It was tucked beneath a giant jacaranda tree, heavy with purple blossoms. If not for the sign out front welcoming us to Gynocare Fistula Center, I'd have thought we were just looking at an old house. Instead, this is where Dr. Mabeya practiced fistula surgery in the western city of Eldoret. I was excited to meet Mabeya, because he'd cured my friend Sarah Omega, the extraordinary woman I first met back in 2007 in London.

As we walked through the front door, Dr. Mabeya emerged from the back to greet us. He had soft eyes and a gentle demeanor like a dutiful minister and bore a passing resemblance to Sidney Poitier. But as he started to talk about his work, healing women with fistula, a steely energy emerged. He said he'd been working in a remote area in northern Kenya as a new doctor, and women with fistula kept coming into the facility. They were desperate, he said, but at that point he didn't know how to treat them and so referred them to a surgeon based in Nairobi. But he soon realized that for many women, the journey to the country's capital, a day's drive away, was beyond their means, so they simply went home to suffer more. He explained that he got training so he could cure them himself. Then he said he found this old, dilapidated home and turned it into a makeshift hospital.

Dr. Mabeya gave us a tour, first pointing out that the reception area we were standing in used to be the living room. Down a hallway we walked into the operating room, which was the former kitchen with a tiny oven built into the wall like you'd see in a pizza restaurant. One of the bathrooms had been converted to a lab. He'd installed a wall on the porch to turn it into a recovery area that had the advantage of cooling, fresh air.

His wife, Carolyn, who was as quietly engaging as her husband, had a master's in counseling. She was helping heal the psychological wounds of the women, providing counseling services, sometimes using the area under the shaded trees that edged the property as an outdoor office.

He said, "The women interact with each other, and they interact with our staff. We've developed a close-knit family that helps these women feel at home."

Mabeya could have easily set up a cushy, lucrative private practice in Nairobi or even in Belgium, where he completed his PhD. But he didn't. Instead, he created this modest but powerful oasis of healing for too-often forgotten women. He had the will, and he'd found a way, to treat women who likely would otherwise have lived lives of misery.

Unfortunately, after seeing what Dr. Mabeya had done to the home, his landlord had forbidden him from building any more structures and had quadrupled the rent. Mabeya was struggling to pay the bills. On top of that, he only had twenty-four beds so women were having to wait to get treatment until bed space was available.

I was moved by Mabeya's humble drive and his ingenuity. He was like an enterprising entrepreneur who also happened to be a gifted surgeon. My obvious thought: we needed to find a way to build a first-rate hospital for Dr. Mabeya, to give him the space he needed to help more women. If we did, we'd also have the center of excellence for fistula surgery training that had been part of our program plan for Kenya from the beginning. We could deepen our already strong partnership with FIGO to train more surgeons from Kenya and surrounding countries.

Now we needed to raise the money to make Dr. Mabeya's dream and our plan a reality. I thought, if we can't raise enough money for this heroic man to build a hospital, I should give my job to someone else.

While in Eldoret, I saw the work of an amazing American woman named Mary Ann McCammon whom I'd met the year before. She was a retired nursing professor, who was also a quilting instructor. When she learned about fistula, she had decided to use her sewing skills to help former fistula patients gain an income-earning skill: sewing. We'd connected her to Mabeya. She engaged two dynamic women: American Christine Fox and Kenyan Nora Otondo, a fistula survivor. Together they taught fistula survivors how to make and sell small quilts that also illustrated their stories of healing. In a classic win-win, we bought some of these quilts to provide our donors with a one-of-a-kind thank you gift. Speaking of one of a kind, that was Mary Ann. She passed away too early, at only eighty in 2023.

Lindsey and I went back to Nairobi to meet the team from Astellas who had flown in from London. Several terrorist attacks in Nairobi suburbs in recent months led Astellas security to conclude that our entourage should include guys with guns—a whole SUV packed with them. We came so armed it felt like we were part of a delegation for a head of state or a drug lord. The advantage of all that security was that the executives from Astellas could focus on the life-changing work their money was enabling. They seemed genuinely moved by the plight of fistula patients and the impact surgery had on the women.

Their branding mavens had trademarked the name "Action on Fistula" to call our new program and thanks to their dogged work and Jessica's, the press conference was well attended. The coverage in the Kenyan media was strong. This would help us get the word out about the availability of free treatment. And we hoped it would give Astellas part of what they sought: visibility for their investment in us.

When the best-selling writer James Patterson referred to his long-gone advertising career, he said he's been "clean for thirty years" implying advertising was a dirty game. I'd shared that low-grade shame about the decade I'd spent on Madison Avenue. But that summer, I found myself at a dais in a massive ballroom at a Washington, DC hotel there to receive an award from The American Marketing Association, "Nonprofit Marketer of the Year." This was the first time that I reflected on just how much I was leaning into my marketing skills to help the Foundation thrive. There was a big silver lining to what I had thought of as my dark, wasted "Madwoman" twenties. The best thing about the awards luncheon was the opportunity it gave me to tell a huge room full of people why fistula and the Foundation were worthy of their support.

Regarding marketing, we ended 2014 stronger than ever, raising more than three times as much money as we raised in 2008 before we went global. The most critical decision we made was to focus on one measurable outcome—surgeries, and then hold ourselves accountable. We were now supporting more than 4,500 surgeries a year with 40 partner hospitals in twenty-one countries. This provided powerful proof that we were delivering on our mission. In addition, the Kenya Network was off to a strong start with the Foundation funding four treatment centers. I'd finally relented, and we were adding staff to our team to accommodate the growth and had moved into a bigger office.

———————————⊥———————————

I awoke on Saturday, April 25, 2015, to news that a 7.8 magnitude earthquake had hit Nepal a few hours earlier. The pictures trickling in showed extraordinary devastation. I reached out to our partner, Dr. Ganesh Dangal, who ran Kathmandu Model Hospital. He was a deeply respected surgeon who'd been trained in fistula surgery by FIGO. I learned that his hospital, like so many other buildings in the nation's capital, had suffered extensive damage. While the ground floor was operational, the upper floors where the fistula operating room was located were unusable. They were taking patients out to the parking lot, fearing parts of the building would collapse. While we were not a disaster relief organization, we wanted to help our partner and ensure that women with fistula would be able to receive treatment. We estimated it would take $150,000 to rebuild their operating room.

Our donors were some of the world's most compassionate people, and I was confident we could raise the funds. But I wanted to give them an incentive to donate. A challenge campaign that we could launch on our website would help us do it. I reached out to a couple of our most generous supporters, Frank Richardson and Kimba Wood. They immediately offered us up to $100,000 for a two-for-one match. They would donate $2 for every dollar donated by our other supporters. We developed a powerful video and launched the campaign two days later.

Within twenty-four hours, we'd raised $50,000, meaning we met Frank and Kimba's match and had raised the entire $150,000 to send to Nepal. The team at Kathmandu Model Hospital had many challenges with the massive damage done by the quake, but at least having the funds to rebuild their operating room wasn't one of them. Like I said, we have the best donors.

30. DOING GOOD BETTER

Shouldn't you put the same amount of effort
into your giving as you might for your for-profit investments?
After all, philanthropy is an investment, and one
in which lives—not profits—are at stake.

—LAURA ARILLAGA-ANDREESSEN

As I scanned the long list of emails on my laptop, one caught my eye. It was from Professor Peter Singer, whom I revered, so I opened it immediately. He was writing to introduce me to Will MacAskill, a Scottish academic. I'd heard MacAskill referred to as the next Peter Singer, a torchbearer for the effective altruism movement. Singer said MacAskill was writing a book and may include fistula in it. Of course, I jumped on this like a hungry dog nipping at a bone and sent MacAskill an email saying I'd be delighted to talk to him.

Crickets.

I followed up with another email to MacAskill.

Again. Crickets.

I moved on, assuming he'd decided not to include us in his book.

When I heard MacAskill was publishing a book titled *Doing Good Better: How Effective Altruism Can Help You Make a Difference*, I pre-ordered it. The day it showed up in my office, I rifled through to the index, finding Fistula Foundation. I flipped to page 41 and 42. I read what he wrote and wanted to scream!

This lauded Oxford-trained professor hadn't bothered to do his homework on us. He described his visit to Dr. Hamlin's hospital, which was moving for him; a reaction I'd had too. But then, he went astray. He asserted that Fistula Foundation was focused on supporting Hamlin's hospital. But we'd changed our mission in 2009 to support hospitals in dozens of countries. His facts were six years out of date, which means they weren't facts, they were errors. Then he used that falsehood to conclude that we were ineffective, by saying: "Should I have donated to the Fistula Foundation, knowing I could do more to help people if I donated elsewhere? I do not think so." We were not only not focused on Hamlin, at that point, exactly $0 of what we were raising was going there. And he had the audacity to then deem us ineffective. I was livid, outraged, angry. This man's sloppy work could hurt us and the women we were in business to help.

My response, after venting my fury with Anne, was to write a clear-eyed piece for the *Huffington Post*. My title: "*Doing Good* Should Have Been Done Better." Here's an excerpt:

Like many people in the Effective Altruism movement, I anticipated this week's release of MacAskill's book *Doing Good Better: How Effective Altruism Can Help You Make a Difference*. But here's a word of caution to readers of the book: beware. If the facts cited and conclusion drawn about my organization—Fistula Foundation— are any indication, the book may contain significant errors, ironic for a field based on the primacy of evidence. . . . MacAskill got our basic mission completely wrong, relying on information from over six years ago. He confined our work to one hospital in one country, and then used that wholly mistaken and outdated view as a reason to not recommend giving us support. What's a girl to do with that, but try to set the record straight? . . . Far from focusing on one hospital in one country, we have become the largest non-governmental funder of fistula surgery in the world, having worked with partners across thirty countries. In the last six years, we've raised more than $27 million USD from donors in more than sixty countries.

I used graphs to display a linear relationship that proved the new funds we raised translated into good done for indigent women measured in more surgeries. I underscored that we were funding nearly ten times as many surgeries as in 2009.

The other thing I did was see who had written blurbs for the book. You know, those quotes on the cover usually from famous people saying the thing is the best book since the Bible. Two well-known writers and thinkers that I admire blurbed the book: Steven Pinker at Harvard and Adam Grant at Penn (no relation, unfortunately). I emailed both my *Huff Post* piece. I said that I respected them but wanted them to know MacAskill's book was wrong about us. I was delighted when both men contacted me. They said they were sympathetic and thanked me.

I sent MacAskill my article and let him know I'd reached out to his blurbers. I got a sheepish apology, and he said he'd investigate fixing the mistake when the book came out in paperback.

Here's the thing: what MacAskill got wrong isn't "insider baseball" or a hidden fact. We post every audit and 990 tax return on our website and have for a decade, along with every annual report, which detail where the funds we raise go. All that Will MacAskill had to do was visit our website. Instead, he used the poor women we help to make his point, even if it was based on malarky. He didn't seem to give a toss about them.

When MacAskill's paperback came out, he had added only the year 2009 in front of his text about our support for Hamlin. That made his statement factually accurate, but still damning and deceiving. He likely led people to embrace his faulty conclusion that we were inefficient and not worthy of support.

This was shocking.

But at least on my paperback copy neither Pinker nor Grant has a blurb. Is that an accident? I hope not.

I had a nagging question with no answer. How many indigent, incontinent women in need of help did not get surgery because readers took MacAskill's analysis at face value and didn't support us because of his negligence?

And, MacAskill said he focuses his research on utilitarianism: the idea that we should "judge right or wrong by their consequences."

Talk about irony.

It was hard not to see this through a gender lens: a careless man once again hurts vulnerable women with impunity.

I'd love to say that this blind spot to the suffering of women was limited to Professor MacAskill. But the same problem plagues a prominent effective altruism group, GiveWell. If you look at GiveWell's recommended charities, you would think that women and men in developing countries had equal rights and opportunities. This is because according to the Foundation's analysis roughly 99 percent of the more than $2 billion they have directed in the last fifteen years has gone to organizations that do not focus on empowering women or girls.

In fact, if you arrived from space and looked at their recommended charities, it would be fair to assume that poverty impacts women and men, girls and boys, the same way. But the simple truth is, it doesn't.

GiveWell seems blind to structural inequality.

There is much to admire about GiveWell's big staff of smart people with impressive degrees. They've raised the bar in the nonprofit sector by focusing rigorously on outcomes—what a charity can prove it accomplishes. This is commendable. But one must question their methodology that ignores the fact that women take all the risks for reproduction. After HIV/AIDS, the biggest cause of death and disability to young women across the developing world is childbearing. Yet, their male-founded and led organization can find few organizations confronting this carnage worthy of support. As a footnote, in 2023, there were reports of troubling sexual harassment of women by men in the effective altruism community reported by *Time* magazine.

We had an engagement with GiveWell that lasted the better part of a year in 2019, answering any and every question they had about our work. The process was so time-intensive that they gave us a $100,000 grant as compensation for our time. When all was said and done, what we got was this: "From an initial cost-effectiveness analysis, our best estimate is that Fistula Foundation may be in the range of cost-effectiveness of our top charities."

Then, radio silence.

No recommendation.

No further analysis.

The million women who have urine, and sometimes feces too, coming out of their vaginas 24–7 were not worth their time.

The key reason for this gender blind spot is likely that addressing gender inequity is daunting. While it is a problem as old as time, trying to attack its root causes and even its symptoms is more complex than providing commodities like insecticide-treated bed nets—a proven approach to help prevent malaria, and the largest beneficiary of GiveWell's work.

I think the time is right for someone to launch an organization that's inspired by the principles of effective altruism yet focused on researching and recommending nonprofits with a proven ability to improve the well-being of women and girls. There's a rising cadre of thinkers and researchers—including scholars such as Emily Oster, an economist at Brown University—who are rigorously applying this kind of gender lens to their work. This new organization could engage and support people like Professor Oster in the urgent task of providing effective altruists with choices of organizations that address the unequal distribution of political and economic resources that harms women and girls. It's not just women and girls who would benefit from applying a gender lens to addressing extreme poverty. Whole families and communities will rise when educated women can earn a greater income and provide better nutrition and healthcare to their families.

———————————

I stared out the large window at Manhattan's glittering skyline and Central Park below. I was in the living room of a successful Wall Street financier and his cookbook author wife.

The occasion: a fundraising dinner for Fistula Foundation, followed by a concert.

The hosts: Professor Peter Singer and me.

The star attraction: Paul Simon.

Singer had met Simon a decade earlier when both were recognized by *Time* magazine as two of their "100 Most Influential People", and the two had become friends. It was Simon that offered to do a concert, and Singer who picked Fistula Foundation. I was both honored and thrilled.

Several years earlier, a pioneering man, named Charlie Bresler partnered with Singer to found an organization called The Life You Can Save. It featured vetted charities like ours that exemplified the values Singer put forward in his book of the same name. Many Foundation supporters found us because of the organization, The Life You Can Save, that wouldn't exist without Charlie.

After dinner, we were all escorted into the spacious living room where Simon was joined by an accompanist on piano. I had goose bumps. I idolized the man sitting a few feet from me. His music had been like a soundtrack to my life. Singer, who I worshiped for different reasons, stood up and gave brief remarks about the Foundation and his friendship with Simon. He also mentioned that the last time Simon performed with Central Park as a backdrop, there were half a million people there to see him. Simon thanked us all for being there, and I willed myself to savor every minute.

Simon began with what he said was one of his favorite songs, the ballad "The Boxer." He said that he wrote the words at a time when he was struggling and felt beleaguered. Then with his next song his voice carried these words across the living room: "When tears are in your eyes, I will dry them all. I'm on your side ... When evening falls so hard I will comfort you ... like a bridge over troubled water." I think "Bridge Over Troubled Water" is one of the most beautiful songs ever written about love and friendship. It's like a secular hymn.

I realized his words described what the Foundation aims to

be—a bridge connecting caring people with women in need and their dedicated doctors. With each verse, my heart soared with a sense of grace and purpose that I had never felt before listening to a song. I was so grateful to have a job that enabled me to engage with amazing people: Simon, Singer, Charlie, and the generous donors sitting around me in that living room, including the Steve that had made the movie *A Walk to Beautiful* possible, Frank Richardson, Kimba Wood, our future board chair, Kelly Brennan, and Peter's wife, Renata.

The hour went by far too fast. And after Simon concluded, Singer asked me to say a few words. I thanked everyone in the audience for coming, Singer for leading the way on effective altruism, the apartment's owners for their hospitality. When I thanked Simon, I know I sounded like a giddy teenager.

As the guests filtered out, I went up to again express my gratitude to Simon. I no doubt babbled on with star-struck wonder. But I had one question that I wanted to ask him.

"What did it feel like to stand on a stage with half a million people in front of you and perform?"

He said, "I'm not focused on the audience, I am focused on getting the music right."

There it was. The reason I can be in a cab in Ethiopia or Bangladesh and hear songs like "Kodachrome" or "Graceland" blaring from the car radio, recorded long before the driver of the cab was born. Simon focused on getting the music right.

On my way back home, I stopped in Chicago to meet with two of our most generous donors, Joe and Sharon Kemper. With Sharon's help, Joe had built a successful business that he had sold for a princely sum. They were both in their seventies but committed to spending their golden years giving away their hard-earned fortune. They'd heard about our work through Singer's book and were inspired to help. Joe had pushed us to do more challenge match fundraising and had put up his own funds to match gifts from our donors. Joe and Sharon were true partners in every sense of the word.

When I drove up to their home, I was surprised. While the lot was large, the house wasn't. It was built in the 1970s and was modest. When we sat down in their kitchen to catch up, Joe said he had just made a Costco run and offered me a root beer. They'd recently returned from a trip to Nepal to visit a school they'd funded and would be off soon on another trip to Honduras. I enjoyed their company and was sad that our time when by too fast. As I said good-bye, my heart was gladdened by deep affection for this selfless pair.

When I got back to the office Bill Mann, one of our newest board members, reached out to me. He said that his organization, the financial firm Motley Fool, had selected Fistula Foundation to be their featured charity for their year-end giving program, "Foolanthropy." Throughout December, employees and members of the Motley Fool community created their own individual fundraising campaigns online. We met our stretch goal of $100,000, helping make 2015 our best year ever.

31. BLIND SPOT

The willingness to change comes when the pain
of staying where you are is too great.

—Anne Lamott

As I walked into our office, it felt like a weekend rather than a Monday morning. Usually, the place buzzed with energy as spontaneous meetings happened in doorways. But today all I heard were leaf blowers from the gardeners outside. What I saw, were mainly closed doors.

Our team had grown a lot in last two years. We were raising more money and increased the number of women we treated by nearly 50 percent in just the last year. I was pushing everyone hard and I wrote off the shut doors to diligence.

There's an African proverb that fits where we were: don't think there are no crocodiles just because the water is calm.

There were indeed predators waiting for me.

They were ones I'd created through a combination of blindness and hubris.

I was tempted to leave this bit out, but like most painful chapters, this one produced profound growth. So here goes.

This is a memo I wish someone had sent me at the time:

To: Kate
Wake up. Your job has changed. Your team is huge, and you barely know their names. You need to spend a lot more time caring about how these good people are doing their jobs and have what they need from you to thrive. Do not write off the lead in the air. This is not normal. Figure out what's wrong. Then, fix it. Because guess what? The it, is you.

A few weeks later, a junior member of the communication team left the Foundation to take a new job. She was likable, earnest, and hard-working. I was surprised when she left. After she did, I learned the reason: me.

Now, I have my glaring weaknesses. I can be sloppy with details I don't care about, which doesn't mean they don't matter. I talk too much, taking way too long to say far too little. I am demanding. But in a letter that our former employee sent to the board she portrayed me as something else: a relentless and driven dictator, and she said others felt the same way.

When I read the letter, my first instinct was defensiveness. I was simply doing my job so the Foundation would grow. But, as my rationalizations faded, I had to admit that many of her words rang true, producing a flash of clarity that pierced my ego and my heart.

A few months earlier, a male board member had told me that I needed to tone down my intensity, that I was intimidating. Of course, I had simply chalked that up to sexism. But maybe the real culprit here was my arrogance, and lack of awareness my own failings. I had long ago gotten over the tyranny of trying to be liked by everyone, because you can't lead if you try to make everyone happy. But I'd obviously taken that basic idea way too far.

I always considered my drive one of my key strengths, the will-power to keep plowing through bad situations such as my divorce, like a sled in a blizzard. That voice could enable me to accomplish a lot, but also could push me to the breaking point, as it had a few years before when I ended up in the hospital. Had I now done that to my team?

My sense of shame ran deep. So much for being the kind of leader that people want to follow. I was the kind of boss who drives people to leave. That unhappy employee would turn out to be one of my greatest teachers. If I was pushing myself and others so hard that I had created this kind of animosity, I was in trouble.

After my face-plant on my first speaking engagement when I was on the Hill, a retired marine I worked with told me to "embrace the suck." I realized that's what I had to do now, but it was painful. One lesson I had managed to absorb from work and life was that if I assumed that I created the problem, rather than simply blaming it on someone else, I gave myself the power to try to fix it.

———————————————

There's another fitting African proverb: If you want to go fast, go alone. If you want to go far, go with others. I wanted the Foundation to continue to go far, and the only way to make that happen was for me to become a better leader. But how would I do that?

I talked to my good friend Suzanne, who had been so helpful during my divorce. She said something like, "Why don't you get yourself a coach, someone who you can really talk to?"

Through a colleague, I found Jeff Balin, at that point teaching at the business school at University of British Columbia, who had coached other nonprofit and private sector leaders. I never met him face to face, but for the at least six months, I had a call with him every week or two. He was like a therapist but for work, and proved to be an ideal sounding board, giving me insights into how my actions rippled through the team in ways I hadn't considered. Our weekly calls got me to slow down and focus both on what my team needed and how best to drive results.

I learned to be more nurturing of our staff, while doing a better job of taking care of myself. It's funny how that works—the demanding, critical voice I was too often using with others was the same one I used on me. Over time, I tried to quiet that voice and both the team and I grew happier and more productive in our roles.

Jeff also got me to recognize that part of the problem was our staff had nearly quadrupled in just a few years. I'd approved hiring a bunch of people without considering the unique culture we'd built. Because I had little nonprofit experience, I had hired people with loads of it, thinking we needed it. But I learned the hard way that our dynamic, always iterating, never-done approach could produce anxiety in people who'd spent their work lives at your average risk-averse nonprofit organization that grows modestly year after year.

The business guru Jim Collins, in his bestseller *Good to Great*, had wise advice that I had at some point read and promptly forgotten. "The adage 'people are your most important asset' is wrong. People are not your most important asset. The right people are." The big problem was, I'd given precious little thought to the core attributes I felt had enabled us to grow. That was on me.

Completely.

Totally.

Painfully.

For the Foundation to thrive, I would have to do a better job of getting the right people on the bus. I realized that the people I wanted were "climbers" not "campers," people wired for growth and smart risk-taking.

To do that, I needed help hiring people, so I reached out to a dedicated local recruiter, Susannah Sallin. She worked hard to find people who were a strong fit for us, such as a brilliant woman, Pam Lowney, now our Chief Operating Officer. After a three-hour, no-holds-barred lunch, I lured Pam away from Stanford Medicine, where she'd been the lead digital strategist. When Anne retired, Pam was able to step up to help fill her enormous shoes.

Even with Susannah's help not everyone would work out. Finding talented, creative people who wanted to reach for the stars proved to be my greatest challenge. Over the years I've hired people who oversold their abilities and others who talked a good game about working hard, but underdelivered. The notion that the charity world attracts only diligent, ethical people is unfortunately wishful thinking. But we've gotten better at finding exceptional people who can help us meet our ambitious goals.

One tangible outcome of this difficult chapter was that, as a team, we developed our own credo, like our friends at J & J. It sits on our website and on the wall in our conference room:

Fistula Foundation Credo:
We believe that no woman should lead a life of misery simply for trying to bring a child into the world. And we dream of a world where women and girls will have the same opportunity for a healthy future as men and boys.

We know that too many poor women give birth without access to critical obstetric care. Too often, these women suffer devastating childbirth injuries, such as fistula, that leave them incontinent and outcast from their communities.

We serve as an essential bridge between women who suffer needlessly and selfless people who want to help them. Across that bridge flow resources to doctors who perform life-transforming surgery and to outreach workers who connect women with the treatment that they deserve.

We recognize that our hospital partners in Africa and Asia know best what will work in their communities. Humility and wisdom demand that we listen to them.

We celebrate the dedicated surgeons and nurses who make miracles of hope and healing happen every day and collaborate with them to ensure that women receive high-quality care.

We are ever grateful to our supporters and treasure the trust that they place in us. We are committed to using their hard-earned money effectively and efficiently to help women reclaim their lives.

We embrace diversity in all aspects of our work. Only by collaborating with people from a wide range of backgrounds and with a rich variety of experiences can we maximize our potential to transform women's lives.

We understand that failure is always part of success, and we learn from our mistakes and grow stronger because of them.

We strive every day to end the suffering of women injured in childbirth—and to ensure that no woman is left behind.

That summer, I found myself at Harvard Business School, for one of the most stimulating weeks of my professional life. Our ardent donor, Lars Bane, had reached out to me in the spring to tell me about a course they offered titled Strategic Perspectives in Nonprofit Management. While it looked appealing, the price was not; it didn't pass my "worth it" test. But it was like Lars read my mind when he said that he and his wife Veronica would pay the fee. The course was taught using case studies of charities facing a range of challenges. These were described in hundreds of dense pages, that we were asked to read before we arrived. About two-hundred nonprofit CEOs from all over the world attended and together we wrestled with these complex cases.

On the plane home, I reflected on the week. While I'd headed off thinking I'd be intimidated, it was after all THE Harvard Business School, I came home feeling more confident than ever that we were on the right track. We had a robust, focused network of hospitals, dedicated doctors, and could demonstrate to anyone who could read a graph that we were scaling efficiently, supporting more high-quality surgeries every year. I started to think about how to strengthen my reporting to our donors. While I knew that our supporters were motivated by their empathetic hearts, it seemed there was more I could do to show them how we were using tough minded strategies to deploy their money.

I started drafting something I've now dubbed my Investor Letters. They are four to five pages long and are a deep dive into the business side of the Foundation, sans patient stories or photos. I send them to our most loyal supporters twice a year. My hope is that the letters reinforce the trust our donors place in me and my team to do what our tagline promises *help give a woman a new life*. The week at Harvard Business School turned out to be well worth the Banes' money and my time after all.

32. FALLEN ANGEL

I think it's got to be okay to mess up in life,
to acknowledge it and notice it and be changed by it.

—SARAH SILVERMAN

When you hear the name, Louis CK, what goes through your mind? Is it his brilliant Emmy, Peabody, and Grammy award-winning writing? His sell-out stand-up shows? Or his Me-Too reconning? If it's the latter, you know Louis had a very public repudiation because of his dealings with several women about twenty years ago. I cannot defend his actions. Having had a couple of my own troubling encounters with men I didn't seek or want, I have empathy for what the women experienced.

Back in December 2011, when few people had heard of Fistula Foundation, we got a call from the company that processed our credit card donations. They said someone was trying to donate $20,000 online and hit a glitch. Since our average donation was then and still is under $100, this created a near panic among our tiny team to get the problem fixed. The donor was Louis. He was giving 25 percent of his proceeds from one of his shows to charity and picked us. How could we thank him immediately? One word: Twitter. Confession: until that day, I was a tweet virgin. So of course we scrambled, and I sent something silly and forgettable, like a high school yearbook entry: WOW TX UR Amazn don't ever change WOW. (There is clearly an art to these things, which I haven't come close to mastering.)

I sent an email too, longer, and gushier about how this was a very big deal for us, which it was. So then, he emailed back and said he'd given us another $20,000. Sure enough, like Santa, but better, the money hit our account. That night, he was a guest on *Late Night with Jimmy Fallon*, and he plugged Fistula Foundation in front of millions of viewers. This was huge visibility for us.

Fast forward several years later, and out of nowhere I got an email from Louis. He asked if I could send him Fistula Foundation t-shirts, extra-large, without indicating what they were for. Of course, we sent all the versions we had in stock. Turned out, he was hosting Saturday Night Live. During the close, he wore a Fistula Foundation t-shirt. But the amazing thing was the shirt he had on was not one we had sent him, with discreet logos. He had made one with "FistulaFoundation.org" across the chest in giant white letters against a dark green background. Louis served as a human billboard for us in front of a multitude of loyal SNL fans. How many "A-list" stars would go to that kind of trouble to help us? The answer, not many. Maybe zero.

Then Louis was asked to appear on the celebrity version of *Jeopardy* and made Fistula Foundation his beneficiary charity. They taped the show in Washington, DC, and Bobby and I caught the last flight out of San Francisco to make the taping. The audience was huge and seemed to be rooting for Louis. They did a trial round and let's just say that it was good it was only practice because the smarty-pants journalists Louis was competing against cleaned up.

But finally, Alex Trebek emerged, smooth as a Sinatra ballad. The cameras rolled and the game started. Here, where it counted, for real money, Louis was still not killing it, but he was holding his own. Then, he pulled a "Daily Double," meaning he could double down and wager twice the normal amount. He went for it. The question was a quote from Richard Nixon, with a word missing. The answer, a virtual mantra for that twisted president. What is "illegal"? As they headed into the final round, Louis's lead was solid. He nailed the final question and won the whole $50,000 in front of a cheering crowd that was in his pocket from the beginning.

A woman from the production company whisked us away to the front of the stage to meet Louis. He said something like, "Thank you for coming all this way to see me play." When I replied that I was so grateful because the money would fund surgeries for close to one hundred women, he added, "Thank you for letting me help you." What? He's a big shot celebrity, why is he thanking me? Louis went on Howard Stern's radio show a few weeks later and mentioned that we were "his charity," a definite first for fistula the cause, and for Fistula Foundation to get airtime with Stern. We are still getting gifts from people like Stern who had no idea what fistula was until Louis told them.

Louis isn't a good friend of mine, but he is to the women we are in business to help. He did something only a very small fraction of our donors do: he traveled to Africa to see the work up close. I went with him, visiting hospitals, patients, and outreach workers. I got to see a side of Louis that few people who know him only from his professional work have seen. Fistula patients are very often stigmatized and ostracized. I saw Louis treat these women with caring and kindness, comparing their courage to that of his mother who had raised four children on her own and was confronting cancer. They didn't know he was a famous entertainer, what they saw was a person who was welcoming and compassionate. During our trip, we ate in the simple homes of outreach workers and Louis treated these people with the deference that some would reserve for only the "great and the good."

When the story about Louis's transgressions first hit, I was shocked and dismayed. They showed another side of this human. The worst side. On a practical level, I was also sad because he had been a very effective messenger for us. People had donated hundreds of thousands of dollars because of him. Now he would be out of the limelight for the foreseeable future.

I was interviewed by *The New York Times* about Louis as part of their #MeToo coverage. The reporter asked pointedly if we would return his donations or the *Jeopardy* prize money? I said, in the nicest tone possible, "No way." I am pretty sure we'd be out of business if we only took donations from perfect people who had not made embarrassing, even troubling, mistakes. I try to put myself in the place of a woman with fistula, one who has often suffered for years unable to access or afford timely surgery. Would she turn down a gift made by Louis or enabled by his *Jeopardy* win that could fund her life-transforming surgery? The simple easy answer, I believe, is no.

One of my personal heroes, lawyer Bryan Stevenson, the civil rights champion, said something that resonates with me. "Each of us is more than the worst thing we've ever done." I find Stevenson so wise and forgiving. His adage seems to spring from the same reserve of humility and compassion as the line in the Lord's Prayer: "Forgive us our trespasses, as we forgive those who have trespassed against us." I hope people can forgive me for my many failings. I'm glad that because I'm not famous, mine aren't plastered all over social media.

It's been over seven years since the initial *NYT* reporting, and Louis has continued to support the Foundation. He also introduced Chris Rock and Sarah Silverman to our work. Rock donated part of his proceeds from his sold out "Ego Death" tour to the Foundation, and Silverman is now an ambassador for us with her millions of fans and social media followers. What these people do is magic to me— getting thousands of people laughing in unison, creating waves of profound human joy. Incredible. Something I couldn't do any more than compose a symphony or build a rocket ship to Mars.

33. TAKE THE CHICKEN

*Appreciation is the purest, strongest form
of love. It is the outward-bound kind of love that
ask for nothing and gives everything..*

—KELLY CORRIGAN

I jumped into the passenger seat of a gray SUV and we headed out of Gynocare's parking lot. At the wheel was Habiba Mohammed, our country director for Kenya. We were on our way to visit Mwanatena, a woman who had had her fistula a staggering thirty-three years before she was recently cured by Dr. Mabeya. She lived in a rural village about forty minutes away. As we left Eldoret's single-story commercial buildings behind, the road wound through the highlands with small mud huts and meager farms dotting the arid landscape.

A few months earlier I'd been back in Kenya for the grand opening of Dr. Mabeya's new Gynocare hospital. It was three stories, with two ORs and a modern lab. There, he could both treat fistula and other childbirth injuries and prevent them by offering hospital-based deliveries and C-sections. It had become the first FIGO Fistula Surgeon Training site in Kenya with Mabeya serving as a master trainer. Thanks to our deep-hearted donors, we'd raised close to $1 million to build it, since this wasn't in the plan Astellas had paid for.

The biggest portion came from our largest donor, dear Paula Weil. When I asked her about naming the hospital after her, she said something like, "I don't want that. Please have the people who will use it name it something meaningful to them." Big money donors in New York or LA, angling for their name on a new concert hall or college building, could learn a thing or two from our donors about what genuine generosity and true humility look like. This selfless woman would also leave us a large bequest when she passed away the next year.

Along with Astellas' VIPs who'd flown in from Tokyo, hundreds of Kenyans had showed up for the grand opening. There were speeches from every relevant local politician, and a dance troupe performed. Then together we cut a massive cake the size of a card table: the CEO of Astellas, Dr. Mabeya, and me. Here was Fistula Foundation, an American nonprofit, partnering with a Japanese pharmaceutical and an African doctor, to bring life-changing care to African women. I wondered what my long-dead relatives who'd fought in the Second World War against the Japanese, would make of this. I hoped they'd view it with the kind of grateful awe I felt that day. Cue, Louis Armstrong's "What a Wonderful World."

We were helping more women get treated than we'd dreamed possible back in 2013 when I pitched our countrywide treatment plan to Astellas. In the first four years our network treated more than four thousand Kenyan women, double our goal. Twelve months post-treatment, 96 percent of the women reported that they were cured.

The patients ranged in age from 14 to 80; the average patient had gotten her fistula at twenty-three. More astounding was that patients had their fistula for an average of nine years before receiving treatment through our program. Can you imagine being incontinent of urine and sometimes feces for nearly a decade for a treatable injury? This demonstrated that without us, they'd likely still be suffering.

Astellas Comms team made sure we won several industry awards for "social responsibility." I'd flown to Tokyo and London and pitched Astellas on additional funding and was delighted when they re-upped for another three years.

One key to our stunning success in Kenya was the strength of the outreach network; the army of men and women who helped ensure women with fistula got life-changing surgery. Lindsey and Habiba led that effort. Habiba's late husband, Yusuf Omenda, even founded a soccer club, nicknamed "Kick Fistula out of Africa." Several players were fistula survivors, and they used their platform to educate fans about fistula treatment.

As Habiba took a quick left turn onto a dirt road, she said we were almost there. It was so narrow that it felt like a wide footpath. We slowed down to a pace not much faster than walking speed because of the many giant potholes. Other than the sound of the car, it was quiet with only the occasional chatter of birds. A welcome gentle breeze brought the smell of fresh earth into the car. After about twenty minutes, Habiba pointed to a small brown hut with a thatched roof in the distance. "That's Mwanatena's home." It was sitting in the middle of a modest plot of land not much bigger than a playground at your average preschool. It was lined by a few rows of parched corn stalks. As we drove up to the hut, the only livestock I could see were three scrawny chickens pecking at the hard ground.

I noticed a mattress, pot and cooking oil, and a small rug— piled outside the hut. I didn't have long to take in our surroundings because Mwanatena and a man that Habiba said was her husband, Mohammed, were waving at us. As we got out of the car and approached them, Mwanatena shook my hand vigorously and introduced me to Mohammed. She was a small woman with bright, sparkling eyes and an infectious smile. Mwanatena invited us into their hut. The only light was the sunshine streaming in through the open door, revealing the dirt floor and a few plastic chairs. Inside she introduced me to several of her neighbors. The space was tiny, and I realized they had moved their belongings out so that there would be room for the group of us to meet.

Mwanatena was beaming and bouncing up and down in her seat. "I am so glad to meet you and thank you in person." She jumped up to hug me, and I met her with a warm embrace. She then continued, "I have my life back. I am so happy." And she again got up to hug me. Honestly, her exuberance made me uncomfortable. I was not the surgeon who treated her. It felt like I was taking credit for what some-one else had done and it felt wrong. But as she talked about her new life, I realized that she was so grateful, she could not contain herself. My job was to share her joy. When she pulled me up to dance with her, I just went with it, and we danced in the dimly lit hut.

I still wanted to hear her story.

She said that before her fistula, "life was good." She and Moham-med had two healthy children, and Mohammed worked as a basket weaver.

Mohammed leaned toward her and added, "She was so beautiful. I have always loved her."

On his income, she said they had enough to meet their basic needs. All that changed with the delivery of her third child. When she went into labor, she said, "The village midwife assured me that everything was fine, but I knew that something was wrong. This was not like my other deliveries. It was the rainy season and pouring outside, and the closest health facility was over ten miles away, and I had no way to get to the hospital. But finally, a neighbor offered to take me on his bike."

I tried to imagine what it must have been like:

Riding on the back of a bike.

While in labor.

In the rain.

On a bumpy road.

For ten miles.

I couldn't.

I said, "You must have been very frightened."

"I was. When we finally got there, all the beds were taken. I was forced to huddle on the floor for another day before I finally saw a healthcare worker. When it was my turn, I pushed for hours, but nothing happened. Then I finally delivered my baby girl, but she was already dead."

"I'm so sorry."

Mwanatena said, "It was a really tough time. When I returned home, I was so sad. I couldn't control my body. My waste kept coming out of me. Mohammed and I agreed it was best to try and hide my problem."

I added, "That must have been hard to do."

"You're right because one day when friends came to visit, I was laughing at a friend's joke, and it happened: I soiled my clothes. News traveled fast. Whenever I would meet people, some would avoid me, while others would tell me straight to my face that I was strange. I started to lose friends."

"That's so hurtful when our friends abandon us."

"Even my family resented me, and so they held a meeting. Mohammed was asked to send me away because I brought a bad name to the family. But he stayed with me instead."

At this point Mwanatena smiled at Mohammed. She explained that together they spent years visiting health centers and trying medications to treat her incontinence, paid for by selling small parts of their meager plot. Nothing worked.

Then she said, "Last fall Mohammed attended a rally in town, and he heard that there was free treatment available for women like me. He took down a hotline number to call."

I looked at Habiba, who smiled. She had been the one to organize the rally and the hotline.

Mwanatena said, "I was so excited that I called the number right way. They asked me a bunch of questions, and a woman arranged for me to travel for treatment. Within a couple of weeks, I went to the hospital and Dr. Mabeya cured me. I came home completely dry. I still can't believe it when I wake up in the morning. It is a miracle!" As she said that, she got up to embrace me and we danced together again.

We stayed a while longer to visit with Mwanatena and her neighbors, but the time came for us to leave. I stood up and walked out of the hut into the bright afternoon sun and looked around once more, taking in the small plot and the struggling rows of corn. When

I turned back to Mwanatena, she was beaming and holding one of her chickens.

She held it out to me and said, "Thank you." It took me a moment to realize that she was giving me the chicken as a gift.

My first thought was pragmatic: she should keep the chicken! Mwanatena and Mohammed had so little, and heaven knows, I didn't need a chicken. They did.

But I looked over at Habiba who knew these chickens were among Mwanatena's most prized possessions, but also knew how grateful she was.

Habiba whispered to me, "Take the chicken."

And at that moment I bent down, took the chicken, and looking into Mwanatena's hopeful eyes said, "Thank you so very much."

I put the chicken in the back of the car, waved goodbye out the window, and we headed back down the narrow dirt road. Each time we hit a bump the chicken let out a cluck in protest, and I couldn't help but laugh. What was I going to do with a chicken?

Our next stop was a support group for fistula survivors. In my most satisfying re-gifting experience ever, I gave the chicken to another former fistula patient. She was thrilled.

We closed out 2019 and set new highs in the number of women treated that year—more than 8,200—and we raised more than $14 million. Compared to when we started our global mission in 2009, we were funding almost sixteen times as many surgeries and raising five times as much money. We were supporting more than 80 partners at 150 hospital sites in 32 countries. We had expanded our team, adding a few new people in the last six months, and were poised for tremendous growth. We were planning to "lift repeat" our successful countrywide treatment network like this one in Kenya into more countries. Our ambition was to end fistula country by country. In the early days of 2020, it felt like nothing could stop us.

34. BLACK SWAN

*We all have an unsuspected reserve of strength
inside that emerges when life puts us to the test.*

—ISABEL ALLENDE

I walked into the house, set my purse down on the kitchen counter, and turned on NPR. It was Wednesday, March 11, 2020, and the World Health Organization had just declared Covid-19 a global pandemic. They cut live to the White House where President Trump announced he was instituting a thirty-day ban on travel to the US from select European countries, such as Italy, beginning that Friday at midnight.

I woke Bobby up with a call to him in London where he was doing a college semester abroad. Now that he was a young adult, I tried to not boss him around. But in this case, I told him he had to get on a flight the next day before the airports were swamped or flights were cancelled. Truthfully, I just wanted my six-foot-tall baby home.

I decided that to keep ourselves and our loved ones safe, we'd work from home starting Friday. I told the team that would be "for the next several weeks." Talk about wishful thinking. We had never all worked together anywhere but the office. Now, we were going fully remote, with only one day to prepare. The good news: we had digital natives on our team. They were more skilled than I will ever be, setting us up for Zoom calls and file sharing so that we could continue our work seamlessly.

That Saturday at about 3 a.m., I was wide awake and staring at the ceiling. I couldn't get images out of my mind of people dying on untended gurneys in overrun hospitals in Wuhan, and body bags in front of hospitals in Italy. How would the pandemic hit our partner hospitals in Africa and Asia? Compared to American hospitals, they often felt understaffed and spread thin. I'm always inspired by how much gets done with so few resources. But how would they confront a potential tidal wave of patients? What, if anything, could we do to help?

I called Anne the next morning and then we reached out to our attorney, Cynthia Rowland, who made time to talk with us that Sunday. She offered to draft revised language to amend our Articles of Incorporation, the legal document that undergirds our work, that would enable us to fundraise for Covid. I called our board chair, Kelly Brennan, who backed this approach, and held an emergency board meeting to get the amended Articles approved. Then we got to work immediately on a campaign for Covid Emergency Relief, promising that every penny we raised would go right to our partners.

To better understand the needs on the ground, we put together a survey and fielded it to the hospitals. While not all were experiencing significant disruption in their ability to treat patients, one thing was clear: most were ill-equipped to confront the pandemic. There was not enough PPE and disinfectants to keep their teams safe. To make matters worse, lost revenue from countrywide lockdowns was forcing many of them to cut salaries and staff, right when they were needed most. It was also clear that most of our partners operated with minimal cash reserves to confront this extraordinary situation.

We developed a direct mail campaign with an online component that went to every one of our donors to fund what we called our Covid Emergency Response Fund. Thanks to our amazing supporters, we raised more than $700,000. We started wiring funds almost immediately to hospitals, based on the needs they documented in our survey. This enabled us to target the funds where they were needed most.

It was becoming clear that the pandemic would have a negative impact on every sector of our economy, and that no corner of the globe would likely be spared. The US stock market had lost close to 30 percent of its value in only one month between the end of February and end of March. The first few waves of massive unemployment in the US signaled we were heading into the fastest financial downturn in US history. This turmoil would likely hurt our ability to raise funds for fistula treatment.

We had a healthy reserve. I've run the Foundation the way I was raised—live beneath your means, and you don't have to worry as much about money. That said, no matter what we did this year, we would likely see a decline in revenue. For perspective, when the Great Recession hit in 2008, our revenue dropped by 20 percent in the critical fourth quarter fundraising period, though we bounced back in 2009. It seemed likely that our revenue would drop by at least that much with Covid, given the depth, breadth, and speed of this economic downturn.

We needed to rethink our priorities. It was obvious that we would need to table our ambitious "In It to End It" expansion plan to replicate the successful countrywide treatment network model from Kenya in other countries. We put the highest priority on making sure we could continue to meet our obligations to our existing hospital partners. That part of our budget would not change. We didn't want to cut back on our ability to fund surgeries, but we could cut other costs.

The biggest line item in our budget after surgeries is Foundation salaries. So, I cut them by 10 percent across the board. I'm the highest paid employee, so I whacked mine by 20 percent. (But so you don't think I'm more selfless than I am, I would restore those salaries once our revenue stabilized.) I also cut our team so we could return to being a leaner organization. It was brutal, but it cut our "run rate" and gave us breathing room to support our hospital partners. Anne reminded me that it wasn't that long ago that there were fewer than ten of us. We could make it work. And, like so much else Anne had said over the years, she was right.

Several months later, our partner in Kathmandu reached out to me because they were overrun with Covid patients who had returned from doing migrant labor in India and brought the virus back with them. They were desperate and needed to purchase oxygenators to keep people alive. We'd depleted the Covid fund, so I reached out to one of our most generous supporters, I'll just call Stacy the Mensch. Within an hour, she was back to me saying she'd wire us $125,000 to help keep people alive on the other side of the planet. We have the most amazing donors.

That fall another selfless donor in Singapore provided an additional $1 million in Covid support. She enabled us to fund more PPE and provide salary support for many of our partners through the worst days of the pandemic. That same donor also came to the aid of our partner in Afghanistan after the Taliban took over. One of the very best parts of my job is getting to engage with selfless people who use their precious resources to help some of the poorest people on the planet. This exceptional woman prefers to remain anonymous. She reminds me of the saying that you can tell the character of a person by how they treat someone who can do nothing for them. That's our saint in Singapore.

———————————⊹———————————

By early 2021, we were back to pre-pandemic surgery totals. This is a testament to our incredible partner hospitals, their resilience, their tenacity, their dedication, and the generosity of our supporters. They enabled us to provide critical PPE and disinfectants to more than six thousand doctors, nurses, and healthcare workers to help prevent the spread of Covid. We were also able to help pay salaries for hundreds of workers at our partner hospitals. This way they could keep their doors open, so women could continue to receive life-transforming surgery. We got a message from the general manager of SALFA, our biggest partner in Madagascar, that brightened my day: "Tears are flowing in my eyes. Tears of joy because God is taking care of SALFA through your support."

My worst nightmares about how our friends and colleagues in Africa and South Asia would be impacted by Covid were not realized. It felt like a miracle given the comparative paucity of hospitals and doctors in both places, that the pandemic's impact was less severe there than in the US. Even with official death rates likely underestimating the true death totals, far fewer people died as a percentage of the population in countries in Africa and South Asia than in the US. The heartbreaking truth is that even with our wealth and the wide availability of the vaccine, the US leads the world in deaths from Covid. More than a million American families have lost loved ones. And long Covid, with the fatigue, brain fog, and respiratory problems it produces, continues to plague millions of people, disproportionately women. Covid was a once-a-century pandemic that killed millions. And yet, it could have hit Africa and the poor parts of Asia harder than it did.

35. THE OTHER HALF

*The golden moments in the stream of life rush
past us, and we see nothing but sand; the angels come to
visit us, and we only know them when they are gone.*

—George Eliot

Earlier this year, Bobby said that he thinks the Foundation is like my second child. At first, I was taken aback, thinking that he resented the time I'd devoted to work. But, as we talked, I realized that far from wounding him, he thought my work had enriched both our lives. The more I thought about it, I realized he was right in thinking of the Foundation that way. That's because growing the Foundation over the last two decades has been like parenting in critical ways. It's demanding, produced humiliating mistakes, forced me to grow, and yielded immense satisfaction to see the work we do together truly change the lives of women.

That's also why the idea of "work/life balance" is not a goal I embrace. My work is central to my life. It is something I love for a selfish reason: it brings me joy, makes me feel alive and propels me forward. It is not something that I want to put in opposition to the non-work part.

This book is largely about the work half of my life, but I wanted to spend a little time on the other half. That starts with Bobby, my first and only child. My love for him is deeper than what I think

Darwin envisioned. Or, to steal a line from Cormac McCarthy, "If he is not the word of God, then God never spoke." Yet parenthood also created a sustained sense of vulnerability, as my terror and gladness walked hand in hand. I am continually humbled, as every chapter is so different. In each I am getting things wrong as I struggle to get it right.

When my divorce was final, I got custody of Bobby. And here, as my missionary friends would say, "grace stepped in." Mom and Dad were sixty-eight and seventy, respectively, when Bobby was born. They each had been retired for years but were still active and healthy. At that point, their other grandchildren were nearly teenagers who lived an hour away. By contrast, I bought a house about ten minutes from them.

Moving back to my hometown, a place as a teenager I only wanted to flee, and staying throughout Bobby's childhood, enabled Mom and Dad to become deeply engaged in my life and Bobby's. Their weekly calendar put a priority on attending any event in which Bobby was involved. Little league games. Cub scout jamborees. Middle school basketball games. High school plays and improv shows. You name it, they were there, right next to me, cheering Bobby on. If they hadn't seen him in a week or so, I'd get a call from Mom wanting to set up a time for him to come over. They gave him something truly invaluable: unconditional love. Of course, this made it possible for me to devote energy and time to the Foundation and to travel extensively. My parents' place was Bobby's second home. When I dropped him off, I could focus completely on work without any worry about how Bobby would fare while I was gone.

I'd been a serial monogamist in my twenties and thirties. By the time Bobby came along, he was the main event. While he was growing up, I saw a couple of doctors, a lawyer, and a brilliant math genius whose deep integrity was compelling. But when he said that he was always third on my list—after Bobby and the Foundation, I realized he was right, and the relationship wouldn't last. While my younger self would have been sad with this outcome, my wiser older self viewed it as a choice. I put my energies in the things I loved most: my son, my parents and the Foundation. My heart was full and so was my life.

The years went by too fast. I tried to take it all in and not miss any of it, and yet it can feel like a dream. Was the man who visits me now ever crawling, saying the word "Mama" in a way that melted my heart, hugging me tightly at preschool pick up, screaming with joy as he learned to ride a bike, smiling nervously in his first suit for a middle school dance? When he left for college, it felt like a wild roller coaster ride that came to an abrupt stop.

As for my dear parents, our roles switched in the last few years. After they had spent a lifetime being there for me and for Bobby, it was now time for me to be there for them. I am beyond grateful that the passage of time had sanded down painful memories from my teenage years. They'd been replaced with new ones from their chapter as Bobby's grandparents. I finally grew up enough to appreciate them and could try to give back a fraction of what they gave me.

I had time to see them as full beings, with their own strengths and weaknesses; to take them off that pedestal I'd put them on long ago. Why did my younger self think I should have flawless humans for parents? With Mom I could finally see her anxious perfectionism as being driven by the unforgiving demands placed on women of her generation to be the impossible: ideal wives, hostesses, and mothers responsible for creating a Hallmark-movie life. I know I was too slow to forgive but, thankfully, I came to realize before it was too late that whatever they had failed to provide me was nothing compared to the wealth of invaluable intangible gifts I'd been given.

I found them both an empathetic gerontologist and started going to their doctor appointments. After Dad got wedged in the back seat of my VW Bug and couldn't get up without help from a burly stranger in the Safeway parking lot, I bought an SUV to drive them places. I helped run errands and tried to be there for them when they needed something. When Covid hit, I did my best to keep them out of any place they could become infected. I was so fearful they would face the cruel fate of too many, dying alone in a hospital.

Dad was diagnosed with leukemia, and it gradually seized his life. A few weeks before he died, I told him, "I can't think of a time when I ever saw you lie about anything to anyone." He looked at me with a twinkle in his eye and said, "Not that you know of." He was always uncomfortable talking about himself, and pushed back compliments the way a narcissist pushes away criticism. He was stoic and fearless—at least outwardly—to the end. He passed away peacefully in the fall of 2021, just shy of his ninety-second birthday, in the same house in which I'd grown up and where he'd lived with Mom for nearly six decades.

The week Dad died, our twelve-year-old rescue mutt Carly, started coughing. I wasn't too concerned because she would still jump up like a dolphin when I'd come home from the store. I assumed she likely had something called kennel cough that she'd picked up at the dog park. But, when I took her to the vet the next week, it turned out it was lung cancer. After a flurry of appointments with a dog oncologist, surgeon, cardiologist, a CT scan, echocardiogram, and a king's ransom in bills, operating on her didn't make sense because her heart was failing. Right after New Year's, as I petted her on my bedroom floor, her tail flicked then stopped, taking another part of my heart with her.

Losing both Dad and then Carly in a matter of months gutted me, but I still had Mom. I tried to savor the tenderness of Mom's company with growing awareness that time together was precious.

She seemed amazingly resilient after just losing her husband of more than sixty years and spent time with her "band of sisters" from the Sunnyvale chapter of American Association of University Women. Winter was finally turning into spring as pink blossoms burst on the branches of plum trees in our neighborhood. We had a lovely Easter at my house with an egg hunt for my cousins' kids and Mom was in good form. She thanked me when I drove her home saying, as she often did lately, "I love you a bushel and a peck," with a sweetness that touched my soul. The next day, in the cruelest month of April, she called me from the Emergency Room. She'd gone because of abdominal pain, and the next day they removed half her colon.

Mom survived the surgery and I was planning to bring her home. One minute I was on the phone to get a hospital bed delivered to her house. Then I was at her bedside as she slipped out of consciousness. Over the next few hours, my siblings, cousins, and nieces rushed to say goodbyes. I called Bobby who was away at college and told him what was happening. He said he wanted a few minutes to compose his thoughts. When he called back, I wasn't sure she could even hear him. But as he expressed his love in words that were so eloquent and thoughtful I felt both pride and piercing sorrow as I watched tears stream down Mom's cheeks.

When evening fell and everyone left, I nestled beside her in her bed. I wanted to be next to her as she left this world, as I'd been a part of her until I entered it. I whispered "I love you" over and over into the darkness. For so long, I heard those same words echoed back from her—words I knew she'd never say to me again. As her breaths became slower and uneven, I murmured "I am so lucky to have you as my mother. . . . Thank you . . . I love you." She died at about 5 a.m.

The room was still. As I walked down the hall toward the hospital's entrance, I could see the horizon turning gold awaiting the rising sun. The only sounds were my whimpers and the wheels of her walker as I dragged it against the sparkling linoleum. I was now nobody's daughter.

———————————⊹———————————

For me, Joan Didion was spot on when she said, "Grief is a place none of us know until we reach it." For the first few weeks after Mom died, I was numb as I went through the motions planning her memorial service.

I'd had decades to build a solid foundation for my own adult life, to live as the independent woman teenage me had dreamed of. But I'd taken for granted the love that was there for me and for Bobby. My parents' emotional support was like the earth beneath me. Yet now that was gone, and I was hurtling toward an unknown and unseen bottom. I would be glad when the day was over and look up at the night sky and feel the moon was mourning with me. The love I had for them was still there, haunting me, because there was no place to put it.

For so much of my life, my focus had been tomorrow not today. This was how I ran the Foundation, always looking to connect the next dot. It was how I parented too, trying to be prepared for the next step in Bobby's life. But with the loss of my parents, I hit a wall. There would be no more tomorrows with them or todays, only yesterdays. This left me stalked by unanswerable questions. Had I done enough for them? Had I told them often enough how grateful I was for all they'd given me? For the enduring love they'd given Bobby?

I took long drives up the coast and hiked through Point Reyes, north of San Francisco. It's a stark, wind-swept peninsula surrounded by rugged coastline on three sides and the Pacific Ocean stretching out like a wild blue carpet as far as you can see. I'd gaze out at the white capped waves and try to comfort myself with the knowledge that neither of my parents suffered significantly. I should be grateful. And yet, selfish me struggled to view it that way. What I saw and still see is a vast hole that will never be filled.

After Mom died, I had to sell their home where I grew up. While my teenage memories from those turbulent years were painful, they'd been replaced by many new ones in the last two decades. It was where we made Sunday dinners and implicit promises to take care of each other. Memories lined the walls like fingerprints. Saying goodbye to the house was one more painful loss. A nice Chinese family bought it to live out their own version of the California dream. I can't bring myself to even drive by the place.

I knew my parents would hate, even despise, the idea of me being immobilized by grief. So, I found a deeply empathetic therapist named Deidre, who'd arrived at her compassion through heartbreaking loss of her own. I leaned on my close friend Tammy, whose son has been good pals with Bobby since second grade. In the most brutal twist of fate, she'd lost her dear husband, Tim, the week Mom died. We became soul sisters, unified in loss, both knowing that you grow into not out of grief.

I also got a new dog from a rescue named Lizzy. She was a clingy black poodle, fifty five pounds of jittery energy. She'd been relinquished by her owner because of anxiety, so the folks at the rescue had put her on dog Prozac. Who knew such a thing even existed? She clung to me with such tenacity that I nicknamed her Velcro and brought her to the office with me. We made a very needy pair.

Work proved to be a lifeline during this wicked time. It gave me a reason to get up and moving in the morning. With Lois and Bob's voice echoing in my head telling me not to wallow, I started writing this book.

36. RECONSTITUTE THE WORLD

Love is the strongest kind of army
because it generates no resistance.

—David Brooks

I was standing in line at Costco. My cart was overflowing with paper towels, a massive bag of dog food, and a case of yogurt. The big clock on the wall above the snack bar said it was 6:30 p.m., and I was kicking myself for shopping during the store's rush hour. As I waited, I checked email on my phone. Along with a few messages from my team there was one from a name I didn't recognize I'll call, Victoria Hart, from a firm called Bridgespan. It was short, unremarkable, and asked for a Zoom call with me to discuss our work on behalf of one of their clients.

A few years ago, this would have produced a prompt affirmative response and not much else on my part. Often meetings generated by emails like this go nowhere, but this one caught my attention immediately. That's because, as anyone paying attention in the charity space in the last few years knew, Bridgespan was the consulting firm advising MacKenzie Scott, the pioneering philanthropist who had promised to give away her entire fortune. But I'd heard that trying to break into the inner circle at Bridgespan was impossible. A dear friend, David Callahan, who is the founder and publisher of *Inside Philanthropy*—the *Wall Street Journal* for the giving sector—could not even get an interview with anyone at Bridgespan to discuss Scott's giving. He described it as like Fort Knox, completely locked down. Adrenaline surged through my fingers as I typed a response, agreeing to a call.

Hart asked me to forward a strategic plan, if we had one, and any other documents that would help them understand our work.

We had annual reports and audited financials.

We had peer-reviewed published research about our program in Kenya.

We had a powerful online database with the tens of thousands of surgeries we'd funded.

We even had an engaging short film about the Foundation's impact.

What we didn't have was a current strategic plan.

We did have a detailed strategic plan years back. But we kept blowing past our own goals; the detailed plan felt like a waste of time and was about as much fun to update as doing your taxes.

What we did have was a rough outline of something we were calling "In It to End It." This was our moon shot—an ambitious plan to provide access to fistula treatment to most women in Africa and Asia. It was designed to take our proven country-wide treatment network that we piloted in Kenya and replicate the model into dozens of countries. The goal over the next fifteen years was to make treatment accessible to women in 90 percent of the impacted countries in Africa and Asia. After that we wouldn't stop until every woman injured in childbirth had access to restorative surgery.

It was audacious.

It was bold.

It was also doable.

We could make this happen if we could get support from someone with a big heart and a very deep pocket like MacKenzie Scott, and then get others to follow her lead.

The problem was the plan at that point was a very rough working draft; more spread sheets, and projections than anything. It was not an "i's dotted and t's crossed" plan fit for a billionaire and her Ivy League advisors. It was clear that we needed to push the accelerator fast and hard to get a polished plan done and in Bridgespan's hands ahead of our call. And that's just what we did over the course of the next week with vital help from Michael Slind our talented communications leader.

Then another email came in from Bridgespan. They asked that if we submitted a strategic plan, we needed to specify if it had been board approved. My thought was *DRAT!*—though with more colorful language. We had reviewed a high-level version of the plan with the board, but it wasn't strictly board approved. So, I called our board chair, Ling Lew, and got her help organizing a boarding meeting over Zoom that Saturday. Every board member showed up—across fourteen times zones and three continents—to review the plan. After a thorough discussion, we got what I wanted: enthusiastic and unanimous approval.

We called on our talented graphic designer, George Chadwick. I'd worked with him at FCB decades ago and he did a masterful job with our annual reports. I knew he could make this look professional, rather than like a college term paper. On Tuesday afternoon, ahead of our first Wednesday call with Bridgespan, I pushed SEND. We'd gotten it done, and "left it all on the field." The upside was that even if we didn't get a penny from Scott, we had a rock-solid plan that we could share with other possible funders.

Over the next few weeks, we had a series of one-hour calls between me, our senior program staff, and the Bridgespan team headed by Hart. They asked a series of insightful questions to understand our work, with a commendable combination of confidence in their abilities and humility to what they didn't know about us. Between calls, we followed up with forty pages of due diligence information about our finances, results, and staffing. It was the most thorough process we'd ever been through.

But the weird thing was, there was no mention of MacKenzie Scott. Not once. There was no discussion of money, let alone the potential amount we would get if we cleared all their hurdles. There was an elephant in the room; we just had no idea how big it was. And, by the end of the three calls over the next few weeks, we didn't know if the elephant had left the room! It was unnerving. The Bridgespan team thanked us for our time and effort and told us we wouldn't hear anything for months.

And that's what happened: radio silence.

I tried to forget about it.

Three long months later, I had just finished streaming the latest episode of *Last of Us* and picked up my phone. I pulled up a message from a woman I'd never heard of, from an email address I didn't recognize and thought I'd wait until morning to respond. But then I saw the words "donor" and "Bridgespan" in her message. She wanted to have a phone call. One on one. It would be confidential. This was it. I emailed her back immediately and gave her times the next day, starting first thing in the morning.

I turned off the light and lay gazing at the ceiling with angst-ridden anticipation. I finally fell asleep and had a dream where I stood in front of a faceless panel of judges like you'd see at the Olympics for gymnastics or diving. But when it came time to get my scores, the judges' cards were blank. Would we get a large gift? Or would we hear once again some version of *The Foundation is doing amazing work, but you don't meet our funding priorities. Good luck.*

I got an email the next morning, saying I should expect a call at 2:30. I decided to do the call at home, so if it was bad news, I could sulk in crushed sadness without witnesses. The day dragged on, and the minutes between 2 and 2:30 ticked by like hours.

Finally, my phone rang. The woman on the other end was professional—not warm, not cold. Her voice was impossible to read, like you'd expect from someone doing a survey about your internet service. I was practically holding my breath at this point as she asked if I knew who MacKenzie Scott was. Then she explained Scott's approach to giving. Her goal was to find good organizations doing meaningful work, evaluate their potential and then give funds to those who are the true experts without conditions. She continued, saying that they based their conclusion on a range of sources. Scott trusted the groups she funded to use her donations effectively. Then she asked if I had any questions. No. So far so good. She hasn't yet said the dreaded words "I'm sorry..."

Instead, she said something like, "Ms. Scott is impressed with your work and wants to support Fistula Foundation. And give you fifteen million dollars." I wonder if I heard her correctly. I am usually a nervous chatterbox. I have energetic conversations with my dog. But now, as I tried to speak, words were not coming out of my mouth. It was like someone hit a pause button on my face.

I finally stammered, "Oh my God! Fifteen million dollars!"

My mind flashed through a kaleidoscope of faces—to women I'd met like Hanna back in Addis, and Sarah Omega and Mwanatena, to their healers Catherine Hamlin, Edna Adan, Hillary Mabeya.

My voice was cracking as I sputtered out, "Thank you so much. This is going to enable us to help thousands of women." The words were replaced by sobs. When she said she would put all of this in an email, I stopped taking notes.

Bobby was home for spring break and I ran to his room to share the news. He hugged me and then looked me in the eyes and said, "Mom, I am so happy for you." At that moment, I felt like Jimmy Stewart in the last scene of *It's a Wonderful Life*. But the people I most wanted to share the news with were gone.

I said, "I so wish I could call your grandparents. Can you imagine how happy they'd be?"

So instead, I called Anne. Though she'd retired a few months earlier, she'd been my wing woman, my ride or die gal, and I wanted her to be the first one at Fistula Foundation to hear the news. And of course, Anne being Anne, said something like, "But I didn't have any part in the process with Bridgespan."

I said, "Yeah, but you helped build this. You've got to come with us to celebrate."

Then I called Ling, who responded with over-the-top joy. I called an all-team meeting to tell everyone at the same time. I blasted Pharrell Williams' "Happy" on my phone and the room exploded with cheers and hugs. I then said, "Let's head to Zona Rosa," a small

Mexican restaurant down the street. "Margaritas on me." I was so happy I was smiling at billowing clouds, chirping birds, and willowy trees. In my head I was skipping.

When it wasn't the middle of the night in Africa, I reached out to our dedicated team there and the rest of our devoted board, to share our joy and appreciation for all they've done to get us here.

That night I sent an email to the extraordinary woman who made this transformative gift:

Dear Ms. Scott,

This afternoon I received the most joy-inducing call of my life from a member of your team telling me that you had decided to give Fistula Foundation $15 million. I sat stunned before sobs took over as my heart burst with gratitude. Even as I type this message, I can hardly believe it is true.

I wanted to reach out to you today and thank you for this profound gift that we will use to help tens of thousands of women in Africa and Asia left incontinent from childbirth get their lives back. You are helping rescue multitudes of women from a lifetime of misery and isolation. I am honored by your trust and deeply moved by your generosity.

You are using your extraordinary power to help those too often marginalized or forgotten. My hope is that others will follow in your bold pathbreaking footsteps.

This is one of my favorite poems and I thought you may like it if you haven't already seen it.

My heart is moved by all I cannot save:
so much has been destroyed
I have to cast my lot with those who age after age, perversely,
with no extraordinary power, reconstitute the world.
—Adrienne Rich
With my heartfelt gratitude,
Kate Grant

EPILOGUE

Addis Ababa, Ethiopia

What you leave behind is not what is engraved on stone monuments, but what is woven into the lives of others.

—Pericles

The cab pulled away from the entrance of the now-familiar Hilton Hotel. I was on my way to see Dr. Hamlin one last time. Over the years, I had written to her on several occasions and received gracious replies. But I had not seen her since that fateful week back in 2008. She was now ninety-five, and I had heard that her health was failing.

I didn't want our last face-to-face meeting to be one fraught with tension. While I had jumped into the labor battle with her Ethiopian doctors with good intentions, I'd likely done little to help, and I knew I contributed to pain she didn't need. While she'd let men cause extraordinary damage to the hospital she had dedicated her life to building, there was no doubt that she had changed tens of thousands of women's lives, including mine.

That morning the street was still gleaming, wet from a rain that had ceased as the sun rose. Everything seemed clean and the city bustled with energy, as cars rather than streams of tattered and weary humans fought for space on the crowded road. The air crackled with competing horns and the sound of car engines and motorcycles. Out my window I could see a flock of giant one-hundred-foot-tall cranes dominating the skyline to build more of the high-rises that dotted the city center. The place brimmed with prosperity, in stark contrast to the destitution that was everywhere on my first trip in 1994. Soon the cab descended the same narrow lane with the green and white sign that pointed the way to the Fistula Hospital.

When I got out of the cab, the glorious shade trees, bright bougainvillea, and the smell of freshly cut grass reminded me of my first visit decades earlier. The murmur of conversations of patients enjoying the morning sun on the green lawn and a few chirping birds made the place feel as tranquil as I remembered. I walked to the end of a stone path leading to the small cottage made of mud mixed with straw where Dr. Hamlin had lived for nearly fifty years.

Mamitu greeted me and took me into the living room to see Dr. Hamlin. It was love in action as I watched Mamitu help Dr. Hamlin stand to welcome me. She seemed fragile; her face lined by a lifetime of making critical decisions for her patients. Her voice was soft and warm. She still radiated the kindness, and for lack of a better word, divinity, that she had the first time I met her. Her living room was also as I remembered it. It was a nest feathered with simple belongings—a floral sofa, framed photos, and cheerful mementos. She'd spent her life in the service of others, and her home was as modest as she was.

We sat down, and after a few pleasantries about the cooling rain that morning, Mamitu brought out tea and biscuits. I pulled out snapshots I'd taken on earlier visits, some with her much-loved only child Richard, others with me and several of our board members. Then I shared with her the Foundation's most recent annual report. I pointed out a map indicating the many countries across Africa and Asia where we were supporting fistula treatment. I also shared a bar graph that showed the expanding number of surgeries we were funding, more than twenty times as many as when we started.

What I didn't say was that we focused our efforts on supporting and empowering dedicated African and Asian doctors, including a few that left her hospital feeling defeated and unappreciated. We believed they know best how to help women in their own communities.

What I did say was something like, "It was you and Reg who pioneered fistula surgery and trained a generation of other surgeons. The Foundation was founded to support your work. Without you, there would be no Fistula Foundation. We all stand on your shoulders."

As I expected, she seemed somewhat uncomfortable with the praise. But I wanted to break through her humble shell, more for me, perhaps, than for her. Most of all, I wanted her to know the difference she'd made in my life and in the lives of multitudes of women we were helping. So, I went on. "We've funded nearly one hundred thousand surgeries for women in more than thirty counties in Africa and Asia. That wouldn't have happened without you."

She smiled, taking my words in, but not saying much. Then she changed the subject to ask if I wanted more tea. I said yes, as I stalled for more time and struggled to find the right words.

We chatted about the expansion of the hospital, the growing physiotherapy program, and the tasty biscuits. I didn't want to overstay my welcome or tax her energy, but there was one more thing I wanted her to know. I set down my empty teacup, I looked into her watery blue eyes and reached for her delicate hand. "Before I go, I want you to know that you changed the course of my life," I said. "You gave me a path to travel that has given me something invaluable: meaning and purpose."

I paused as I struggled to convey what I was feeling deep in my soul. "My words are inadequate to capture my gratitude to you." She smiled as I persisted. With my voice cracking, I added, "I mean every word of it and more . . . from the very bottom of my heart." Now it was her eyes along with mine that glistened with tears.

As I stood up to leave, Mamitu helped Dr. Hamlin stand. I wished them both well and thanked them again. Then Dr. Hamlin gave me a kiss on the cheek. After I walked across the small living room to the doorway, we waved gentle goodbyes. I closed the door behind me. Then I headed toward the hospital where a movement to help women injured in childbirth was born fifty years earlier.

A FINAL WORD

As this book goes to press, every penny of the $15 million dollars donated by MacKenzie Scott has been spent to provide thousands of women with life-transforming surgery. This is a testament to both the profound need for fistula treatment and the dedication of the surgeons and our team. While this is powerful proof that money can truly change women's lives, we have a long way to go.

At a press conference in 2022, President Joe Biden embraced and then dismissed fistula. He said, "I feel badly also about the fistulas still taking place in eastern Congo. I feel badly about a whole range of things around the world. We can't solve every problem." Fistula Foundation is in business to help the women whose governments, including my own, have too often chosen to neglect.

I am hopeful about the future for a couple of reasons. For starters, we have the know-how to end the needless suffering of women left incontinent by childbirth. This isn't a disease for which there is no cure. Surgery can give a woman back her health and her future.

When I first went to Africa in 1992, few Africans had college educations and the literacy rate was roughly 50 percent. Thankfully, that is not true today. Nearly 70 percent of Africans are literate and more than ever they are accessing higher ed to help build the human infrastructure to confront fistula and other health challenges. In Kenya, for instance, in 2000 just 3 percent of the population was enrolled in post-secondary education; by 2022 that had skyrocketed to 20 percent. Our program team in Africa is staffed entirely by Africans. Most of the hospitals we fund in Africa are run by Africans and in Asia are run by Asians. These dedicated people are the future of healthcare in their regions.

My optimism is strengthened by a growing community of people that demonstrate that being your sister's keeper is a privilege, not a burden. Everyday life asks each of us: what kind of person am I? I believe our answer is shown by how we treat other people. Our donors' selfless empathy is the rocket fuel that drives everything we do. I am inspired by the countless people who give amounts large and small to help women they will never meet, in places they will likely never visit, get their lives back. We share a reverence for the courage of women with fistula, who against the odds, persevere to emerge the heroes in their own story as their despair is turned into hope and healing. I feel so lucky to spend my days surrounded by such compassion and courage.

A woman with fistula is like you and me—she is someone's daughter, sister, wife, aunt, or friend. She wants what you'd want for yourself—a healthy future. Her story is unique and her own. Her struggles are deeply personal. And yet, there is one element that is the same: surgery provides a hard-won opportunity for a new life—a rebirth. But the promise of curative surgery is a dream for far too many women. It doesn't have to be this way. Together we can create a world where no woman suffers needlessly for trying to bring a child into the world. My hope is that you'll join us in our efforts to ensure that every woman injured in childbirth gets the care she needs to thrive, so that there is no woman left behind.

It's folly to measure your success in money or fame.
Success is measured only by your ability
to say yes to these two questions:

Did I do the work I needed to do?
Did I give it everything I had?

—CHERYL STRAYED

ACKNOWLEDGMENTS

I've described Fistula Foundation as a bridge. On one side are grievously injured women and their doctors, and on the other side are compassionate people who want to help those women get the priceless gift of health. It's been the privilege of a lifetime to work with a tireless group of people to build the bridge linking them together.

This is my first and very likely only book. One of its underlying themes is my growing awareness of luck I've too often taken for granted. So here I'd like to recognize many of the people I've been fortunate to know who have made our story possible.

The expertise of scores of fistula surgeons, nurses, and health care workers make miracles of healing happen. They enable resilient women with fistula to get their lives back. The list of our dedicated partners is vast, and I unfortunately can't celebrate each by name here. But I wanted to thank a few people that made a permanent mark on my heart and from whom I've learned so much. They include: Steve Arrowsmith, Nrinmoy Biswas, Andrew Browning, Ganesh Dangal, Serigne Gueye, Brian Hancock, Edna Adan Ismail, Ruth Kennedy, Sinan Khaddaj, Joe Kinahan, Carolyn and Hillary Mabeya, Iftikher Mahmood, Rick Manning, Denis Mukwege, Mulu Muleta, John Omboga, Sarah Omega, Naren Patel, Charlotte Polle, Tom Raassen, Lauri Romanzi, Hamid Rushwan, Shershah Syed, Igor Vaz, Kees Waaldijk, Said Ahmed Walhad, and Ambaye Woldemichael.

Without our donors most of the women we've helped would likely still be suffering needlessly. There are so many kind people who have supported us over the years. I have deep appreciation for each of the nearly seventy-thousand donors who have stepped up and stepped in to help women they will likely never meet.

I want to recognize those who've gone above and beyond by making exceptional contributions to drive our growth: Doris Apel, Brad Aronson, Kelly and Sean Brennan, D'Anne Burwell, Linda and William Chamberlain, the late Serena Connelly, Seamus Connolly, Ethel Cook, Sandra Crowder and Andrew Grant, Phyllis Dixon, The Dreitzer Foundation, Susan Guthrie Dunn, Anne Emmet, Caroline Fisher and the Craig Family, Annemarie Fontaine, Tom Franeta, Vince Gallagher, Linda Gottlieb, Dona Bolding Hamilton and Roger Hamilton, George Hanby, Justine and Erin Hastings, Ronnie Hawkins and Nigest Getahun-Hawkins, Head Family Charitable Foundation, Carol Judd, Kassy Kebede, Joe and Sharon Kemper, Rachel King, John Larkin, Peter Laventhol, Mary Stobie Lechman and Lily Ribeiro, Terry and Laurie Ledbetter, Sara Gaviser Leslie and Josh Leslie, Darren and Ling Lew, Gilbert L'Italien, the MacFarlane Foundation, Albert Malvino, Bill and Judy Mann, Leslie and Colin Masson, the late Betty McFerren, Gordon Murphy and Marie Steinthaler, Susan and David Ogden, Rebecca Perry, Virginia and Roger Perry, Sara Poston, Kathy Rall and Larry St. Pierre, Monika Reed, Frank Richardson and Kimba Wood, the Saul Foundation, The Semkiw Family, Micah Shea Trust, Diane Sherman, Mason Smith, Soroptimist International, Ellen Spertus and Keith Golden, Wendy Strgar and the team at Good Clean Love, Rob Tessler, Spyridon Triantafyllis, Matt Winkler, Paul and Pamela Wood, Sally Woodhouse, and our indefatigable late volunteer, Jerry Goldstein. My gratitude for you is boundless.

Everything we've accomplished at Fistula Foundation has been because of our truly extraordinary staff team. Their creativity and commitment to our mission are invaluable. I'd like to thank these current and former staff members for their critical contributions: Kimberly Adinolfi, Michael Juma Aduol, Kelly Anderson, Steven Armstrong, Clement Lofumbwa Balilo, Anjana Bhattarai, Caleb, Darren and Melisa Blankenship, Carol Brill, Ashley Burke, Victor

Chibale, Martin Chiyana, Jordan Chileshe Chomba, Bwalya Chomba, Jesse Chu, Shaun Church, Sally Cole, Emmanuel Dhiluba, Linda Edwards, Jhoanna Enriquez, Niki Friedman, Renee Gardner, Hannah Garone, Ahana Gunderson, Shelly Helgeson, Sharon Howe, Nicole Huelar, Kristin Intlekofer, Melissa Johnson, Kalumba Kaputo, Jameson Kaunda, Robyn Leslie, Jessica Love, Pam Lowney, Debbie Mancuso, Mirabel Miscala, Habiba Mohamed, Florence Changwe Mulenga, Nelson Musa, Clement George Ndahani, Katie Nerod, Esther Njoroge-Muriithi, Gerald Kennedy Okada, Violet Okwaro, Jaya Patten, Lindsey Pollaczek, Kee Rajagopal, Jackelen Renteria-Bustos, Terry Rodriquez, Joop Rubens, Jing Shi, Mike Slind, Patricia Nyawa Tempo, Sajira Mae The, Carol Tillman, Pascal Vahwere, Lara Veldman, Alyssa Vu, Tarah Walker, Morgan Walter, Donalda Watson-Walkinshaw, and Katie Weller. I also want to do one last shout out to Anne Ferguson, my tried-and-true deputy. Her myriad contributions to the Foundation are truly indelible.

We strive to manage the Foundation like a dynamic, driven, and highly successful business. To do that, we've relied on the expert legal, financial, technical, recruiting and creative advice from these talented people: Tracey Canepa, George Chadwick, Ed Chavez, Molly Christiansen, Seble Getaneh, Georgina Goodwin, Perrett Laver, Leah Lococo, Ted Mitchell, Andrew Pierce, Gina Roccanova, Cynthia Rowland, Susannah Sallin, Tanya Slesnick, Mark Strahs, and Brenda Vingiello. They are exceptional professionals and have made the Foundation stronger and better.

We've also been blessed with amazing ambassadors. Nick Kristof and Peter Singer provided us with invaluable visibility and credibility by sharing their well-earned halos. The team at The Life You Can Save, including Charlie Bresler, Amy Schwimmer, and Jon Behar, have enabled us to engage new ardent supporters. I'm also grateful to Oprah Winfrey who played a crucial role in getting the Foundation off the ground twenty years ago, and to Abraham Verghese for his moving foreword to this book and for his beautiful novel, *Cutting for Stone*, that introduced many people to the plight of fistula patients.

I want to recognize Ric and Shaleece Haas, the father–daughter duo that started the Foundation back in 2000. Without them, the Foundation would not exist. I'd also like to thank our amazing board members who all served as volunteers. They've each contributed their precious time, talent and treasure to help the Foundation thrive. They've also given us life's most precious commodity: wisdom. Thank you to our board chairs: Kelly Brennan, Suzy Elneil, Kassy Kebede, Cleo Kiros, Ling Lew, Bill Mann, and our other directors: Abaynesh Asrat, Lisa Bloom, France Donnay, Deborah Harris, Thomas Huntington, Darren Lew, Sarah Omega, Linda Paul, Charlotte Polle, Denis Robson, the late Allan Rosenfield, Steve Saunders, Jerry Shefren, Gillian Slinger, Mary Tadesse, Vanessa Taylor, Rob Tessler, Whitney Tilson, Linda Tripp, Mal Warwick, Teri Whitcraft, Larry William, and Susie Wilson.

This book benefited enormously from gifted editors, Barbara Milbourn, Kai Flanders, and Leslie Wells. They each gave me many thoughtful ideas for improving my prose. Reminding me of the quote attributed to Mark Twain, "a successful book is not made of what is in it, but of what is left out of it," they encouraged me to trim my draft. This book is far from perfect, but it is nearly eighty pages shorter than my first version. I so appreciate their kindness, candor, moral support, and patience.

I'm extraordinarily grateful to have publisher Brooke Warner, as well as Lauren Wise, and the team at She Writes Press guiding me. Brooke is a champion for writers, and I so appreciate her expertise and tenacity. Thanks also to the team at Simon and Schuster for helping get this book into readers' hands and to Leah Lococo for the terrific cover design.

I'm lucky to count as friends, successful writers Peter Singer, David Callahan, and Evan Mandery. I appreciate their encouragement and gentle warnings about the challenges of bringing this book to publication. Thanks, also, to our donors, Daniel Pink and Jessica Lerner, for giving me the invaluable suggestion to read my draft out loud enabling me to catch a boatload of mistakes. I'm also grateful to a diverse group of caring and dedicated people who've kept me and Bobby thriving and our household going: Fernando and Leo Ibarra, Pari Jahanafard, Melody Lowman, Aqualino Marcos, Blanca Motta, Deidre Popolizio, Joni Walters, and Casey Weber.

While at Princeton, the late Professor James Trussell gave me something invaluable: the recognition that I belonged in a place where I initially felt intimidated. He was a mentor and a true warrior for women's health; the world is better for his indefatigable work. I am also grateful to the faculty at The Princeton School of Public and International Affairs and the UC Berkeley Haas School of Business for providing me with a priceless education. Thanks, too, to the Robertson Family, for endowing the Princeton program, enabling me to graduate with only minimal debt and my IRA intact.

Lastly, I want to thank the people to whom this book is dedicated, my late parents, Lois and Bob Grant, and my son, Bobby Houston, as well as my extended family in California and Montana and dear friends for their caring support and encouragement. As Franklin Jones said, "Love doesn't make the world go 'round. Love is what makes the ride worthwhile."

SELECTED READINGS

These nonfiction books have given me something precious: the knowledge and wisdom of their authors.

If you haven't read hundreds of books,
you are functionally illiterate, and you will be
impotent, because your personal experiences alone
aren't broad enough to sustain you . . . *

—GENERAL JAMES MATTIS

International Development/Medicine

- *Poor Economics,* Abhijit V. Banerjee and Esther Duflo
- *Behind the Beautiful Forevers,* Katherine Boo
- *Sometimes Brilliant,* Larry Brilliant
- *A Doctor in Africa,* Andrew Browning
- *The Bottom Billion,* Paul Collier
- *The Great Escape,* Angus Deaton

---

* The second half of General Mattis's sentiment: "Any commander who claims he is 'too busy to read' is going to fill body bags with his troops as he learns the hard way. The consequences of incompetence in battle are final." Fortunately, most of us don't kill people with our arrogant blunders.

- *Guns, Germs and Steel*, Jared Diamond
- *White Man's Burden*, William Easterly
- *To Repair the World*, Paul Farmer
- *The Forever War*, Dexter Filkins
- *The Moment of Lift*, Melinda French Gates
- *How to Prevent the Next Pandemic,* Bill Gates
- *A Hospital by the River*, Catherine Hamlin
- *Complications*, Atul Gawande
- *Lords of Poverty*, Graham Hancock
- *A Woman of Firsts*, Edna Adan Ismail
- *Mountains beyond Mountains*, Tracy Kidder
- *Half the Sky*, Nicholas Kristof and Sheryl WuDunn
- *Road to Hell*, Michael Maren
- *Dead Aid*, Dambisa Moyo
- *The Power of Women,* Denis Mukwege
- *The Blue Sweater*, Jacqueline Novogratz
- *The Business Solution to Poverty,* Paul Polak and Mal Warwick
- *Factfulness*, Hans Rosling
- *Epic Measures*, Jeremy Smith
- *Tears for My Sisters*, L. Lewis Wall

Business/Management/Leadership
- *The Way of Integrity*, Martha Beck
- *Oath and Honor*, Liz Cheney
- *Good to Great*, Jim Collins
- *Principles: Life and Work*, Ray Dalio
- *Leadership is an Art*, Max Depree
- *Measure What Matters*, John Doerr
- *Originals: How Non-conformists Move the World,* Adam Grant
- *Only the Paranoid Survive*, Andy Grove
- *No Rules Rules*, Reed Hastings and Erin Meyer
- *Made to Stick*, Chip and Dan Heath
- *Shoe Dog*, Phil Knight
- *Call Sign Chaos*, Jim Mattis and Bing West

- *Playing Big*, Tara Mohr
- *Uncharitable,* Dan Pallotta
- *The Lean Start-up*, Eric Ries
- *Start with Why*, Simon Sinek
- *Zero to One*, Peter Thiel
- *Fast Forward*, Melanne Verveer and Kim K. Azzarelli

Effective Altruism

- *Strangers Drowning*, Larissa MacFarquhar
- *The Life You Can Save*, Peter Singer
- *The Most Good You Can Do*, Peter Singer

Thought Provoking/Inspiration

- *Everything Happens for a Reason*, Kate Bowler
- *The Second Mountain*, David Brooks
- *The Givers*, David Callahan
- *The Middle Place*, Kelly Corrigan
- *Excellent Sheep*, Willian Deresiewicz
- *Man's Search for Meaning*, Viktor Frankel
- *Thank you for Being Late*, Thomas Friedman
- *The Algebra of Happiness,* Scott Galloway
- *Checklist Manifesto*, Atul Gawande
- *Winners Take All*, Anand Giridharadas
- *My Life So Far,* Jane Fonda
- *Sapiens*, Yuval Noah Harari
- *Thinking Fast and Slow*, Daniel Kahneman
- *When Breath Becomes Air*, Paul Kalanithi
- *The Art of Memoir,* Mary Karr
- *Bird by Bird*, Anne Lamott
- *A Beginner's Guide to the End,* BJ Miller and Shoshana Berger
- *Becoming a Dangerous Woman,* Pat Mitchell
- *The Road Less Travelled*, M. Scott Peck
- *Regret*, Daniel Pink
- *Better Angels of Our Nature*, Steven Pinker

- *How to be Perfect*, Michael Schur
- *I've Been Thinking,* Maria Shriver
- *Men Explain Things to Me*, Rebecca Solnit
- *Just Mercy*, Bryan Stevenson
- *Awakening,* Meighan Stone and Rachel B. Vogelstein
- *Caste,* Isabel Wilkerson
- *A People's History of the United States,* Howard Zinn

TOPICS AND QUESTIONS
FOR DISCUSSION

1. The book opened as Kate described her trip around the world in her twenties. How did it impact her? Have you had an experience that changed the course of your life? If so, what was it?

2. Kate's parents were "first gen"—the first in their families to graduate from college. How did her parents' experience and their values shape her initial career aspirations? How did your upbringing impact your career choices?

3. David Foster Wallace is quoted: "There is no such thing as not worshipping. Everybody worships. The only choice we get is what to worship." What was Kate worshipping while working on Madison Avenue? How did she change over time? Have you had a similar experience where your goals and values shifted?

4. Kate realized that she had let a relationship impede her ability to find a more fulfilling career path. Have you had a similar experience?

5. Kate said she experienced "imposter syndrome" while working in political jobs in Washington, DC. Have you ever had a similar experience? If so, how did you manage it?

6. Women with fistula are often clinically depressed before they are treated. Their psychological healing starts with sharing their experience with other patients and with health workers. Why

do you think that's important? Have you had an experience that is similar?

7. Kate came to see diversity of thoughts, perspectives and backgrounds in a team as a force for better decision making. Has that been your experience?

8. Soon after the Foundation adopted its global mission, they chose to focus on one measurable outcome: surgeries, to become "the Smile Train of Vaginas." How did that choice impact the Foundation's growth and effectiveness? Was that narrow strategy a smart move?

9. Kate pushed hard for "invitation only" selection of their hospital partners. Why was this so important to her? Do you think it was the right decision? Why or why not?

10. Kate recounted several incidents of sexism. What does that reveal about the challenges of being a female leader? Have you faced similar situations? If so, how did you handle them?

11. Writer Ariel Levy is quoted: "This thinking you can have every single thing you want in life is not the thinking of a feminist. It's the thinking of a toddler." Why do you think she chose that quote? How does it apply to Kate's life choices? Is it relevant to yours?

12. Fistula Foundation has grown at a rate that is multiples faster than most US charities. What do you attribute that to? What did the Foundation do differently than other charities that enabled it to become so successful?

13. How did Kate's relationship with her mother evolve over time? How does that compare with your experience with your parents?

14. Kate described empathy as the "rocket fuel" that drives the Foundation forward. What does she mean by that? How has empathy helped the Foundation thrive? What role does empathy play in your life and with your charitable giving?

15. Kate underscored the vast difference between the deaths and injuries due to childbirth and pregnancy in the poorest developing countries and in the US. Why do you think this differential is so vast? What would be necessary for this situation to change?

16. Trust is a core value with Fistula Foundation and informs how they work with the hospitals and doctors they fund. Philanthropist MacKenzie Scott also indicated that she trusted Fistula Foundation and other organizations she's chosen to support. How does trust benefit both Fistula Foundation and the hospitals doing surgeries?

17. One of the themes of the book is Kate's increasing awareness of blessings, privileges, and other advantages that she had too often taken for granted. Does that resonate with you? Are there elements of your life that you take as a given, when you know others struggle to obtain them?

ABOUT THE AUTHOR

KATE GRANT is the founding CEO of Fistula Foundation, the world's largest charity devoted to treating childbirth injuries. She joined the Foundation in 2005, expanding the Foundation's global footprint from one country to more than 30 in Africa and Asia. Grant is a graduate of UC Berkeley's Haas School of Business and earned an MPA from Princeton University. She lives in the San Francisco Bay Area.

Looking for your next great read?

We can help!

Visit www.shewritespress.com/next-read
or scan the QR code below for a list
of our recommended titles.

She Writes Press is an award-winning
independent publishing company founded to
serve women writers everywhere.